Cycles, Trends, and Turning Points

Practical Marketing & Sales Forecasting Techniques

John V. Crosby

NTC Business Books
NTC/Contemporary Publishing Group

Library of Congress Cataloging-in-Publication Data

Crosby, John V.
    Cycles, trends, and turning points : marketing and sales
forecasting techniques / John V. Crosby.
        p.   cm. (American Marketing Association)
    At head of title: American Marketing Association.
    Includes index.
    ISBN 0-8442-3244-0
    1. Marketing research.   2. Sales forecasting.   I. American
Marketing Association.   II. Title.
HF5415.2.C77   1999
658.8′02—dc21   98-34338
                                                                        CIP

Cover design by Nick Panos
Cover image copyright © 1997 PhotoDisc, Inc.
Interior design by Precision Graphics

Published by NTC Business Books (in conjunction with the American Marketing Association)
A division of NTC/Contemporary Publishing Group, Inc.
4255 West Touhy Avenue, Lincolnwood (Chicago), Illinois 60712-1975 U.S.A.
Printed in the United States of America
International Standard Book Number: 0-8442-3244-0

00 01 02 03 04 05 LB 19 18 17 16 15 14 13 12 11 10 9 8 7 6 5 4 3 2 1

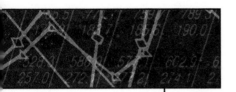

Contents

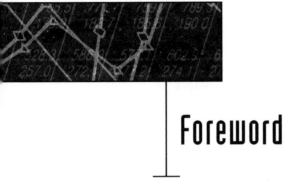

Foreword

AS GEOFFREY MOORE ONCE NOTED in a foreword to one of my books, "Computer technology is rapidly sweeping back-of-the-envelope methods of forecasting into a well-deserved oblivion." John Crosby continues this sweeping action with his book on the practical forecasting techniques for marketing and sales. Crosby acknowledges that effective forecasting is both art and science, and his emphasis on a graphical approach is amplified by his effective use of the computer. In my opinion, there is simply no substitute for good graphics!

What distinguishes Crosby's work from the work of other forecasters is his relational model of marketing and sales. This means that the roles and responsibilities of marketing and sales are defined in terms of the other's needs and from the perspective of the customer. Crosby defines how the contributions of strategic marketing, tactical marketing, and sales differ and illustrates how the various forecasting techniques can be applied in the context of each of the three functions. He illustrates how the high-level and longer-term forecasts by strategic marketing are useful for forecasting macro-economic trends and linking economic forecasts with industry and market forecasts. He demonstrates how the short-term revenue and billings forecasts by tactical marketing focus on specific product lines and serve to keep the company flexible and responsive to change in the marketplace. His presentation of the sales forecast, as a bookings forecast, is especially novel. In the context of the relational model, sales forecasts consist of specifically defined opportunities that are "somewhere in the selling cycle." This level of specificity eliminates guesswork on the part of the salespeople and provides the most accurate description of near-term sales.

Forecasting is about change. If there is no change, then there is no need to forecast. Crosby has both complicated and simplified this notion. He has complicated the notion of change by introducing the different perspectives and contexts of strategic marketing, tactical marketing, and sales; and paradoxically, he has also simplified the forecasting of change.

Robert L. McLaughlin
Former chief of acquisition research
for Malcolm Baldridge, Chairman
of Scovill, Inc., and member of the
Economic Advisory Board during
the Nixon administration
Editor Emeritus, Micrometrics Press, LLC

Preface

NEARLY ALL COMPANIES forecast in one form or another. Some companies rely on a bottom-up forecast from field sales, while others place their confidence in a top-down approach from central planning. Few companies, however, have adopted a systematic and well-organized approach to forecasting that accommodates forecasts from different parts of the organization with different levels of detail and different horizons. This book is about such a system. It is written as a practical guide for marketing and sales professionals as they face the day-to-day forecasting demands of economies, industries, market segments, and product lines. This is a practical book in which mathematical notation has been kept to a minimum.

The centerpiece of the book is the Average Recession Recovery Model (ARRM), pioneered by my friend and colleague Robert L. McLaughlin and carried forward here in the context of the relational model of marketing and sales. The ARRM is a simple yet incredibly powerful approach to forecasting. The age-old question of which time series approach yields the greatest accuracy is rendered moot by adopting the philosophy and methodology of the ARRM. The ARRM methodology parses the cycles, trends, and turning points of continuous data series into simple patterns of change that are practical and useful in forecasting.

The structure of the book reflects the different types of forecasts generated by strategic marketing, tactical marketing, and sales. Part I advances the notion that forecasting is both art and science and sets the stage with a discussion of the various forecasting schools of thought. Part II proposes a graphics-rich approach as an aid to understanding forecasts and forecasting. It also provides a brief review of time series, seasonal adjustment, and the Average Recession Recovery Model.

Part III begins with a discussion of the cycle of business and continues by exploring the forecasting situations and tasks appropriate for strategic marketing. This part includes how the economy is structured, how to link industry and company data to the broader economy, and how to construct a long-term forecast.

Part IV addresses the short-term and near-term forecasting demands of tactical marketing and how to forecast new products using the Average Experience Model (AEM), a variant of the ARRM. In Part IV we also explore how tactical marketing monitors turning points, or changes in the economy, and how these changes can influence commerce. The revenue forecast, a key contribution of tactical marketing, is presented in the context of bookings, backlog, and billings.

Part V reviews marketing and sales as a relational approach and focuses on how to track sales opportunities. Bookings forecasts that are generated from defined opportunities that are "somewhere in the selling cycle" are specific and most likely to materialize into an order. This contrasts sharply with the more conventional sales forecasts in which field salespeople are required to generate unconstrained demand forecasts for their current and prospective customers. The different functions of strategic marketing, tactical marketing, and sales can each contribute their different perspectives on future demand.

Part VI concludes the discussion with a recap of a few simple ways of monitoring forecast accuracy and illustrates how forecast accuracy can be improved through a detailed review of the forecasts created by the three functions: strategic marketing, tactical marketing, and sales.

PART I

Introduction

1

Forecasting— Art or Science?

TIMELY AND ACCURATE FORECASTS are singly the most valuable contribution that can be made to the success of a business. Whether formal or informal, statistical or judgmental, every business decision is based on some sort of a forecast. Even the businessperson who claims that forecasts are not required is, in fact, employing a de facto forecasting model known as *naive forecast 1* (NF1). NF1 is a "no change" model and holds that today will be the same as yesterday and tomorrow will be the same as today.

While most businesspeople recognize the need for effective forecasts, there is a tendency to view forecasting as either a black art or an impossible task. These extreme views are often amplified by competing vocal factions within the company who take the position either that "you can't forecast, so why try?" or that "your forecast has to be by part number and cover a three-year period by month, and you can't change it." Neither of these extreme views is correct.

Part of the difficulty comes from not recognizing that businesses often require several different types of forecasts, at different time periods, at different levels of detail, for different horizons, and for different purposes. For example, there are long-range strategic forecasts that influence new-construction decisions; mid-range tactical forecasts that support new-product development and expansion efforts; and short-term operating forecasts that influence quarterly revenue and profitability goals. Each of these special-ized forecasts requires different perspectives and often employs different methods. Creating a total forecasting system that acknowledges these dif-ferences is the key to effective forecasting.

This book presents some practical forecasting techniques for market-ing and sales and illustrates how these methods can contribute favorably to the success of the business. Some of the tangible and intangible benefits of a successful total forecasting system follow.

TANGIBLE BENEFITS

- Increased profits from operations
- Decrease in nonproductive cash consumption
- Increased factory utilization
- Decrease in excess and obsolete inventories
- Increased inventory turns
- Decrease in negative manufacturing variances
- Increased performance to "customer request date" (CRD)
- Decrease in number of stock-out situations
- Decrease in cost of purchased items
- Decreased time-to-market for new products

INTANGIBLE BENEFITS

- Improved customer relations
- Reduced level of frustration (internally and externally)
- Reduced meeting time
- Critical resources freed up from expediting tasks
- More frequent and more accurate views of the marketplace
- Increased organizational flexibility

FORECASTING AND CHANGE

Forecasting is about anticipating change. Change can be gradual and con-tinuous, or it can be rapid and discontinuous. Understanding the patterns of change can be very helpful in planning forecast activities. For example, if there is no change from one period to the next, then NF1 becomes the most accurate forecasting method. Clearly, NF1 is also the lowest-cost fore-

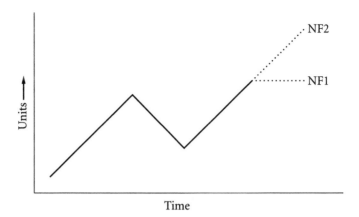

EXHIBIT 1.1 The Naive Forecasts

casting method, requires the least amount of knowledge, and requires literally no mathematics. It can play a valuable role, however.

There is also a second type of naive forecast, *naive forecast 2* (NF2). NF2 holds that change occurs at a constant rate. Using NF2, the rate of change from today to tomorrow will be the same as the rate of change from yesterday to today. NF2 can be either positive or negative. Many companies unknowingly employ NF2 in their annual strategic-planning activities as they forecast annual sales to increase at a constant rate of, say, 15 percent per year.

The two naive forecasts may appear frivolous, but each can play a useful role in evaluating the effectiveness of more costly and more complex methods. Later on, we will explore how the two naive forecasts can be used as part of a total forecasting system.

One of the fundamental challenges we face as forecasters is the accuracy of our forecasts. NF1 and NF2 provide the low-cost, low-effort, fastest baseline measures. If we cannot beat NF1 or NF2, how can we justify the additional time and expense required for more complex methods? The simple answer is, we cannot!

Given that forecasting is about anticipating change, as forecasters we should strive to achieve two broad goals: one, get the direction of change correct, and two, predict successfully as much of the change as possible. Percent change successfully predicted (PCSP) is a concept that we will explore in greater detail in Chapter 20.

A MEANS, NOT AN END

Forecasting is really decision support. In and of itself, forecasting has no intrinsic value. The value is found only in the conclusions reached by the users of the forecast. It is a dangerous and arrogant game to argue for the universal superiority of one forecasting method over another, especially when research supports the claim that there is no one best forecasting method applicable to all forecasting tasks. The method providing the best results depends on what is to be forecast, the context, the level of detail involved, and the forecast horizon of interest. For example, when forecasting product groups or divisions, the greater the level of product aggregation, the more accurate the forecasts.

As we introduce the generation of forecasts from the multiple perspectives of strategic marketing, tactical marketing, and sales, we can essentially parse potential forecast errors by creating forecasts that have different applications, rather than requiring that one forecast fits all. The "one-forecast-fits-all" approach usually compromises some details in the forecasting process and burdens all users with unnecessary error generated by a single forecast. The key is to use a wide range of methods to yield timely and accurate forecasts and to choose the method or methods appropriate for the task at hand.

A RANGE OF METHODS

An effective total forecasting system must have access to a range of methods. For ease of discussion, we have organized these methods into three broad categories: basic models, organization factors, and judgmental inputs. The first category includes models developed by different forecasting disciplines: for example, the naive and moving average models developed by practicing forecasters, the decomposition models developed by the U.S. Census Bureau, the exponential smoothing models of the operations researchers, the Autoregressive Moving Average (ARMA) and Autoregressive Integrated Moving Average (ARIMA) models of the statisticians, the filtering models of the engineers, and the regression models of the econometricians.

Organization factors include data and methods that contribute to a more eclectic approach. This category comprises the objective models described in the first category plus other factors such as the raw tabular data from finance or accounting, graphs of raw and adjusted data using different combinations of variables, surveys of major customers or sales force composites, economic variables, and leading indicators.

The third category includes the critical element of judgmental inputs. This very important element has more to do with the art of forecasting than with the science of forecasting. Forecasts containing judgmental inputs usually result in more accurate forecasts than those generated strictly mechanically.

ART AND SCIENCE

The message of this book is that a total forecasting system that is effective and contributes favorably to the success of the business is worth its weight in gold. Any such system must contain elements of both art *and* science. The art element refers to how the total forecasting system can be designed and constructed to yield accurate, timely, and low-cost forecasts. This includes knowing how to organize and present data graphically to organization members who may have a wide diversity of knowledge and experience. The art element also relates to the selection and communication of a measure of forecast accuracy that is appropriate for the organization and the management team.

The science element refers to how the individual methods are structured and manipulated numerically to deliver the actual forecast. This includes understanding the assumptions behind different types of forecasting models, how series are computed and centered, the mechanics of seasonal adjustment, and how to move quickly and easily from seasonally adjusted to non–seasonally adjusted forecasts. The science element also includes knowing how to apply and compute the various measures of forecast accuracy.

2

A Total Forecasting System

A TOTAL FORECASTING SYSTEM, to be effective, must not only have access to a wide range of methods but must also view the forecasting task from the multiple perspectives of the economy, the industry, and the company and, within the company, from the multiple perspectives of strategic marketing, tactical marketing, and sales. This means being forever curious about what the many possible futures might hold and then following up that curiosity through a variety of analyses that include the economy, the industry, the company, and the company's products and services.

Being familiar with the different perspectives involves being familiar with the various schools of thought and how they can be blended in ways that contribute to the art and science of forecasting.

VARIOUS SCHOOLS OF THOUGHT

Three broad schools of thought influence the practice of forecasting: the macro- and microeconomics school (economic), the production and inventory control school (statistical or operations research), and the sales force composite or executive opinion school (judgmental). Each of the three schools of thought contributes to the forecasting process.

9

Economic School

The economic school of thought emerged from the economics departments of colleges and universities and emphasizes the use of "causal or explanatory models" that are constructed from simple and complex regression analyses of key economic variables. The analytical techniques perhaps most frequently employed include regression and correlation analysis. As analytical techniques, *regression analysis* defines the nature of the relationship between variables, while *correlation analysis* quantifies the nature or strength of that relationship. Although the economic school refers to regression models as "causal models," correlation does *not* imply causation. It is simply a tool used to illustrate the relationship between variables of interest.

To illustrate, regression analysis could be used by a residential home builder interested in understanding the relationship between housing starts and his company's sales. In this case, regression analysis can be used to explore the relationship between the dependent variable, the company's sales, and the independent variable, housing starts. By measuring and understanding the historical relationship between the two variables, you can predict the future value of the dependent variable, using an estimated value of the independent variable.

The accuracy of this approach depends on how highly the two variables correlate over the history of the observations: the higher the correlation, the more accurate the approach. The two dominant measures used to assess how well the two variables correlate are the *correlation coefficient* and the *coefficient of determination* (more on these in Chapter 8). Analysis involving a single independent variable is called *simple regression*, and analysis involving several variables is called *multiple regression*.

Econometric models are a subcategory of the economic school and utilize the results of regression analyses to construct simple and complex equations that describe various sectors of the economy. It is not uncommon for an econometric model to consist of several hundred different mathematical equations. The U.S. Department of Commerce employs an econometric model to explore the impact of proposed changes in fiscal or monetary policy.

Statistical School

While economic forecasting often proceeds from the general to the specific, the statistical or operations research school, on the other hand, proceeds from the specific to the general. This school of thought proceeds from the individual part types and sums them, or "rolls them up," to produce a company or industry forecast. This approach is largely mathematical, often mechanical or automatic, and originated in the industrial engineering colleges, applied sciences, and production management departments of business colleges. The advent of computers has brought this school of thought into the forefront. Today most companies' production and inventory control departments generate automated computer analyses of specific part types based on order rates, ship rates, and actual versus desired inventory levels. It is not uncommon to encounter this approach in companies that maintain active parts catalogs or data books with part types numbering in the tens or hundreds of thousands.

Judgmental School

The judgmental school is perhaps the most pervasive and includes such practices as the sales force estimate, the jury of executive opinion, and a group forecasting approach called the Delphi Technique.

The *sales force estimate*, or *composite estimate*, is widely practiced and involves asking each salesperson the type and quantity of product each plans to sell in the coming months or quarters. The individual salesperson's forecast is then combined with other salespersons' forecasts to generate a composite sales force forecast. Frequently these forecasts are subject to being "scrubbed" by various levels of sales management, so the final number may or may not have any resemblance to the salesperson's original estimate. Salespeople are generally optimistic and are subject to sales quotas, so the challenge for this approach is how to control for bias.

The *jury of executive opinion* is more of a top-down approach and involves one or more knowledgeable executives, generating and agreeing on the probable demand for their company's products and services over the next few fiscal periods. In companies with a large number of product lines and an even larger number of products, this approach is, by necessity, limited to the critical few product lines that generate most of the company's revenue. Forecasts resulting from this approach can be accurate or inaccurate, depending on the level of detailed knowledge possessed by the executives. Similar to the case with the salesperson estimate, the challenge in this approach is controlling for the dominant opinion contributed by the ranking executive.

The *Delphi Technique* is a more organized and iterative group process that employs anonymous written responses in an attempt to control for the influence of the more dominant members of the group. Each round of participation employs group data. The iterative nature of the technique provides feedback to all participants and allows them to see their responses within the context of the group's responses. In each successive round, they are asked to reevaluate their respective contributions and to submit a new response. The process continues until the range or variability in the responses reaches an acceptable level. The average of these data then becomes the forecast. As with the jury of executive opinion, the knowledge level of the participants influences the process and the result.

The *eclectic* approach is a school of thought in which all methods are welcome as long as forecast accuracy and reliability are not sacrificed. This school of thought is populated by pragmatists who are interested in providing timely and accurate forecasts regardless of the methodology employed. The eclectic approach calls on methods from economics, statistics, and the judgmental schools. Our approach in this book is eclectic in that we borrow concepts freely from economics, statistics, and the more subjective judgmental methods.

A BROAD ECONOMIC VIEW

Having a broad economic view involves understanding the structure of the economy, patterns in business cycles, short- and long-term trends, and turning points or changes in direction of key business indicators and how these factors influence your company. General business activity is seldom static and usually increases and decreases at varying rates and amplitudes over time. Sometimes these variations are correlated with national economic events, or with seasonal factors such as the start of a new school year, summer family travel versus winter or spring business travel, major holidays, and so on. The resulting increase or decrease in business activity contributes to the cycle of business. Adjusting for seasonal factors and comparing changes from one period to another is essential when seeking information about possible trends. A turning point occurs when there is a change in the direction of a trend. This could be a decreasing trend that turns up or an increasing trend that turns down.

A major contribution from the economics school, and the centerpiece of our work, is the economic indicator approach to forecasting. Indicators can be direct measures of output such as industrial production, or they can be discrete measures such as weekly labor hours, level of unemployment, interest rates, or the money supply. They can also be either computed ratios or composites of one or more discrete measures. Literally hundreds of different indicators are used to track various sectors of the economy over different time periods. There are time series that monitor Gross Domestic Product (GDP) on a quarterly basis and time series that monitor GDP on an annual basis. For example, quarterly series may be expressed in percent change from the previous quarter, percent change from the same quarter a year ago, or at an annualized rate. Annual series reflect year-over-year percent change. Other indicators, such as interest rates, are tracked minute by minute, although such historical data are seldom available in raw form. Different indicators can be constructed, selected, or grouped that tend to lead, coincide, or lag historical peaks or troughs in the general business or economic cycle. These indicators, together with other techniques, can be useful in anticipating or forecasting future turning points.

Although criticized initially as "measurement without theory," the indicator approach was defined by the early work of Wesley Mitchell, Arthur Burns, and Geoffrey Moore at the National Bureau of Economic Research (NBER). The NBER is a private nonprofit economic research organization which, since its founding in 1920, has studied, developed, and published information on a wide range of economic and social topics. The National Bureau dedicated itself early to the pursuit of factual and informative information about the workings of the economy. It is the organization that defines, through its Business Cycle Dating Committee, the official peak and trough dates that describe the onset and end of U.S. economic recessions. Contrary to statements often reported in the financial press, a decline in GDP for two successive quarters does *not* define a recession. The peak and trough dates are defined through the detailed analyses of key indicators such as real income, real sales, nonagricultural employment, and industrial production.

The two individuals who were most influential in the formation of the NBER were also motivated to seek a more eclectic path to understanding the economic issues of the day. Malcolm C. Rorty, an AT&T engineer turned statistician, and Nahum I. Stone, a social-minded economist, had begun meeting five years prior to the actual founding of the NBER, to discuss the benefits of having an organization that would devote itself to "fact finding on controversial economic subjects of great public interest."

During their early meetings, the two men concluded that the group should be started by well-known economists who represented individually the full spectrum of political and economic thinking. They also believed that other organized interests such as financial, industrial, agricultural, and labor should be associated with their work.

The National Bureau's early attempts to organize centered around the hot topic at the time: the distribution of income among individuals and families. The First World War interrupted their early attempts to organize and also served to point out "the appalling lack of the quantitative information needed to cope with the urgent mobilization and reconstruction problems facing the nation." These observations broadened the original thinking and pointed out the need for some sort of national economic accounting. This early work led to the formalization of our National Income and Product Accounts (NIPA), which remain as the core structure of the U.S. economy. The NIPA tables shown in Exhibits 2.1 and 2.2 illustrate this structure. Later chapters explore the NIPA structure in much greater detail.

Line		Line	

Account 1.—National Income and Product Account

Line			Line		
1	Compensation of employees	2,921.3	31	Personal consumption expenditures (2–3)	3,296.1
2	Wages and salaries	2,443.0	32	Durable goods	437.1
3	Disbursements (2–7)	2,443.0	33	Nondurable goods	1,073.8
4	Wage accruals less disbursements (3–8 and 5–4)	0	34	Services	1,785.2
5	Supplements to wages and salaries	478.3			
6	Employer contributions for social insurance (3–16)	247.8	35	Gross private domestic investment (5–1)	793.6
7	Other labor income (2–8)	230.5	36	Fixed investment	777.4
			37	Nonresidential	545.4
8	Proprietors' income with inventory valuation and capital consumption adjustments (2–9).	324.3	38	Structures	182.0
			39	Producers' durable equipment	363.4
			40	Residential	232.0
9	Rental income of persons with capital consumption adjustment (2–10)	4.3	41	Change in business inventories	16.2
10	Corporate profits with inventory valuation and capital consumption adjustments.	365.0	42	Net exports of goods and services	–108.0
			43	Exports (4–1)	444.2
11	Profits before tax	347.5	44	Imports (4–4)	552.2
12	Profits tax liability (3–13)	137.0			
13	Profits after tax with inventory valuation and capital consumption adjustments.	228.0	45	Government purchases (3–1)	918.7
			46	Federal	387.0
14	Dividends (2–12)	115.3	47	National defense	295.6
15	Undistributed profits with inventory valuation and capital consumption adjustments (5–5).	112.6	48	Nondefense	91.4
			49	State and local	531.7
16	Inventory valuation adjustment	–27.3			
17	Capital consumption adjustment	44.7			
18	Net interest (2–15)	387.7			
19	National income	4,002.6			
20	Business transfer payments	25.6			
21	To persons (2–20)	20.8			
22	To rest of the world (4–9)	4.8			
23	Indirect business tax and nontax liability (3–14)	385.3			
24	Less: Subsidies less current surplus of government enterprises (3–7)	10.9			
25	Consumption of fixed capital (5–6)	534.0			
26	Gross national income	4,936.7			
27	Statistical discrepancy (5–6)	–28.4			
28	Gross national product	4,908.2			
29	Less: Receipts of factor income from the rest of the world (4–2)	128.7			
30	Plus: Payments of factor income to the rest of the world (4–5)	120.8			
	GROSS DOMESTIC PRODUCT	4,900.4		GROSS DOMESTIC PRODUCT	4,900.4

Account 2.—Personal Income and Outlay Account

#	Item	Value		#	Item	Value
1	Personal tax and nontax payments (3–12)	527.7		7	Wage and salary disbursements (1–3)	2,443.0
2	Personal outlays	3,392.5		8	Other labor income (1–7)	230.5
3	Personal consumption expenditures (1–31)	3,296.1		9	Proprietors' income with inventory valuation and capital consumption adjustments (1–8).	324.3
4	Interest paid by persons (2–18)	93.7		10	Rental income of persons with capital consumption adjustment (1–9)	4.3
5	Personal transfer payments to rest of the world (net) (4–7)	2.7		11	Personal dividend income	108.4
6	Personal saving (5–3)	155.7		12	Dividends (1–14)	115.3
				13	Less: Dividends received by government (3–6)	6.9
				14	Personal interest income	583.2
				15	Net interest (1–18)	387.7
				16	Interest paid by government (3–5)	229.9
				17	Less: Interest received by government	128.1
				18	Interest paid by persons (2–4)	93.7
				19	Transfer payments to persons	576.7
				20	From business (1–18)	20.8
				21	From government (3–3)	555.9
				22	Less: Personal contributions for social insurance (3–17)	194.5
	PERSONAL TAXES, OUTLAYS, AND SAVING	**4,075.9**			**PERSONAL INCOME**	**4,075.9**

EXHIBIT 2.1 National Income and Product Accounts (NIPA) structure (in billions of dollars)

Account 3.—Government Receipts and Expenditures Account

Line				Line		
1	Purchases (1–45)		918.7	12	Personal tax and nontax payments (2–1)	527.7
2	Transfer payments	566.2		13	Corporate profits tax liability (1–12)	137.0
3	To persons (2–21)	555.9		14	Indirect business tax and nontax liability (1–23)	385.3
4	To foreigners (net) (4–8)		10.4	15	Contributions for social insurance	442.3
5	Net interest paid		101.8	16	Employer (1–6)	247.8
6	Less: Dividends received by government (2–13)		6.9	17	Personal (2–22)	194.5
7	Subsidies less current surplus of government enterprises (1–24)		10.9			
8	Less: Wage accruals less disbursements (1–4)		0			
9	Surplus or deficit (–), national income and product accounts (5–7)		–98.3			
10	Federal		–136.6			
11	State and local		38.4			
	GOVERNMENT EXPENDITURES AND SURPLUS		1,492.4		GOVERNMENT RECEIPTS	1,492.4

Account 4.—Foreign Transactions Account

Line			Line		
1	Exports of goods and services (1–43)	444.2	4	Imports of goods and services (1–44)	552.2
2	Receipts of factor income (1–29)	128.7	5	Payments of factor income (1–30)	120.8
3	Capital grants received by the United States (net) (5–8)	0	6	Transfer payments to foreigners (net)	17.8
			7	From persons (net) (2–5)	2.7
			8	From government (net) (3–4)	10.4
			9	From business (1–22)	4.8
			10	Net foreign investment (5–2)	–118.0
	RECEIPTS FROM REST OF THE WORLD	572.9		PAYMENTS TO REST OF THE WORLD	572.9

Account 5.—Gross Saving and Investment Account

1	Gross private domestic investment (1–35)	793.6	3	Personal saving (2–6)	155.7
2	Net foreign investment (4–10)	–118.0	4	Wage accruals less disbursements (1–4)	0
			5	Undistributed corporate profits with inventory valuation and capital consumption adjustments (1–15).	112.6
			6	Consumption of fixed capital (1–25)	534.0
			7	Government surplus or deficit (–), national income and product accounts (3–9).	–98.3
			8	Capital grants received by the United States (net) (4–3)	0
			9	Statistical discrepancy (1–27)	–28.4
	GROSS INVESTMENT	675.6		GROSS SAVING AND STATISTICAL DISCREPANCY	675.6

NOTE.—Numbers in parentheses indicate accounts and items of counterentry in the accounts. For example, line 3 of account 1 is shown as "wage and salary disbursements, [2–7]"; the counterentry is shown in account 2, line 7.

for Federal Government receipts and expenditures are shown in table 3.2 and for State and local government, in table 3.3 (quarterly and annual).

Most of the estimates corresponding to the entries on the left-hand side of account 1 are shown in table 1.14 and table 1.9. Estimates corresponding to the entries on the right-hand side of account 1 are shown in table 1.1. Most of the estimates corresponding to the entries in account 2 are shown in table 2.1.
Most of the estimates corresponding to the entries in account 3 are shown in table 3.1 (annual only). Estimates

Estimates corresponding to the entries in account 4 are shown in table 4.1.
Estimates corresponding to the entries in account 5 are shown in table 5.1.

EXHIBIT 2.2 National Income and Product Accounts (NIPA) structure (continued)

AN INDUSTRY VIEW

All businesses and all industries are interconnected in one form or another. In a total forecasting system, it is essential to be aware of the many different types of industries and their interrelationships. The U.S. government is a rich source of information on just about any type of industry. The government gathers and reports business and industry information organized around such topics as revenue, profits, employment, and taxes, to name a few. Understanding the classification structure used for these activities can help guide your efforts in accessing information meaningful to forecasting.

At a very broad level, the Standard Industrial Classification (SIC) system was developed to classify establishments by the type of activity in which they are engaged. This classification scheme covers the entire field of economic activities and facilitates the uniform collection, tabulation, presentation, and analysis of establishment data. The SIC system includes: agriculture, forestry, fishing, hunting, and trapping; mining; construction; manufacturing; transportation, communication, electric, gas, and sanitary services; wholesale trade; retail trade; finance, insurance, and real estate; personal, business, professional, repair, recreation, and other services; and public administration.

The structure of the SIC system makes it possible to access data at the division level—for example manufacturing—two-digit major group, three-digit industry group, or four-digit industry code, depending on the degree of data resolution desired. In some cases a greater degree of resolution is available in data series on industrial production and consumer and producer price indexes. See Appendix A for a complete listing of two-digit major groups, three-digit industry groups, and four-digit industries.

The SIC system, however, is not the only industry classification system employed by the U.S. government. The Commerce Department also employs a classification system for use in its Benchmark Input-Output (I-O) Accounts. The I-O Accounts show the production of commodities by each of nearly 500 industries. At a macro level, the structure of the I-O Accounts is: Agriculture, forestry, and fisheries; Mining; Construction; Manufacturing; Transportation; Communications; Utilities; Wholesale and retail trade; Finance; Insurance; Real estate; Services; Government enterprises; Noncomparable imports; Scrap; General government; Household; and Inventory valuation adjustment. The I-O structure is based on the SIC system, and there is considerable similarity between the two. However, the I-O structure provides for other industries for which the SIC system does not. See Exhibit 2.3 for the macrostructure and principal data sources.

The I-O Accounts report which industry "makes" the commodities and which industry "uses" the commodities. The accounts also show the commodity composition of GDP and the industry distribution of value added. This structure permits a variety of statistical and analytical uses. For example, the I-O Accounts can be used to study industry production and consumption patterns. These patterns can be a valuable source of information when examining the long-term impact of a shift in demand for a particular commodity. An increase in automobile demand, for example, increases the production of cars and, secondarily, increases the demand for steel which, in turn, increases the demand for chemicals, iron ore, limestone, and upholstery fabrics. The increase in upholstery fabrics increases the demand for natural and synthetic fibers, which in turn increases the demand for cotton and wool, polymers, and so on. See Appendix A for the industry classification of Benchmark I-O Accounts and related SIC Codes.

Each of the industries in the foregoing example of the cascade effect of increased automobile demand belongs to some sort of industry association. These associations, in turn, typically publish industry statistics that can be used to supplement the government's data. These additional data increase the level of resolution, thereby permitting more specific analyses and forecasts to be realized. Useful sources of industry association information can be found in the *Encyclopedia of Associations* and in *National Trade and Professional Associations of the United States.*

The U.S. Census Bureau implemented a new system of classification called the North American Industry Classification System (NAICS) sometime in 1998–1999. The NAICS was developed to provide common industry definitions for Canada, Mexico, and the United States to better compare economic and financial statistics in a changing economy. The new NAICS will replace each country's separate classification system. In the United States, NAICS will replace the SIC system. See Exhibit 2.4.

Other nongovernmental sources include the Dow Jones Industry Groups, Investor's Business Daily Industry Groups, and the S&P 500. The S&P 500 has been around since 1923 and is made up of companies that tend to be leaders in important industries. The S&P 500 is structured into four broad segments: Industrials, Financials, Utilities, and Transportation. These four segments are further divided into ten sectors, composed of eighty-eight industries, with 500 individual companies. The Investor's Business Daily Industry Groups contain 197 industry groups and include each group's market value. Each of the 197 industry groups comprises several companies. A subset of the companies in each group is used to compute an industry index for that group. The Dow Jones Industry Groups are organized into nine

The U.S. Input-Output Accounts

MAKE TABLE: INDUSTRIES PRODUCING COMMODITIES

		COMMODITIES									TOTAL INDUSTRY OUTPUT
		Agricultural products	Minerals	Construction	Manufactured products	Transportation	Trade	Finance	Services	Other*	
INDUSTRIES	Agriculture										
	Mining										
	Construction										
	Manufacturing										
	Transportation										
	Trade										
	Finance										
	Services										
	Other*										
TOTAL COMMODITY OUTPUT											

USE TABLE: COMMODITIES USED BY INDUSTRIES AND FINAL USES

		INDUSTRIES													FINAL USES (GDP)							TOTAL COMMODITY OUTPUT
		Agricul-ture	Mining	Construc-tion	Manufac-turing	Transpor-tation	Trade	Finance	Services	Other*	Noncomparable imports	Total intermediate inputs			Personal Consumption expenditures	Gross private fixed investment	Change in business inventories	Exports of goods and services	Imports of goods and services	Government purchases	GDP	
	Agricultural products																					
	Minerals																						
	Construction																						
	Manufactured products																						
	Transportation																						
COMMODITIES	Trade																						
	Finance																						
	Services																						
	Other*																						
	Noncomparable imports																						
	Total intermediate inputs																						
VALUE ADDED	Compensation of employees																						
	Indirect business tax and																						
	Other value added*																						
	Total																						
TOTAL INDUSTRY OUTPUT																							

TOTAL COMMODITY OUTPUT

PRIMARY PRODUCT OF THE INDUSTRY

TOTAL INDUSTRY OUTPUT

* The I-O accounts use two classification systems, one for industries and another for commodities, but both generally use the same I-O numbers and titles. "Other" includes government enterprises and I-O special industries; for more information, see "Appendix B – Classification of the 1987 Benchmark Input-Output Accounts."

** For most industries, this item includes consumption of fixed capital, proprietor's income, corporate profits, and business transfer payments. For banking and for credit agencies other than banks, it also includes net interest. For owner-occupied dwellings and for real estate agents, managers, operators, and lessors, it also includes rental income. For the six industries covering the "Federal Government and State and local government enterprises, it also includes current surplus less government subsidies.

U.S. Department of Commerce, Bureau of Economic Analysis

EXHIBIT 2.3 Macrostructure of the benchmark input-output (I/O) accounts

Table 1: 1997 NAICS Matched to 1987 SIC	Table 2: 1987 SIC Matched to 1997 NAICS
Agriculture, Forestry, Fishing and Hunting	Agriculture, Forestry, and Fisheries
Mining	Mineral Industries
Utilities	Construction Industries
Construction	Manufacturing
Manufacturing	Transportation, Communications, and Utilities
Wholesale Trade	Wholesale Trade
Retail Trade	Retail Trade
Transportation	Finance, Insurance, and Real Estate
Information	Service Industries
Finance and Insurance	Public Administration
Real Estate and Rental Leasing	
Professional, Scientific and Technical Services	
Management of Companies and Enterprises	
Administrative and Support, Waste Management and Remediation Services	
Educational Services	
Health Care and Social Assistance	
Arts, Entertainment and Recreation	
Accommodation and Food Services	
Other Services (except Public Administration)	
Public Administration	

EXHIBIT 2.4 New North American Industry Classification System (NAICS)

major segments: Basic Materials, Conglomerate, Consumer Cyclical, Consumer Noncyclical, Energy, Financial, Industrial, Technology, and Utilities. The major segments are subdivided into ninety-six industry groups, with each group comprising several companies.

The structure and content of these industry groups differ somewhat from the government's classification schemes because they were constructed for stock investment purposes. Being aware of these differences and knowing that each of the industry groups comprises several similar companies, with each followed by one or more investment analysts, adds yet another dimension to a total forecasting system.

A COMPANY VIEW

The company view completes the third leg of the information triangle. Companies almost always belong to associations of one sort or another and often contribute detailed data. The associations, in turn, aggregate the companies' inputs, disguise or assign codes to specific companies, and report comparative data back to the member companies. Data of these type are useful to individual companies as they seek to assess their industry or association rankings.

Specific company sales, in units and dollars, are useful as the forecaster seeks to determine the relationship between the company's sales and the more general industry or economic data. Knowing these relationships is necessary to developing meaningful leading indicators for any individual company. In this case regression and correlation analyses could be used to explore the many possible relationships among the key independent and dependent variables. In exploring these possible relationships, it is important to employ a classification scheme that is similar to if not the same as the classification scheme employed by the associations to which your company belongs and those employed by the government. If this is not done, you run the risk of spending a lot of time and money gathering company data but having no reference base with which to compare the data.

The industry groups such as the S&P 500 or the Dow Jones provide a valuable starting point when you're searching for company data. Another source for company data is the on-line electronic filing service of the Securities and Exchange Commission (SEC) called EDGAR (Electronic Data Gathering, Analysis, and Retrieval). EDGAR involves the automated collection, validation, indexing, acceptance, and forwarding of reports by companies required by law to file forms with the SEC. We explore these issues further in Chapter 8.

BUSINESS PLANNING

For an effective total forecasting system, it is essential to have in-depth knowledge about the company's internal strategic business-planning activities. We recommend a level of knowledge that spans the full spectrum of the business and includes information about the industry in which your company competes, the total market, served market segments, product/service portfolio, marketing, sales, operations, research and development, human resources, and critical risks and contingencies. In this section, we explore the marketing and sales elements only. For additional information, please see Chapters 3 and 4 in my book *Managing the Big Sale* (Lincolnwood, Ill: NTC Business Books, 1996).

Business planning can address the following broad issues:

- What are the marketplace and the market segments served by our company?
- How do we compare against our competition?

- What are our major product lines? What are the key trends for each?
- What is the size of the total market and each of the market segments served?
- What is the quality of our existing products? What are the trends?
- What are the current selling prices for our goods and services? Are they holding steady? Going down? Historically, what has been the slope of the selling price curve for those products that account for 80 percent of our revenue? How do our prices relate to those of our competition? How do we know?
- Who are our major competitors? Are they gaining or losing share of market? What can we expect them to do in response to our planned activities?
- What are our projections for another plant or store? When will it be needed?
- Will our projected sales growth support a new facility?
- What gross and net margins can we expect? What margins do we need? How do the two compare?
- What is our revenue per employee? How does this figure compare with our competition's? What is our target? What is their target?
- What product mix should we have? At what volume?
- What are our planning procedures? How do they compare with those of our competition?
- What are the critical risks we face? How can we anticipate them?

The more people know about the major trends occurring within the industry, the more they are able to contribute their perspectives on the future. What are the major trends that are emerging currently, and how do they impact your company's product lines? Are cost and price considerations driving product integration? Does your industry lead or lag the general economy? Does your company lead or lag the industry? How do your industry trends relate to national economic trends?

Additional questions expand the knowledge:

- What trade associations maintain information on the history of the industry?
- Which major stock brokerage firms have market analysts who follow the industry?
- Which newspapers and magazines have trend information? For example, special feature articles could be used to help identify significant events or describe new technologies.
- How can this information be integrated with the specific company data to help the company develop its view of the future?

MARKETS

As we look more closely at the marketplace, there are three aspects of the market that are of interest to the forecaster: total available market, served available market, and share of market.

The *total available market* (TAM) describes the broader market and is usually subdivided into many smaller and more specific segments. For example, if your company manufactures and sells notebook computers, the served market might be portable computers, but the TAM would be electronic computers. The structure and organization of the markets influence how your products and services are marketed and sold. Important questions relate to how the market is segmented. What are the major segments? How were they determined? Who are the major competitors by segment? In our example, the TAM for electronic computers might be segmented further into large-scale general-purpose computers, midrange general-purpose computers, personal computers and workstations, portable computers, and other computers.

The *served available market* (SAM) refers to the portion of the total available market that is defined by the products and services sold by your company. When your company is active in one or more market segments, it is important to look at both TAM and SAM to get a sense of how big a player your company is in the overall scheme of things and the rate at which each is growing.

Determining *share of market* (SOM) is always important. A small share of market in a rapidly growing market segment means that you will probably encounter a growing number of competitors. A large share of market in a slower-growing market segment means your company's product lines can grow only as fast as the market segment. To be most accurate, define SOM as a percent of the served available market (SAM) and not as a percentage of the total available market (TAM).

The following questions can help in understanding market organization and structure:

- What are the size and annual growth rates of each of the total markets of interest?
- What are the major trends or developments occurring in the markets, and how can they impact the company and the markets it serves?
- What are the major economic factors, and how do they influence the markets?
- What are the cyclical and noncyclical components of the markets?
- Do the critical indicators lead or lag the company's revenue? How can this be used as a competitive advantage?
- How do the growth rates of the markets relate to the desired growth rate of the company?

Markets can be segmented any number of ways. How the market is segmented, however, impacts the availability and use of marketing research information. For example, if your markets are segmented differently from your competitors, from the industry association to which you belong, or from the government, then you are less able to make direct comparisons of the marketing data. Privately funded marketing research information can become very expensive.

Additional questions include:

- Who are the major customers served, and what are their applications?
- What are our competitors' major product lines?
- What segment names are being used in the trade press?
- What are the size and growth rates of each segment?
- What is our target or potential share of market for each segment served? How do our plans relate to these?
- What are the critical seasonal factors, such as holidays, that might dominate the segments?

PRODUCTS AND SERVICES

Your understanding of the products and services offered by your company can help structure your approach to forecasting. Are the groups defined in such a way that people understand which market segments they serve? How do your product groups relate to those of your competition? If different, how different are they, and why are they different? How are they the same? How do they relate to your industry association groupings?

The following questions may be helpful in your product/services analysis:

- How were the product groups defined? Were they defined by the industry, or were they defined by the customer base?
- Are the product groups also categorized by application? Are they categorized by major type of customer? How are the products organized? What is the purpose of the organization?
- Who are the company's major competitors and how do they forecast?
- Where are each of the company's major products in the product life cycle? What information is available on customer returns? Warranties? Competitive comparisons? Customer complaints?

MARKETING AND SALES

The marketing plan defines your company's road map for the future. It consists of both strategic and tactical elements and serves as the foundation for all subsequent planning activities. The sales plan is generated from the marketing plan. Factories are sized and people are hired based on operations managers' interpretation of the marketing plan. New technologies are funded and research projects initiated based on the projected product-line performance and cost forecasts contained in the marketing plan. The marketing plan is the central element in the business planning process.

In the context of a total forecasting system, there are really three different types of forecasts: strategic marketing, tactical marketing, and sales. Following is a discussion of each type of forecast.

STRATEGIC MARKETING

The Role of Strategic Marketing

The primary role of strategic marketing is to develop the long look ahead and communicate that look to the wider organization and, specifically, to tactical marketing. Together, the two marketing functions continually view both the present and the future. An equally important role of strategic marketing is to obtain feedback from the marketplace through the organization's business won/business lost analyses and quarterly account reviews. Staying in touch with the marketplace enables marketing strategists to determine the outcome of their plans. In other words, did the critical events occur as planned? Were they close? Were they far different?

Major Responsibilities

Major responsibilities of strategic marketing forecasts include identifying the many possible served markets for the company's products and services and discussing the relationship of the markets served currently to those anticipated for the future. Another is defining new products and services for each of the served markets together with the required technologies and product development pathway. Strategic marketing is also responsible for defining the profitability and share-of-market goals for each of the major product lines anticipated. This includes anticipated selling prices and cost targets that must be met at critical milestones if the projected profitability and share-of-market goals are to be realized. Strategic marketing's responsibilities also encompass defining criteria for the selection of prospective target accounts. This involves profiling the most likely competitors and providing an estimate of their response to the company's planned activities.

Although strategic marketing is almost always viewed from the perspective of positive growth, the perspective of defensiveness is equally important. A key responsibility of strategic marketing's long look ahead is to detect any potential threat to the company's employees, physical facilities, technologies, products, services, and markets and to devise solutions.

Scope

Scope—the level of detail involved in strategic marketing's planning efforts—is necessarily restricted and involves the projection of activities some five to ten years into the future. Typically planning involves the broad definition of technologies needed to manufacture the planned products at the quality and cost levels required by the served markets as well as the definition of new product groups to be designed.

Relationship to Tactical Marketing and Sales

Strategic marketing has a direct relationship to tactical marketing and sales and an indirect relationship to customers. For example, its relationship to tactical marketing involves the feeding of information about the products and services anticipated for each future served market. This includes analysis of the appropriate price and cost points that must be met if the revenue, margin, and share-of-market goals are to be met.

Tactical marketing's relationship to strategic marketing is to provide feedback regarding desirable refinements to existing products and services, customer satisfaction in each of the served markets, actual versus planned market penetration, what the competition is doing, confirmation of projected price and cost trends, and the actual position of each major product line relative to its planned position.

Strategic marketing's major relationship to sales consists mainly of listening and learning about the current marketplace and what is working and not working. Detailed business won/business lost analyses are presented and discussed during regularly held account reviews. These analyses include information about the sales kit, selling cycle, customers' needs and wants, served markets, products, applications, pricing, competition, quality, reliability, lead times, and customer service. When effective relationships are in place and representatives of strategic marketing, tactical marketing, and sales are present during the account reviews, an incredible number of issues can be addressed in a remarkably short time period.

Planning Level and Horizon

In terms of products, the planning level of strategic marketing is restricted to the product group or the product family. Expected quantities and their dollar value are derived from market growth rates and share-of-market assumptions. This takes advantage of the principle of aggregation, using product mix and market research data, and provides ample leeway for tactical marketing planners to expand the planning process as new information becomes available.

The planning horizon for strategic marketing is typically five to ten years. This means a minimum of a five-year revenue and profit plan is required for each of the major product families or product lines involved. If new technologies are to be developed, the five-year plan must take that into consideration and show the source and application of funds to pay for the new development. Planned cost reductions would also have to occur for the margin goals to be met. The plan would also describe the slope of the cost improvement curve.

Forecast Level and Horizon

Forecasting at the strategic marketing level must include knowledge of what's happening in the national economy. The following questions must be considered: How is the economy structured? Which microsectors of the economy contain data about our products? What is the relationship of the projected product groups or product families to the national economy? Do the product families move in a procyclical fashion, or do they move in a more contracyclical manner? What is the impact of any recessionary periods that may occur while we bring the new products to market?

It is recommended that the forecast be in constant dollars to agree with the U.S. government data and to control for the effects of inflation. Constant dollars can then be converted to current dollars using the Implicit Price Deflator. Two key concepts that are useful in forecasting are the Average Recession Recovery Model and the Average Experience Model which we explore later in much greater detail.

Impact of Information

The planning and forecasts generated by strategic marketing have the greatest impact on the future of the organization. This information is used by senior management to drive major expansion or contraction decisions, including the opening or closing of factories, strategic partnering, mergers, acquisitions, and divestitures. The weight given to the information generated by strategic marketing is incredible. Basically top management is betting the organization's future on how accurately the strategic marketing people view the future! The long lead times involved in this type of planning can exacerbate the inherent problems, however, especially if strong and effective relationships are not in place among strategic marketing, tactical marketing, and sales.

TACTICAL MARKETING

While marketing *strategists* are responsible for the definition of the product lines, the markets to be served, and the longer-term forecasts, marketing *tacticians* are responsible for converting those plans and forecasts into shippable product that satisfies the customers' needs and wants at a price and quality that are satisfactory to both the customers and the company.

The Role of Tactical Marketing

Broadly speaking, the primary role of tactical marketing is to refine the product lines that were defined initially by marketing strategists, develop specific products, and bring them to market in a cost-effective manner. This means tweaking product features to modify fit, form, and function and adjusting planned price, cost, and volume requirements to meet the needs and wants of the current and near-term markets. Tactical marketing may also be known as *product management* or *product line management*. It is a key function that requires continuous dialogue with sales and strategic marketing to be effective.

Major Responsibilities

Working within the categories of planned product lines and the capabilities of current and future technologies, marketing tacticians validate the needs and wants of the served markets and develop specific products for each of the served market segments defined. This check-and-balance function serves two purposes: it verifies or refutes the accuracy and foresight of the earlier efforts of marketing strategists, and it builds maximum flexibility into the organization's ability to respond to the changing needs and wants of the marketplace. This flexibility and shared responsibility also tends to minimize the chances of product marketing's becoming overly invested in a specific product design that may no longer be suitable.

Marketing tacticians build upon marketing strategists' earlier research to reaffirm or redefine the performance, price, and cost parameters for their products. This includes conducting any additional market and marketing research that may be required, as well as test marketing. Marketing tacticians also provide feedback to marketing strategists regarding their findings. Marketing strategists use this feedback to update their position on the next generation of product lines. This feedback is especially valuable for the timing and scope of product-line migration plans.

Another key responsibility of marketing tacticians is to define, for each product line, the prospective target accounts and projected product applications within each of the accounts. This involves understanding the business in which each prospective account is engaged and the markets they serve. Together with the sales organization, marketing tacticians also define the selling cycle for each product line and establish introductory and subsequent pricing needed to meet or exceed the planned volume, share-of-market, and profitability goals established by marketing strategists. Any differences between strategic and tactical marketing plans are reconciled before proceeding.

Marketing tacticians are also responsible for constructing the sales kit, providing new-product training to the sales force, and establishing the engagement strategy. The sales kit contains a summary of the needs and wants of the prospective accounts embedded in a series of slide or overhead presentations constructed with standard presentation software such as Microsoft PowerPoint or Lotus Freelance Graphics. The sales kit also contains product data sheets and sales support documentation that fits with how the prospective accounts structure their decision-making process. This includes a summary table of the features and benefits of your company's products compared with those of your major competitors.

When marketing tacticians use their knowledge of the products and of the target market and generate a short list of prospective accounts with suggested application ideas, the salespeople no longer have to prospect their territories to locate the most likely customers. Eliminating this prospecting task allows the field salesperson to increase face-to-face selling time by about 20 percent! Marketing tacticians also assume responsibility for the revenue forecast, but more on that later.

Relationship to Strategic Marketing and Sales

Tactical marketing has a direct relationship with strategic marketing and sales and an indirect relationship with the customers. Tactical marketing's relationships with the other two functions are pivotal. With marketing strategists, marketing tacticians exchange information about any refinements to previously planned products and provide feedback on planned versus actual penetration, acceptability of the pricing structure adopted, plan versus actual share of market attained, and updates on the activities of major competitors.

Tactical marketing's relationship with sales is more hands-on and involves product training, technical support, and assistance in engaging prospective accounts. Also, the primary marketing interface for salespeople is the tactical marketing group, which is an information source and their partner in the factory. It is the responsibility of marketing tacticians, not salespeople, to present the company's future products and product migration plans; we will explain why in Chapter 18. The salespeople "own" the accounts, so it is their responsibility to arrange and schedule meetings for these future-product presentations and to identify who is to attend from the customers' company, set the agenda, open and close the meetings, and follow up with the customers.

Scope

The scope of tactical marketing describes the level of product detail and the time period covered in planning and forecasting activities. Marketing tacticians plan and forecast product families and product lines. They are knowledgeable about and monitor specific product configurations but do not plan or forecast at the part-number level.

All planning and forecasting activities involve both units and dollars. When the forecast is generated in units, it can be used by operations managers for capacity planning. Marketing tacticians are also responsible for planning and forecasting their product lines' elasticity in each of their served markets, replacement markets, and saturation levels, and they should have a sense of what the competition might be expected to do in response to the company's actions.

Planning Level and Horizon

Tactical marketing's planning level involves product families and product lines. The planning horizon must be long enough to allow for the successful development of the products and their positioning in the marketplace and yet be short enough to maintain a focus on revenue and profit generation. Plans should accommodate at least two generations of the product to maintain continuity in the marketplace. For high-technology products such as microcomputers that have a life of six months or less, a planning horizon of two years is appropriate. This means that marketing tacticians are primarily responsible for revenue, capacity utilization, share of market, and profitability for two years in this case.

Using the example of microcomputers, marketing tacticians are interested in forecasting demand that is driven by their share-of-market assumptions rather than unit demand generated by the sales force. Tactical marketing must know the probable demand so that the factory can install adequate capacity. The tactical marketing forecast is at a high level of aggregation—for example, product line or product family—and is useful for capacity planning, revenue projections, and profitability forecasts. It is also extremely valuable in forecasting conversion from one product family to another.

Forecast Level and Horizon

Within the context of the relational model, marketing tacticians are responsible for the revenue forecast for their respective product families and product lines. The term *revenue forecast* is used rather than *sales forecast* to avoid confusion with a sales forecast generated by the sales organization. It saves a lot of time and eliminates a lot of confusion when there is only one revenue forecast and that forecast is generated by marketing tacticians, not the sales organization. (See Chapter 19 for a description of what the sales organization should forecast.)

The revenue forecast should be in units and dollars by product line by month, span a two-year horizon, and be updated quarterly. Some companies may publish the unit and dollar forecasts in separate reports. If you do this, label them prominently to prevent confusion. Think and work in units, and then bring the units and dollars together in the profit-and-loss statement or in a summary report.

Monthly, as actual revenue is reported, enter the actual data, and compute the monthly forecast accuracy. When the first quarter's actuals are in, compute the quarterly accuracy, and update the forecast. See Exhibit 16.1 for an example of a quarterly tactical marketing forecast. The horizon then becomes a two-year rolling forecast. This two-year detailed forecast by quarter or by month coupled with the strategic marketing group's five- and ten-year forecasts gives adequate time for capacity planning. The same format can be used for the monthly forecast.

Impact of Information

Of the three functions, the information generated by tactical marketing directly impacts the near-term health and vitality of your company. This information drives the construction of annual budgets, staffing levels, capacity planning, and capital equipment purchases. Tactical marketing defines near-term revenue and profitability.

If effective relationships are not in place between marketing tacticians and marketing strategists, then marketing tacticians may be surprised by the direction of the product lines and may find themselves playing catch-up as they seek to serve a market that won't wait. When effective relationships are in place, unexpected changes in the marketplace or aggressive acts by the competition are anticipated and dealt with accordingly. When effective relationships are in place between marketing tacticians and salespeople, there is a smooth exchange of product information, and marketing's identification of the various prospective accounts and the establishment of a strategy for engagement greatly facilitate the sales organization's development of the accounts.

SALES

We have described marketing's role as business analysis and planning. Sales builds on the work of marketing and calls on, qualifies, penetrates, and services the target accounts, both existing and new.

The Role of Sales

The salesperson is the primary contact with the customer. Rarely, if ever, should there be any contact with the customer that does not include the salesperson responsible for the account. The salesperson "owns" the account and is focused on the here and now. Based on the type of account and the engagement strategy adopted, the salesperson utilizes the sales kit and his or her knowledge and experience to qualify, develop, and service the target accounts. The primary role of sales is to sell *existing* products and services at a level of price, quality, and performance that is acceptable to customers.

Major Responsibilities

The initial responsibility of sales is to understand the strategies and tactics crafted by marketing for each of the prospective target accounts. This understanding makes the salesperson most effective and is fundamental to the relational model and the account development cycle. For example, when sales is dependent on marketing's identification of prospective target accounts, the salespeople gain about a 15 to 20 percent increase in face-to-face selling time because they are no longer required to prospect.

The salespeople are responsible for using the engagement strategy and sales kit to call on the target accounts and to begin or extend the account development process. The sales kit contains an account profile, data sheets, white papers, testimonials, and sales history if applicable. The salesperson knows who the key persons are, knows about the potential sales opportunities, and knows about possible competition before ever calling on the account.

With an account profile in place, account qualification shifts quickly to identifying or verifying the identity of the key decision makers in each of the potential sales opportunities. The salesperson is responsible for clarifying the needs and wants of the customers and matching those needs and wants to the features and benefits of the most appropriate products. The salesperson is also responsible for tracking each of the developing sales processes through its respective selling cycle. This becomes very important when the time comes to generate bookings or order forecasts. The salesperson is also responsible for improving or refining the selling cycle. For example, the salesperson may find through experience that additional steps in the selling cycle would result in increased success.

The sales organization is responsible for chairing and presenting a detailed review of all target accounts on at least a quarterly basis. This includes a brief statement of the business conditions at the account, the position of the supplier, some insight on the competition, and a detailed review of each of the sales opportunities. During the account reviews, the salespeople articulate their approach to develop, penetrate, and service the account.

Last, but not least, is the responsibility the sales organization has as a resource manager for tactical and strategic marketing. You should *never* ask salespeople to sell future products before they are developed and released for sale. The salesperson's role is to sell existing product at a price that is acceptable to the customer. For future products, the salesperson is to function as a resource manager and to arrange the necessary meetings for marketing tacticians (and marketing strategists if needed) with the customers to discuss the company's plans for the future. In addition to scheduling the meeting, the salesperson knows who is to attend and what sorts of questions they will have. The salesperson opens the meeting and reviews its purpose before turning the session over to the marketing people. The salesperson also closes the meeting and takes responsibility for any follow-up.

The reason the salesperson should not be responsible for presenting future product plans is that he or she has no control over when or if a planned product is to be introduced. When salespeople present future products, the customer holds them responsible if those products are late to market. When the salesperson functions instead as a resource manager and allows the marketing people to present the new-product plans, his or her credibility is not put at risk.

Relationship to Strategic and Tactical Marketing

Sales's relationships with strategic and tactical marketing are many, varied, and complex. As salespeople develop the target accounts, they are intimately involved with marketing tacticians and depend heavily on them for product training, prospective target-account identification, product availability, product positioning, sales kits, and engagement strategies. Salespeople build and maintain their relationships with marketing tacticians through dialogue. For example, salespeople communicate, via the target account reviews, their progress in developing the accounts and how well the engagement strategies and sales kits are working. Their relationships are highly complementary.

Marketing strategists should be present during the target account reviews to learn firsthand about the customers' current and projected needs and wants and how the company's product lines are or are not satisfying them. In these meetings, sales and marketing representatives may collectively decide that marketing strategists should visit a number of customers to learn more about them.

Scope

Salespeople work in the detailed here and now. The scope of their work involves specific part numbers and specific units and dollars for specific customers. Their world consists of countless phone calls, E-mail messages, voice mail messages, written notes, faxes, and documents.

Planning Level and Horizon

The planning horizon for sales consists of multiple time periods. The fiscal year is usually the longest time period and relates more to annual quotas and commissions than to specific target-account planning. Some companies pay sales commissions on a yearly as well as a quarterly basis. Within the account development model, it is appropriate to use the fiscal year as a longer-term planning horizon for developing and penetrating specific target accounts. By doing so, the salesperson can keep track of planned sales levels for each major target account.

The next planning horizon is quarterly. Typically the salesperson is asked to make a commitment to achieving a specific sales revenue for each of the fiscal quarters. With the product selling cycles being about a quarter in length, the better salespeople plan when they want their sales to close and work backward to identify the specific starting point for each opportunity.

Monthly planning is just a refinement to the quarterly planning horizon. Months are important but not as important as quarters. Once again, the more effective salespeople break down their quarterly goals into monthly goals and seek to track their own performance across the months.

Daily and weekly planning horizons are used in conjunction with the longer-term planning. Most of this planning involves making appointments and meeting face-to-face with current and prospective customers.

Forecast Level and Horizon

Many companies require their sales force to generate a detailed forecast each month in units and dollars by customer, product, and month, spanning a horizon of six months to three years. Using the relational model and the account development cycle, this is no longer required.

First, executives ask the marketing strategists and tacticians to generate, each month, a forecast of potential sales or billings. This removes the need for salespeople to generate a similar forecast. Instead, the salespeople forecast when they are planning to book the orders that they are tracking through their respective selling cycles. This bookings forecast is updated monthly. Operations and manufacturing planning managers then generate a response to the forecast, taking into consideration the backlog and important inventory information to produce a revenue forecast. In Chapter 17 we will expand this concept considerably, once again seeking to take advantage of the relational nature of marketing and sales.

Impact of Information

The information generated by the sales organization has the greatest impact on the present and the near term. The success of their account development activities tells the organization how well the customers are accepting the company's product lines. The order booking rate confirms or refutes marketing's forecasts and drives week-to-week manufacturing schedules, staffing, and procurement.

Marketing strategists are expected to take the lead in developing the long look ahead. The more specialized functions of market research, marketing research, and marketing communications are subordinate to the broader functions of strategic and tactical marketing.

As you anticipate developing strategic marketing forecasts, consider the following suggestions:

- Develop a solid data-based approach for your plans and projections.
- Place your plans in context by presenting recent history as a bridge to the future.
- Illustrate and explain how your marketing plan ties in or does not tie in with the major trends in the market.
- Briefly show how the research data were gathered and analyzed.
- List your assumptions, and describe how specific conclusions were reached.
- State the criteria for selecting your key customers and major accounts.
- Describe the broad application categories envisioned for each market segment.
- Discuss the impact of each major account.
- Identify your major competitors by market segment, and briefly describe their expected response to your plans and projections.
- Define the general pricing and cost strategies considered.
- Describe the size and growth rates for each segment, together with your share-of-market assumptions.
- Generate a revenue forecast (units and dollars) for each segment that supports your previous assumptions.
- Build a strong dialogue with tactical marketing throughout the entire process.

The following questions will be helpful in developing your tactical marketing forecasts:

- What are your product development assumptions?
- Is there sufficient capacity installed to support your revenue forecasts?
- What is the current status of your major competitors?
- Are your products performing as planned? What secondary development activities can be exploited?

- Are your product price and cost targets still valid?
- What is your share of market for each product line? How do they compare with the plan?
- Are selling cycles defined for each product line, and are they accurate?
- What is the feedback from the account reviews? Are the engagement strategies working? Are the sales kits working? Are you winning and penetrating the accounts as planned?
- What is the price elasticity for each product line?
- Are the product applications and sales opportunities developing as planned?

CLOSING THE LOOP

A total forecasting system makes use of and applies the knowledge and information generated by each of the marketing and sales functions discussed. It has been our experience that forecasting is least valued when applied in a strictly mechanical fashion or in an environment that suffers from a management and leadership vacuum. It is impossible to consistently generate point forecasts with zero error. The forecasting process must therefore reflect the boundary conditions of the company's zones of uncertainty. These zones of uncertainty include such areas as throughput time, schedule flexibility, capacity trade-offs, and mix limitations. The zones define the acceptable forecast accuracy and level of detail that can be accommodated within the response capabilities of the organization.

The task for the organization is then defining what forecast level and accuracy is "good enough": "good enough" in terms of identifying future demand in sufficient detail, accuracy, and lead time so that adequate capacity can be installed; "good enough" so that operations can plan for the production and shipment of existing and new products; "good enough" to support share-of-market goals; "good enough" to help achieve revenue and profitability goals; "good enough" so human resources can adequately source and hire the necessary people to carry out the business plan; and "good enough" to provide adequate warnings of impending economic turning points that could affect the company adversely.

PART II

Basic Tools

A Graphic Approach

PRItoTHEINTRODUCTION and rapid proliferation of the microcomputer, graphics were either constructed by layout artists or graphic designers within the company's art department or outsourced to advertising and marketing communications firms. Usually a great deal of time was required to sit down with the artist and describe what it was you were interested in graphing. If the content involved a complex mathematical function, then the math, or at least the concepts, had to be explained before the graph could be created. Graphs were very expensive and were usually limited to special presentations and glossy publications.

The introduction of the microcomputer changed all of that when the early DOS-based machines gave us the capability to create our own graphs directly from rows and columns of numbers arrayed in spreadsheets such as Lotus 1-2-3 and Excel. Although rudimentary by today's standards, this newfound capability was an incredible step forward for those of us who worked with numbers continually. Today we take this for granted as we use the now famous GUI (graphical user interface) to search for just the right chart type from what seems like an endless selection of two-dimensional, three-dimensional, and special-format graph and chart types. Recently, full-featured geographical mapping software has extended our capability of looking at large data sets across several variables. The next step is full-featured animation with sound. But for now, let's look at some of the key elements of data as cognitive art.

COGNITIVE ART

Perhaps the foremost contemporary expert in the field of data as cognitive art is Edward R. Tufte. Tufte teaches statistics, graphic design, and political economy at Yale University and has published three important books on the subject. First was *The Visual Display of Quantitative Information*; next was *Envisioning Information*; and most recently, *Visual Explanations*. In *The Visual Display of Quantitative Information*, Tufte establishes a powerful case for data graphics. Following is a quote from the introduction:

> *Data graphics visually display measured quantities by means of the combined use of points, lines, a coordinate system, numbers, symbols, words, shading, and color.*
>
> *The use of abstract, non-representational pictures to show numbers is a surprisingly recent invention, perhaps because of the diversity of skills required—the visual-artistic, empirical-statistical, and mathematical. It was not until 1750–1800 that statistical graphics—length and area to show quantity, time-series, scatterplots, and multivariate displays—were invented, long after such triumphs of mathematical ingenuity as logarithms, Cartesian coordinates, the calculus, and the basics of probability theory. . . .*
>
> *Modern data graphics can do much more than simply substitute for small statistical tables. At their best, graphics are instruments for reasoning about quantitative information. Often the most effective way to describe, explore, and summarize a set of numbers—even a very large set—is to look at pictures of those numbers. Furthermore, of all methods for analyzing and communicating statistical information, well-designed data graphics are usually the simplest and at the same time the most powerful. (Italics added.)*

Tufte's eloquent description of the role of statistical graphics once again calls our attention to the intersection of art and science. Carrying the discussion a bit further, Tufte lays out a set of guidelines for the use of statistical graphics in the display of complex data. He proposes that graphical displays should do the following:

- Show the data
- Induce the viewer to think about the substance rather than about methodology, graphic design, the technology, or something else
- Avoid distorting what the data have to say
- Present many numbers in a small space
- Make large data sets coherent
- Encourage the eye to compare different pieces of data
- Reveal the data at several levels of detail, from a broad overview to the fine structure

- Serve a reasonably clear purpose: description, exploration, tabulation, or decoration
- Be closely integrated with the statistical and verbal descriptions of the data set

Tufte's guidelines are especially relevant for the marketing and sales forecaster. All too frequently, discussions of forecasting, as well as specific forecasts, degenerate into intellectual discussions of the virtues of one forecasting method versus another, with the likely consequence that the overall view of forecasting as decision support is missed.

ENVISIONING INFORMATION

A major benefit of statistical graphics is that the data of interest can be envisioned in ways that contribute to their understanding and use. For example, forecasts are often presented in tabular form only. The usual approach is to use a spreadsheet program of some sort and arrange the months or quarters as column headings and the product lines or part types as rows. The numbers may be in units, although more often than not, they are in current dollars or thousands of current dollars. This presents a problem to people who were not involved in the creation of the forecast and who are not familiar with the numbers. Few people can look at a table of numbers and deduce a pattern. Most, on the other hand, can look at a graph or chart and agree on the pattern or patterns present.

Following Tufte, we have reproduced four data sets known as Anscombe's Quartet to illustrate how much additional information is provided when tabular data are also presented graphically. Exhibit 3.1 contains the tabular data. Note that the sample sizes, means, equations of the regression lines, correlation coefficients, and coefficients of determination are all equal! Now look at the graphic representation of each in Exhibit 3.2.

For complex data sets, it is often helpful to present the numerical set and the graphic. Both can be used quite effectively in conveying a rich amount of information.

Tufte also presents a set of guidelines that enhance the visual quality of data. He proposes that good design has two key elements: "Graphical elegance is often found in simplicity of design and complexity of data." Graphics that are visually attractive are well proportioned, are easy to read and understand, and help convey complex patterns and conclusions not apparent in the numerical data set only.

Series I	N = 11	Series II	N = 11	Series III	N = 11	Series IV	N = 11
X-Axis	Y-Axis	X-Axis	Y-Axis	X-Axis	Y-Axis	X-Axis	Y-Axis
10.0	8.04	10.0	9.14	10.0	7.46	8.0	6.58
8.0	6.95	8.0	8.14	8.0	6.77	8.0	5.76
13.0	7.58	13.0	8.74	13.0	12.74	8.0	7.71
9.0	8.81	9.0	8.77	9.0	7.11	8.0	8.84
11.0	8.33	11.0	9.26	11.0	7.81	8.0	8.47
14.0	9.96	14.0	8.10	14.0	8.84	8.0	7.04
6.0	7.24	6.0	6.13	6.0	6.07	8.0	5.25
4.0	4.26	4.0	3.10	4.0	5.39	19.0	12.50
12.0	10.84	12.0	9.13	12.0	8.15	8.0	5.56
7.0	4.82	7.0	7.26	7.0	6.42	8.0	7.91
5.0	5.68	5.0	4.74	5.0	5.73	8.0	6.89
$\bar{x}$ = 9.00	7.50	9.00	7.50	9.00	7.50	9.00	7.50

EXHIBIT 3.1 Anscombe's Quartet—tabular data

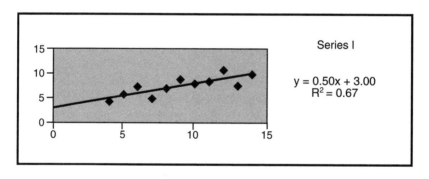

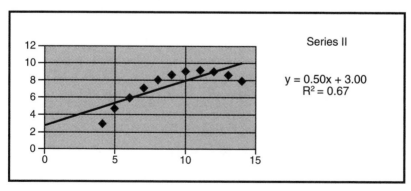

EXHIBIT 3.2 Graphs of Anscombe's Quartet (Series I and II)

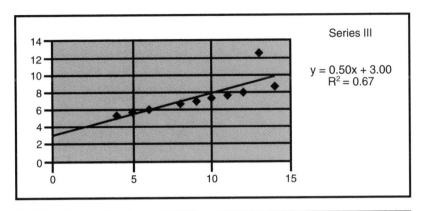

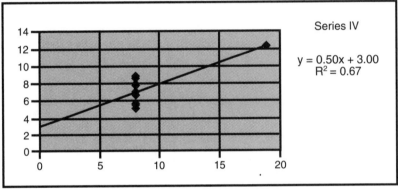

EXHIBIT 3.2 (continued) Graphs of Anscombe's Quartet (Series III and IV)

To enhance the visual quality of information, Tufte suggests the following:

- Choose a format and design that is suitable yet aesthetic.
- Combine words, numbers, and drawing.
- Reflect a balance or sense of relevant scale.
- Display a level of accessibility in the complexity of detail.
- Have the data tell a story.
- Use care in constructing the technical details of the graphic.
- Avoid unnecessary decoration, or "chartjunk."

A very good illustration of these guidelines is found in Exhibit 3.3, a graphic adapted from the January 2, 1979, issue of the *New York Times* and adapted from Tufte. The data are complex and meaningful, yet the design is simple.

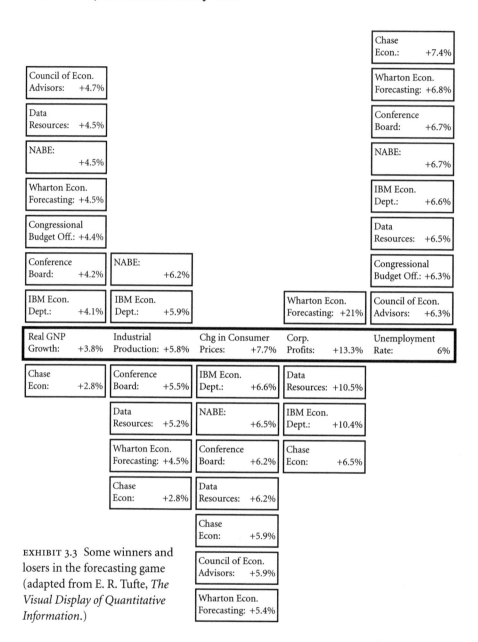

| Real GNP Growth: +3.8% | Industrial Production: +5.8% | Chg in Consumer Prices: +7.7% | Corp. Profits: +13.3% | Unemployment Rate: 6% |

EXHIBIT 3.3 Some winners and losers in the forecasting game (adapted from E. R. Tufte, *The Visual Display of Quantitative Information*.)

The center band in Exhibit 3.3 draws your eye to the critical economic variables presented together with the actual results. Following the accepted perceptual principle that items above a midpoint are perceived as higher and items below a midpoint are perceived as lower, the various forecasters and

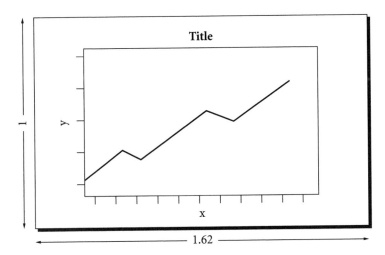

EXHIBIT 3.4 Preferred aspect ratio for charts

their forecast values are arrayed in ascending and descending order from the midpoint for each variable. This array identifies each forecast source and tells a story about the distribution of forecasts for each of the critical variables. The graphic is made more powerful by the combination of words, numbers, and spatial reference or distance from the "target."

One last item on envisioning information has to do with the scale and proportion of graphics. For western cultures, most text is read from left to right, so horizontal graphics are more familiar and perhaps more easily understood than other orientations. The horizontal format is also more compatible with labeling. It is easier to read labels that are consonant with how we read and with the format of the graphic. The continuous nature of time series lends itself to horizontal graphics, and the proportion of graphics most pleasing to the eye approximates the ratio of 1:1.62. That is, for each vertical unit of length of 1, the horizontal unit is 1.62. This gives a pleasing shape, as shown in Exhibit 3.4.

DISPLAYING COMPLEX RELATIONSHIPS

In a marketing and sales environment, displaying complex relationships may involve comparing TAM (total available market), SAM (served available market), and SOM (share of served market) for one or more product lines over a given time period, or it may involve comparing the levels of sales for several product lines within a given fiscal period. Charts intended to convey a sense of change over time are referred to as *time series,* and those intended to compare different parameters within a given time frame are called *period charts.*

Time Series

Time series are probably the most frequently presented graphic and are clearly the dominant format for forecasters. In *The Visual Display of Quantitative Information,* Tufte reports, "A random sample of 4,000 graphics drawn from 15 of the world's newspapers and magazines published from 1974 to 1980 found that more than 75 percent of all graphics published were time series." We believe that this trend not only will continue but will accelerate as society accelerates the shift to the more visually rich Internet and World Wide Web for most of its future information.

The format of time series graphics also contains an embedded story and is therefore easy to understand and remember. In conventional time series format, the vertical or y-axis is typically the dependent variable, and the horizontal or x-axis is the independent variable. Time is the independent variable, and units, dollars, or percent change the dependent variable. The time series chart may consist of either a continuous line or a series of columns. It is also common to see monthly economic data for a year presented in a column format. See Exhibits 3.5 and 3.6.

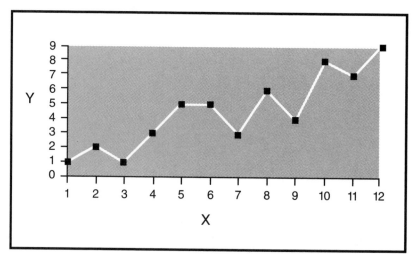

EXHIBIT 3.5 Monthly time series in line format

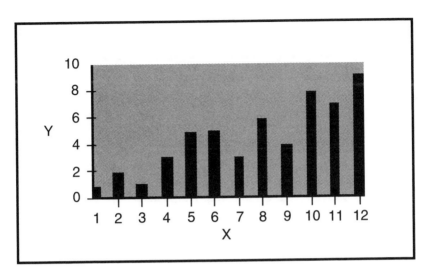

EXHIBIT 3.6 Monthly time series in column format

Time series can be displayed using arithmetic axes or scales, ratio divided scales, or indexed scales. The arithmetic scale has or implies a zero at its origin, and the level increases or decreases in a linear fashion. The same numerical distance is represented by the same interval distance on the axis (see Exhibit 3.7). The ratio scale (also known as a logarithmic scale), on the other

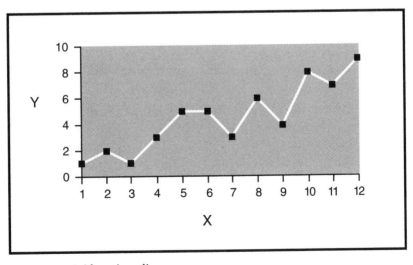

EXHIBIT 3.7 Arithmetic scaling

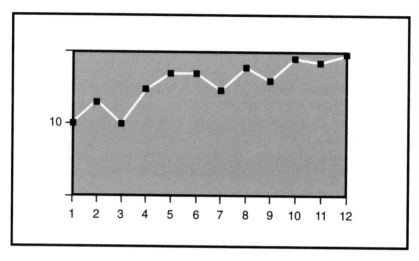

EXHIBIT 3.8 Logarithmic scaling

hand, does not have a zero and increases or decreases at a constant rate (see Exhibit 3.8). A chart with the y-axis as a ratio scale and the x-axis as an arithmetic scale is called a semilogarithmic, or semilog, chart. The third type of format, the index scale, is constructed as a ratio of two numbers and is useful when you are interested in presenting percent change charts, with a base equal to 100 at some time period, without resorting to logarithmic scales. One negative aspect of index charts is that the original numbers are lost during the indexing, so the result is a ratio, and original values are not displayed. A useful component of index scales is that the index number can be read directly as cumulative percent change from the baseline (see Exhibit 3.9).

In marketing and sales forecasting, the majority of charts are created in either a line format or a column format or some combination of the two. Charting guidelines indicate that a line format is to be used when the variable being displayed is of a continuous nature (e.g., stock prices) and a column format is to be used when the data are discrete (e.g., hourly stock trade volume). Occasionally marketing and sales will employ circle or pie charts to illustrate the percent distribution of customers' sales in a given territory or portion of a given market served by competitors, but circle charts are limited in their application.

A modification of circle charts that is useful is bubble charts. Bubble charts are used to convey relative size or importance. A typical example is a

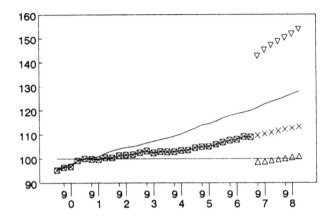

EXHIBIT 3.9 Indexed graph

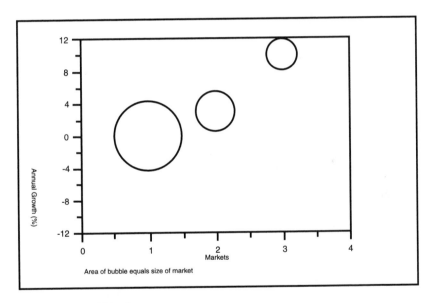

EXHIBIT 3.10 Bubble chart

bubble chart showing the relative share of market for your company and your competitors (see Exhibit 3.10). When you're displaying complex relationships using a bubble format, the critical measure is the area of the bubbles, not the diameters.

Period Charts

Period charts are useful when comparing sales revenue or share of market for a number of companies within a given fiscal period. The time period is finite, and the focus is on similarities and differences between the parameters plotted. Line formats as well as bar and column formats can be employed. Samples of bar and column charts are presented in Exhibits 3.11 and 3.12.

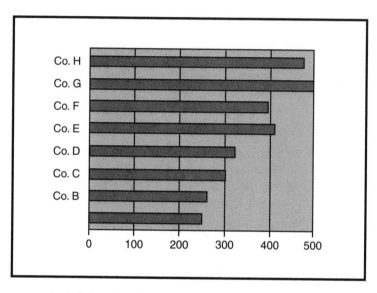

EXHIBIT 3.11 Period chart (rows)

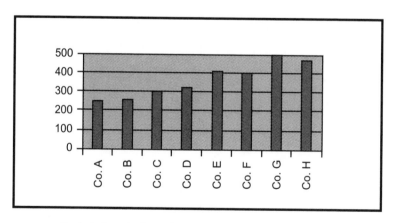

EXHIBIT 3.12 Period chart (columns)

CYCLES, TRENDS, AND TURNING POINTS

Cycles, trends, and turning points are endemic to marketing and sales forecasting. Cycles refer to the repeating but nonperiodic ebb and flow of change. For example, cycles can refer to broad business cycles in which economic ups and downs are marked by the official peak and trough dates, and cycles can also refer to the minor perturbations often encountered within the context of the broader business cycle. Regardless of the official designation of these cyclical changes, they often have consequences for the health or robustness of your firm's business, and analysis and understanding of these patterns will pay handsome dividends when included in the scope of marketing and sales forecasting.

Knowing the cyclicality of key economic variables and their relationship to the firm enables the forecaster to develop a number of possible scenarios to address the possible future course of events.

Trends display the course, direction, and rate of change underlying the broader cyclical patterns. Gradual as well as dramatic changes in cycles and trends are presaged by second-order changes, such as the change in the rate of change. These second-order factors are useful in signaling the onset of a turning point.

A turning point indicates a change in direction. This may be the reversal of an upward trend, the reversal of a downward trend, or an increase or decrease from a no-change trend. The idea behind monitoring rate of change is that the rate of change of a series will change before the level of the series changes. As we continue with Part II, we explore how effective marketing and sales forecasting encompasses the continual gathering, analyzing, and displaying of complex relationships involving economies, industries, companies, divisions, and product lines.

To illustrate the rich complexity of a graphic approach to cycles, trends, and turning points, Exhibit 3.13 reproduces a chart from the July 1996 issue of *Survey of Current Business*.

The chart, "Real GDP and Its Components: Trends and Cycles," is published monthly in the *Survey of Current Business* and illustrates many of the concepts presented in this chapter. Note the nearly thirty years of economic data for each of ten major economic variables that make up the U.S. economy. Each variable is labeled clearly, and the ratio scales provide for the immediate comparison of each variable's rate of change within the context of the whole. The shaded vertical bars signify recessions, with the official peak and trough dates referenced at the top of the chart.

As we examine Exhibit 3.13 more closely, we observe that each of the ten major variables has behaved somewhat differently over the course of history

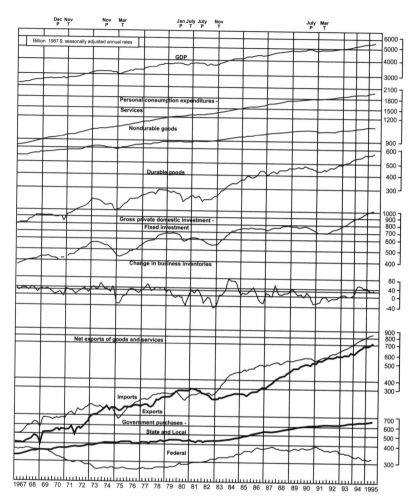

EXHIBIT 3.13 Real GDP and its components: trends and cycles

shown. In terms of cycles and trends, for example, services have been much
less reactive to recessions than have durable goods. The timing and ampli-
tude of changes in individual series can also be helpful in anticipating turning points in the general economy. Look at durable goods. Note that the
durable goods series turned down several quarters before the onset of each
of the prior five recessions. Does this mean that it will behave this way in the
future? No! Later we explore ways of linking your company's performance
to the economy and also how you can employ various economic indicators
to monitor changes in economic cycles, trends, and turning points.

4

Time Series

OUR DECISION TO DESCRIBE TIME SERIES first and not correlation and regression analysis may come as a surprise to many readers. Because we are interested in punctuating the relationship between time series and the Average Recession Recovery Model, we chose to cover correlation and regression as a support methodology in Chapter 8, "Linking Economic and Company Data," in the context of exploring relationships. Our primary focus is time series and, specifically, two special cases of time series, the Average Recession Recovery Model (ARRM) and the Average Experience Model (AEM).

Time series, most simply put, is the graphic display of chronological data. The data are sequential in nature and ordered along a uniform time scale measured in days, weeks, months, quarters, or years. Less frequently encountered, although equally valid, are time series involving units of time measured in milliseconds, seconds, minutes, or hours. Displaying data as it occurred sequentially in time can tell a story in terms of distant history, near history, and the present. Using the patterns shown in the historical data, we can project or forecast the *likely* future for the variable of interest. We use the term *likely* because we cannot forecast the future without error! A "good" forecast is one in which the error (forecast versus actual) falls within the response capabilities of the organization. Forecasts of this type involve the short term (usually less than a year), the near term (one to three years), and the long term (greater than three years).

From a marketing and sales perspective, the most interesting time series include monthly or quarterly series of various economic variables together with key company data such as orders received (bookings) and shipments made (billings). Additional time series may include the order and shipment performance of various product lines or share-of-market trends for each product line. We are also interested in the forecasts published by various market researchers regarding the total available market (TAM) and served available markets (SAM). These forecasts are often in the form of time series and usually employ annual data.

A General Model

The general model for time series treats the data series as a black box (see Exhibit 4.1), as there is no attempt to assign causality. This notion holds that there are certain patterns in the source data that may be apparent or hidden through some sort of *transformational process*. The general model further holds that these patterns can be detected and approximated mathematically and that these mathematical approximations can then be used to forecast future values of the variable or variables of interest. The presence or absence of certain types of patterns in the historical data is influenced by the assumptions made for each data series.

Assumptions

As was stated previously, the purpose of describing the past performance of a variable is to predict or approximate its future performance, using knowledge gained about its past. A word of caution, however: While we may be able to describe the past performance of a variable quite precisely, there is no guarantee that we can predict the future with equal precision. All forecasts are probabilistic statements about some future event, and as you might expect, there are different tools and techniques to use, depending on the assumptions.

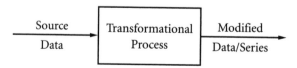

EXHIBIT 4.1 Time series general model

In some data series the degree of variability can be so regular and predictable that simply extending the series using the prior rate of change will yield the most accurate forecast. On the other hand, data series that are more variable and more irregular require additional mathematical operations and transformations before yielding an acceptable forecast. It is also important to note, as we shall see later, that increased sophistication of forecasting models does not equal increased forecast accuracy.

Following are a few assumptions that are critical to the use of time series:

- Units of the independent variable (time) are consistent throughout the series.
- Units of the dependent variable (e.g., unit sales) are consistent throughout the series.
- Data are ordered sequentially in time (chronological) and progress from the earliest observations to the most recent.
- The data series is continuous (no missing values).

Structure

The structure of a time series refers to the form and content of the data series. A data series can consist of irregular data; increasing or decreasing trends combined with irregular data; cyclical and irregular data; or increasing or decreasing cyclical trends combined with irregular data. Exhibit 4.2, an illustration from the American Institute for Economic Research, describes a number of different time series. As we shall see in the next section on time series models, various investigators have developed different approaches that are most suited to working with various time series structures.

The Measurement of Change

Forecasting is about the prediction of change. If there is no change, then there is no need to forecast. In other words, tomorrow's values will be the same as today's! But we all know that the world does change, so let's take a few minutes to review how change is measured.

The U.S. Census Bureau measures change as *the percent change from the preceding period*. For example, if February's unit sales were 1,315,000, and March sales were 1,446,000, there is an increase of 131,000 or plus 10 percent. Conversely, if March sales were 1,184,000 (lower than February), then there

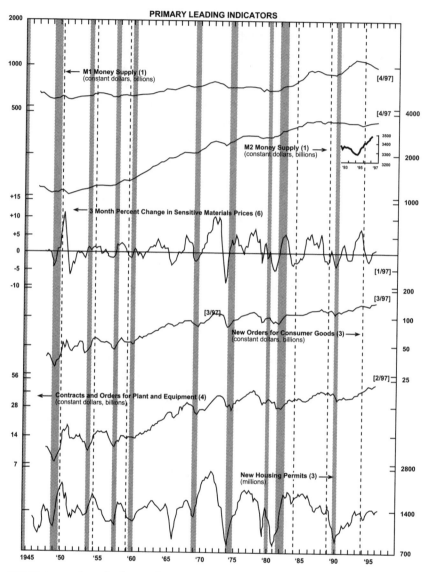

EXHIBIT 4.2 Sample time series

is a minus 10 percent change. But what if we are interested in the average change across the three months? Do we average plus 10 percent and minus 10 percent to arrive at zero percent change? No. We compute the average percent change without regard to sign:

With Regard to Sign	Without Regard to Sign
+ 10%	10%
− 10%	10%
0%	20%
0% ÷ 2 = 0 %	20% ÷ 2 = 10%

To get an average measure of change across a data series, we compute the percent change from the preceding period without regard to sign. The preceding example states that the average change is plus or minus 10 percent per month. A larger sample follows:

Month	Sales	% Change
Jan	9,002	
Feb	9,417	4.6
Mar	13,194	40.1
Apr	12,947	−1.9
May	12,806	−1.1
Jun	15,526	21.2
		68.9 ÷ 5 = 13.78% average change

Percent Change and Forecast Error

In Chapter 20 we explore the many different ways of monitoring forecast accuracy, but our current focus is on understanding the relationship between forecast accuracy and percent change in the underlying data series. The previous section discussed the importance of measuring percent change accurately, and perhaps the most effective way to introduce the relationship between percent change and forecast error is to point out two key concepts in forecast accuracy: one is to get the direction of change correct, and the second is to successfully predict as much of the change as possible.

There is a tendency to conclude that forecasts are good if the forecast error is less than plus or minus 5 percent and not so good if the error is greater than plus or minus 5 percent. Since forecast error, or conversely forecast accuracy, is very much related to the amount of change or fluctuation in the underlying series, then we should consider as more accurate the forecast that successfully predicts the greatest amount of change. To illustrate, assume that we have forecast error data on two forecasters:

	Average Forecast Error	Average Change in Data Series
Forecaster A	4%	1%
Forecaster B	8%	16%

At first blush, it would appear that forecaster A is twice as accurate as forecaster B. But when we consider the percent change in the underlying data series, we see that forecaster B successfully predicted one-half of the change while forecaster A missed the mark.

We will return to discussions of forecast accuracy and percent change successfully predicted in Part VI, "Monitoring Forecast Accuracy." Part of the skill in predicting change is understanding the different types of time series models and how each one seeks to capitalize on percent change in the data series.

MAJOR TIME SERIES MODELS

There are, of course, many different time series models. The purpose here is not to exhaustively review these models nor to argue for the superiority of one over another, but rather is simply to introduce you to the major time series models and discuss the context and structural applications to which they are most responsive. For additional detail on the various models, refer to the primary sources listed at the end of this chapter.

First, the naive models, which were alluded to in Chapter 1.

NAIVE MODELS

Naive models were employed initially as straw-man arguments or accuracy benchmarks in the comparison of one forecasting model versus another. McLaughlin (1984), commenting on the historical development of the naive models, draws on commentary from the famous economist Milton Friedman and suggests that any proposed model of economic change, to have value, must forecast with an accuracy greater than that of naive model 1:

> *The essential objective behind the derivation of econometric models is to construct an hypothesis of economic change; . . . given the existence of economic change, the crucial question is whether the theory implicit in the econometric model abstracts any of the essential forces*

responsible for the economic changes that actually occur. Is it better, that is, than a theory that says that there are no forces making for change? Now, naive model 1 . . . denies, as it were, the existence of any forces making for changes . . . If the econometric model does no better than this naive model, the implication is that it does not abstract any of the essential forces making for change; that it is of zero value as a theory explaining change.

While there is, potentially, an entire family of naive models, the principal models are naive forecast 1 (NF1) and naive forecast 2 (NF2). Other naive models usually consist of various combinations of the two. Conceptually the two naive models are illustrated in Exhibit 4.3.

NF1

Naive forecast 1, the earliest naive model, is simple in its intent and in its interpretation. It holds that the next period's *level* will be the same as that of the preceding period. In other words, it is a "*no change*" model! As my colleague Bob McLaughlin argued in his article, "Forecasting Models: Sophisticated or Naive?": "If our forecasting model cannot do better than NF1, it should be disqualified. NF1, then, becomes the benchmark of the worst permissible error. NF1 can be said to be the ultimate forecast error measurement."

Remember that the primary subject of forecasting is change. As forecasters, we want to focus on constructing models that help us forecast change

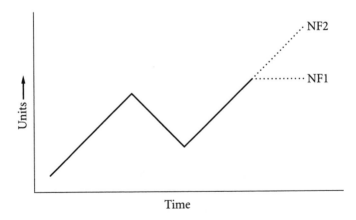

EXHIBIT 4.3 Naive Forecast 1 and Naive Forecast 2 (NF1 and NF2)

accurately. Here, NF1 plays a role. For example, consider the following situation. A company manufactures fuel tanks for large trucks, and we are asked to develop a forecast for the second quarter. The data are as follows:

Fuel Tanks: Second-Quarter Forecast

	Actual			Forecast		
	Jan	Feb	Mar	Apr	May	Jun
Raw data	9,500	10,000	10,500	9,000	11,000	12,000
Seasonal factors (%)	95.0	100.0	105.0	90.0	110.0	120.0
Seasonally adjusted volume	10,000	10,000	10,000	10,000	10,000	10,000

The raw data are the monthly sales volume (units) as reported by the finance and accounting department. The latest month for which we have data is March, and we are asked to generate a forecast for the next three months.

First, divide the raw monthly data by the seasonal factor to get the seasonally adjusted volume. When we compute each of the first three months of the first quarter, we note that the seasonally adjusted volume is flat. In other words, we have an NF1 application for the seasonally adjusted series.

To obtain forecasts for each of the next three months, we forecast a "no change" of 10,000 units per month and multiply each month's seasonally adjusted value by the seasonal factor to get the raw monthly data. The result is a forecast that contains substantial change, but all of the change is due to seasonal factors. Our NF1 forecast assumes "no change" in any of remaining factors of change such as trend, cycle, calendar, or irregular. Note that a graph of the raw data in this example (Exhibit 4.4) does not look like a "no change" model. Usually management sees only the raw data, so without knowledge of the underlying series and the seasonal factors, they would conclude that fuel tank demand was on an upward trend. Also, as we shall see later in this section, NF1 is a special case of Brown's Single Parameter exponential smoothing model.

NF2

While NF1 holds that tomorrow's *level* or *volume* will be the same as today's, NF2 holds that tomorrow's *change* will be the same as the change from yesterday to today. NF1 is a *no-change* model, while NF2 is a *change* model. Change can refer to the unit change from one period to the next or the percent change.

NF2 is useful when the *trend* or *cyclical* component of our data series is increasing or decreasing. If, in our fuel tank example, we were seeing a gradual increase in monthly unit demand through the first quarter, then we may want to employ an NF2-type forecast to the increasing series:

Fuel Tanks: Second-Quarter Forecast with Monthly Incremental Volume

	Actual			Forecast		
	Jan	Feb	Mar	Apr	May	Jun
Raw data	9,500	10,500	11,550	10,350	13,200	15,000
Seasonal factors (%)	95.0	100.0	105.0	90.0	110.0	120.0
Seasonally adjusted volume	10,000	10,500	11,000	11,500	12,000	12,500
Cyclical forecasts		500	1,000	1,500	2,000	2,500
Seasonally adjusted volume	10,000	10,000	10,000	10,000	10,000	10,000

What we have done is to simply extend the recent amount of change into the future. Following this simple arithmetic progression, we adjust the increased data series, using the same seasonal factors used previously. Remember, the seasonal factors did not change; only the cyclical component

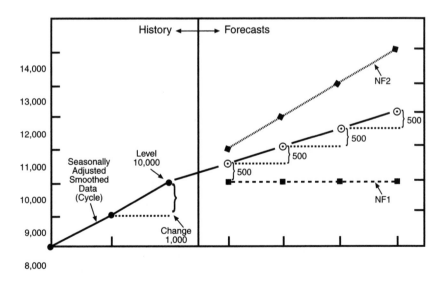

EXHIBIT 4.4 The concept of hedging (in the context of NF1 and NF2)

changed. As was the case in our first example, the raw data are the data that we would present to the management team.

If we were concerned about an upcoming turning point, we could also "hedge" our forecast by using a fraction of the recent change, rather than the full amount. For example, rather than increasing at a rate of 500 per month, we could forecast an increase of 250 per month and then monitor actual versus forecast to determine whether our forecast error was increasing, decreasing, or remaining constant. Exhibit 4.4 illustrates the concept of hedging graphically.

On the surface, NF1 and NF2 seem silly. But if we view them as tools rather than as literal forecasting models, the two naive models take on a whole new dimension.

MOVING AVERAGE MODELS

The basic function of all moving average models is to smooth the irregular components of a data series in such a way that the smoothed numbers can be used to construct a more meaningful forecast. Like other time series, moving average models assume that there is value in historical data patterns and that these patterns, when smoothed, become useful data in the creation of new forecasts. These models are called moving average models because the computed average "moves" as the series unfolds.

There are two moving average subclasses: simple and complex.

Simple Moving Average

A simple moving average consists of the mean or average of a certain number of periods in a data series, say three months. This approach typically assigns an equal weight to each of the periods being averaged. For example, if the values for January, February, and March are 90, 110, and 100, respectively, then the three-month moving average for the first three months is $90 + 110 + 100 = 300 \div 3 = 100$ (see Exhibits 4.5 and 4.6). The number 110 represents the equally weighted average of the first three months of actual data. Note that the three-month moving average is centered in the middle of the three-month period.

The second three-month average is the average of the second through the fourth months—February, March, and April—and its value is centered in the second three-month period. As we progress through the entire data

	A	B	C	D	E	F
Month	Actuals	Prior Month	Center Month	Month After	B + C + D	E ÷ 3
Jan	90					
Feb	110	90	110	100	300	100
Mar	100	110	100	120	330	110
Apr	120	100	120	110	330	110
May	110	120	110	115	345	115
Jun	115					

EXHIBIT 4.5 Three-month moving average

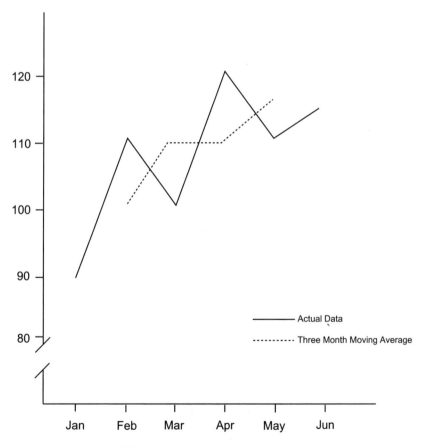

EXHIBIT 4.6 Graph of three-month moving average data

series, the three month-average "moves" as we drop the oldest month and add the newest month to the moving average calculations. A six-month data series and graph, as shown in the exhibits, illustrate how a three-month moving average is computed and presented.

The three-month moving average is often employed because it is easy to compute, the three months make centering decisions straightforward, three-month averages are reasonable approximations of current demand, and the three months provide an acceptable compromise to the "smoothness versus currency" issue. Smoothness versus currency relates to the loss of data points at the beginning and end of the smoothed data series. On the negative side, three-month moving averages lag an increasing or decreasing trend. In other words, the moving average understates the level of an increasing series and overstates the level of a decreasing series. Being aware of this, however, you can adjust your forecast using NF1 and NF2 as decision support tools.

For moving averages that use an odd number of periods—three or five—the placement or centering of the smoothed average is straightforward. What about an even number of periods? How is the moving average centered when the periods are four, six, or twelve? The same basic approach is used but with an additional calculation to adjust for the even number of periods. Assume, for example, that we are interested in a four-month moving average, and we wish to center it as we did with the three-month moving average. We compute the four-period moving average and enter the first average value opposite the fourth month, April. Then we calculate a two-period moving average of the moving average, and this is the value entered opposite March. The process is continued through the data series. The result is two months of missing data at the beginning and end of the series, and the moving average is adjusted for an even number of periods.

It is not uncommon to compute a twelve-month moving average when you are interested in controlling for seasonality. When you compute a twelve-month moving average and center the averages (remember to adjust for an even number of periods), then six months of data are lost at the beginning and at the end of the data series. The result is a very smooth average but one that is not very current. The answer to this dilemma is in classical decomposition, which we will cover in the next chapter. A reminder: Although some forecasters compute a moving average and use the noncentered moving average directly as a forecast, we do not recommend this practice. A noncentered moving average can grossly distort the timing by offsetting a key turning point by the number of periods used in the moving average.

Complex Moving Averages

Complex moving averages are a class of time series models in which moving averages of moving averages are computed. Perhaps the most frequently encountered example is referred to as a "three-by-three" (3×3), which is a *three-month moving average of a three-month moving average*. (See Exhibits 4.7 and 4.8.) The goal of complex moving averages is to increase the smoothness of the underlying data series, like simple moving averages, but without the great loss in current data points.

The decision whether to use a simple or complex moving average is influenced by the structure of the data series and the desired forecast error. Use long-period moving averages with highly irregular or random data series and short-period moving averages for less irregular data series. Moving average models are most appropriate when you are interested in developing greater insight into the underlying pattern for data series that do not have marked trends or seasonality. They can be helpful when used with *deseasonalized data series* that are relatively free from trend and cyclical components. The moving average is *not* the forecast. The moving average is a smoothed data series that minimizes the irregular components in the series so that it can be used as a *baseline from which to generate the forecast.*

EXPONENTIAL SMOOTHING MODELS

Exponential smoothing models were conceived when computer memory was in short supply. Weights are unequal and decay in an exponential fashion as we move from current to past periods. Compared with the moving average models, estimating the number of periods and the smoothing weights necessary for accurate forecasts is simpler and more straightforward with exponential models.

There are four broad classes of exponential models: single parameter, two parameter, three parameter, and adaptive filtering. Each of the models is most appropriate for time series displaying specific underlying structures.

Brown's Single Parameter

The single parameter model is the simplest of the four exponential models, as it employs a single weight or smoothing constant. The logic behind the model holds that the more recent observations in a data series are more representative of the near future than are the older observations in the same

| | | A | F | G |
	Month	Actuals	E/3	3 × 3
	Jan	90		
	Feb	110	100	
	Mar	100	110	103
	Apr	120	100	108
	May	110	115	
	Jun	115		

EXHIBIT 4.7 A 3 × 3 moving average

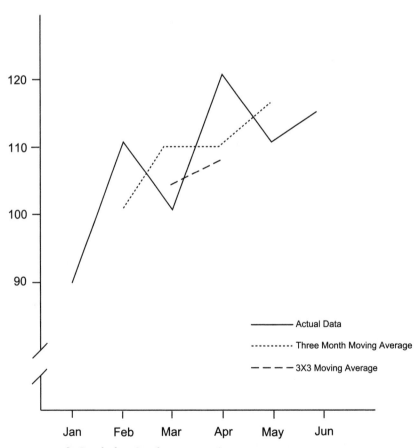

EXHIBIT 4.8 Graph showing the 3 × 3 moving average

series, so they should receive a greater emphasis in the forecast. The *forecast* for period *t* + *1*, is the product of the *actual data* for period *t*, times the smoothing constant, *a*, plus *1* − *a* times the *old forecast number*. Said in another way, the current forecast is equal to the old forecast plus a fraction of the error in the previous forecast. Arranged as a formula, we have:

Forecast = alpha (actual data) + (1 − alpha) (old forecast)

Note that when alpha equals zero, the exponentially smoothed forecast for the next period is the same as the forecast for the prior period. When alpha equals 1, the smoothed forecast is the same as NF1. The value assigned to alpha is key to the analysis. For example, use a high value for alpha when the random variation in the data series is low, and use a low value for alpha when the random variation or irregular component is high.

In their book *Forecasting Systems for Operations Management*, Stephen DeLurgio and Carl Bhame provided a means of approximating the relationship between the value of alpha, *a*, and the roughly comparable number of periods, *n*, in a moving average model. The simple equation is:

$$a = 2 \div (n + 1)$$

By inspection, you can see that a three-period moving average is roughly comparable to an alpha value of 0.5.

Unlike the moving average models, in which each of the data points in the smoothing period is weighted equally, all of the data points in the exponential model are weighted differentially; that is, the weights in the exponential model are unequal. They are the greatest for the most recent data and decrease in an exponential manner for older data. When alpha = 0.3, the weights for a forecast period moving from the most recent to the oldest forecast values, the weights are as follows:

Forecast Period	Weights per Period
Forecast Period = *t*	a = 0.300
Period = *t* − 1	a(1 − a) = 0.210
Period = *t* − 2	a(1 − a)(1 − a) = 0.147
Period = *t* − 3	a(1 − a)(1 − a)(1 − a) = 0.103

Notice how each period is weighted in a decreasing manner as we progress through the forecast. Like the moving average models, the single parameter exponential model lags an increasing or decreasing series. For example, a low alpha level yields a smooth series, but the level of the smoothed series is depressed from the level of the actual data.

Exhibit 4.9 uses a series drawn from DeLurgio and Bhame to illustrate how three different alpha levels differ from the shape and level of the underlying data series. Note when alpha = 0.1, the series is very smooth, but it is also not responsive to incremental increases in new data; it is slow to respond to a sharp increase. An alpha = 0.9, on the other hand, is quick to respond to a sharp increase, but it is less smooth. Note also that the timing of the data is altered as well. The exponentially smoothed values are offset in time. Like the moving average models, the single parameter exponential smoothing models are best suited for data series that consist largely of irregular components and display no prominent trend or seasonality.

To use exponential smoothing models that adjust for trend, we turn to Holt's model.

Holt's Two Parameter

Previously we saw that moving averages or exponentially smoothed averages will always lag behind an increasing or decreasing trend. Therefore, to include the trend values in our forecast, the trend must be estimated and the series adjusted accordingly. Holt's Two Parameter model provides a convenient way to do this.

There are three equations used in Holt's model. The first equation is similar to Brown's equation, with a term added for trend:

Forecast = alpha (actual data) + (1 – alpha)(old forecast + trend)

The trend estimate is the difference between two successive exponentially smoothed forecast values. Since the successive values have been smoothed for irregularity, their difference is an estimate of the trend:

Trend = (forecast for period t) – (forecast for period $t – 1$)

or

Trend = forecast (t) – forecast $(t – 1)$

A second parameter, *beta*, is used to smooth the trend estimate in the same manner that *alpha* is used to smooth the actual data. The second equation is used to update the trend estimate. The equation states that the estimate of the trend, *forecast (t) – forecast (t – 1)*, is multiplied by *beta* and added to the old estimate of the trend, *(t – 1)*, multiplied by *(1 – beta)*. The equation appears as follows:

Update Trend = beta [forecast (t) – forecast $(t – 1)$] + [$(1 – beta)(t – 1)$]

The final equation is used to calculate the new forecast value that is adjusted for trend. The equation states that the *trend adjusted forecast, F,*

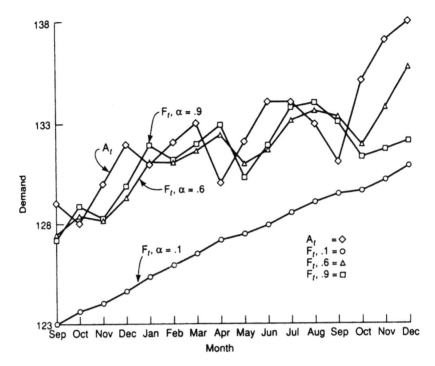

EXHIBIT 4.9 Comparison of alpha weights (reprinted from DeLurgio and Bhame)

equals *forecast* (*t*) plus the *trend estimate, T,* at *forecast period, p.* The equation appears as follows:

$$F = f(t) + Tp$$

Holt's Two Parameter model permits the forecaster to smooth both level and trend with separate smoothing parameters, alpha and beta. See Exhibit 4.10. Holt's model is appropriate for data series with increasing and decreasing trends.

Neither Brown's Single-Parameter nor Holt's Two-Parameter model is appropriate for data series containing seasonal components. For this, we turn to Winters's model.

Winters's Three-Parameter Model

Winters's linear and seasonal exponential smoothing model extends Holt's model and is used with data series that exhibit trend *and* seasonal patterns. See Exhibit 4.11. The model consists of four equations, one additional equation

Holt's Two-Parameter Exponential Smoothing

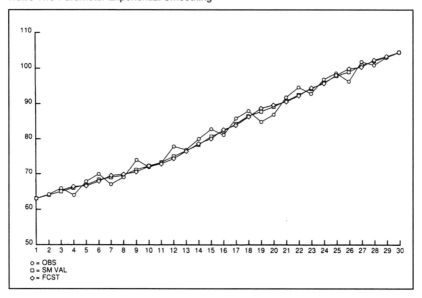

EXHIBIT 4.10 The effect of added beta weights for trend (reprinted from DeLurgio and Bhame)

Winters's Three-Parameter Exponential Smoothing

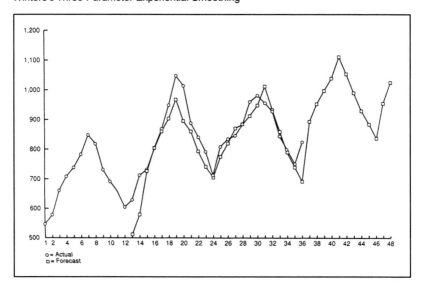

EXHIBIT 4.11 Data series with trend and seasonal patterns (reprinted from DeLurgio and Bhame)

to estimate the seasonality. The first equation is similar to Holt's first equation, except the smoothed data are divided by a smoothed seasonal index, thus removing the seasonal component in the original data series.

$$\text{Forecast} = \text{alpha}\ \frac{\text{(actual data)}}{\text{seasonal index}} + (1 - \text{alpha})(\text{old forecast} + \text{trend})$$

The seasonality estimate appears as follows:

$$\text{Seasonality} = \frac{\text{actual data in period}}{\text{exponentially smoothed data in same period}}$$

Once the seasonality index is computed, the seasonality is updated with the following equation:

$$\text{Update Seasonality} = \text{beta}\ \frac{\text{(actual data)}}{\text{smoothed data}} + (1 - \text{beta})(\text{prior period's seasonality index})$$

Finally, the last equation is used to calculate the new forecast value that is adjusted for trend and seasonality. The equation states that the *trend and seasonal adjusted forecast*, *F*, equals *forecast* (*t*), plus the *trend estimate*, *T*, at *forecast period*, *p*, multiplied by the seasonality estimate, *S*, at *period, p*. The equation appears as follows:

$$F = [f(t) + Tp]\ S(t)$$

As you can see from this brief overview, the various exponential smoothing models have been created to address the different patterns and structure of the underlying data series. We saw how Brown's Single Parameter model is useful in smoothing data series in which there is neither trend nor seasonality. Holt's Two-Parameter model was presented for use with data series that contain a trend but not seasonal components. Finally, Winters's Three Parameter model was discussed as an exponential smoothing model that adjusts for trend and seasonality.

Before completing this chapter with a discussion of the Box-Jenkins ARIMA model, a brief comment on adaptive models is appropriate.

Roberts-Reed Adaptive Response Model

The prior moving average and exponential smoothing models have treated the various smoothing parameters as constants. Adaptive response models (of which there are many) are a special case of exponential models and are often referred to as Adaptive Response Rate Exponential Smoothing (ARRES) models. This class of smoothing models seeks to reduce forecast errors by automatically changing or adjusting the weighting constants used to forecast the time series. The reasoning is: if the forecast error in a continuously monitored data series is increasing, then it is appropriate to adjust the weighting factors to reduce forecast error. This approach adapts, or "learns from," the error rate and adjusts the weighting constants accordingly.

The many different models refer to the many different approaches to adaptive response rate smoothing. Some models use a *tracking signal*, which is itself a ratio of exponentially smoothed error terms, to adjust the series forecast. Tracking signals are a subclass of forecast error monitoring tools which we will cover in more detail in Chapter 20.

Another model, pioneered by Chow and extended by Roberts and Reed, is more of an evolutionary approach. This approach requires that three forecasts be generated for each period. One forecast is based on the alpha weights referred to in the exponential smoothing models discussed previously. However, two additional forecasts are generated by using the primary alpha weight plus 0.05 and minus 0.05. For each period, the forecast error is calculated. If the forecast error using the primary alpha weight is less than the error of either alternate weight, then the alpha weight is left unchanged. On the other hand, if the error is greater than one of the alternates, the primary weight is adjusted to the appropriate alternate value for the next period's forecast. New alternate weights are used in the next period's calculations.

On the surface, adaptive response models would appear to yield more accurate forecasts, as the error rates are monitored continuously and adjusted accordingly. The results are mixed, however. It appears that the adaptive models suffer from the same malady as the conventional smoothing models, and that is lag. Another factor that comes into play with highly irregular series is oscillation.

Box-Jenkins ARIMA Model

The final model we present is the Box-Jenkins Autoregressive Integrated Moving Average (ARIMA) model. This model is different from the prior models presented, and while it is arguably the most flexible, it is also the most complex and most difficult to apply. It is popular among academicians and requires substantial statistical knowledge and experience to understand and use. Since the emphasis of this text is on practical forecasting techniques for marketing and sales, we will limit details to a description of the model and its underlying assumptions. As a practical matter, computers and ARIMA software are required to use this model.

Experience shows that most statistical concepts are better understood when people first understand the vocabulary used to describe the processes. ARIMA models combine three processes: *autoregression* (AR), differencing for the *integration* (I) of the series, and *moving averages* (MA), and are a special case of linear filter models. Linear filter models define a class of processes that either transform "white noise" (a spectrum in which all frequencies are present) into a time series or, conversely, transform a time series into white noise. These processes make the assumption that successive data points in a series are acted upon by random factors and that these random factors influence the level of the series. It is these random factors that are described by the ARIMA models. The notation used to describe the three ARIMA processes is AR(p), I(d), and MA(q), where p is the order of regression, d is the differencing, and q is the order of the moving average employed. The formal ARIMA notation is ARIMA(p,d,q). Let's look at each of the three processes separately before considering applications.

Autoregression

The autoregression process assumes that each data point in a series is a linear function of the preceding point or points. Autoregression involving only a single preceding value is called a first-order process, and autoregression involving two preceding points is called a second-order process. The notation for strictly the autoregressive process is AR*(1)* and AR*(2)*, respectively. The complete ARIMA notation for a first-order autoregression and no differencing or moving average is ARIMA*(1,0,0)*.

Integration

Most time series increase or decrease over time as cumulative factors contribute to changes in the series. A series that measures the cumulative effect is an integrated series. That is, the long-term trend in a series is more stable than the short-term changes or perturbations. The degree of integration can be approximated through the process of differencing. When a data series deviates from its trend, the deviations are usually small; thus, the difference observed from one data point to the other is usually small. These small differences relate favorably to the stationarity of the series. Stationary data series are constructed through the process of differencing and are essential to the application of ARIMA models. The notation is I*(1)* for integration involving a single difference and I*(2)* for differences of differences. The formal ARIMA notation for single-difference integration is ARIMA*(0,1,0)*.

Moving Average

The last of the three processes is similar to the exponential smoothing models presented previously, but with a key distinction. Each smoothing value in the prior models is a *weighted average of the most recent data points* in the series. Moving averages in the ARIMA model, on the other hand, are *weighted averages of the most recent disturbances* in the series. In the exponential smoothing models, the weighting process decays over time. In the ARIMA model, the moving average influences the data series for a finite number of periods equal to the order of the moving average process. The order specifies the number of previous disturbances that are averaged into the new value. Once again, the notation for a single-order moving average is MA*(1)*. The formal ARIMA notation is ARIMA*(0,0,1)*.

Using the Model

ARIMA applications are constructed using a model-building approach that encompasses three major steps: identification, estimation, and diagnosis. It is a largely a trial-and-error process that begins with the identification of the three processes, *p*, *d*, and *q*, that are contained within the data series. The estimation step involves the iterative calculations required for the various coefficients. The last step involves checking for acceptable error rates and, if the error rates are excessive, redoing the model.

Box and Jenkins combined autoregressive, differencing, and moving average operations to propose a class of models defined as autoregressive integrated moving average models. The methodology makes no assumption about the pattern on the underlying data series. It uses an iterative approach to identify a potentially satisfactory model based on the shape and distribution of the autocorrelations and how well they fit the theoretical models. The methodology is appropriate for short-term forecasting of virtually any series. Some disadvantages are: a large number of data points are required (36 to 72, depending on the investigator); the methodology requires substantial statistical knowledge, experience, and time; the parameters are difficult to identify; and finally, the methodology is simply not cost effective for a large number of series.

WHICH METHOD IS THE BEST?

The simple answer to the question of which is best is, *none of them*, and the more complex answer is, *it depends!* The conventional wisdom and experience is that there is no "one best" time series model or methodology suitable for all applications. Spyros Makridakis and his colleagues, in their book *The Fore-casting Accuracy of Major Time Series Methods*, place the issue in perspective:

> *It is important to understand that there is no such thing as the best approach or method as there is no such thing as the best car or the best hi-fi system. Cars or hi-fis differ among themselves and are bought by people who have different needs and budgets. What is important, therefore, is not to look for "winners" or "losers," but rather to understand how various forecasting approaches and methods differ from each other and how information can be provided so that forecasting users can be able to make rational choices for their situation.*
>
> *In forecasting, accuracy is a major, although not the only factor that has been dealt with in the forecasting literature by empirical or experimental studies. Summaries of the results of published empirical studies dealing with accuracy can be found in Armstrong (1978), Makridakis and Hibon (1979), and Slovic (1972). The general conclusions from these papers are: (a) Judgmental approaches are not necessarily more accurate than objective methods; (b) Causal or explanatory methods are not necessarily more accurate than extrapolative methods; and (c) More complex or statistically sophisticated methods are not necessarily more accurate than simpler methods. (p. 104)*

Perhaps the most extensive empirical study ever undertaken was the forecasting competition conducted by Makridakis and his colleagues, which later became known as "the Big Mak." The competition included the following features:

1. Time series were drawn from 1,001 different data series.
2. Several different forecasting methods were compared.
3. Experts in each methodology analyzed and forecasted the time series.
4. Various data series were employed, such as macro, micro, industry, and demographic data, at monthly, quarterly, and yearly time intervals (see Exhibit 4.12).
5. The forecast horizon was eighteen periods for monthly data, eight for quarterly data, and six for yearly data.
6. Initial values were generated by "back-casting."

Extensive accuracy measures were computed; the conclusions are summarized here:

1. For shorter forecasting horizons (one period and two periods ahead) deseasonalized Brown, Holt, and Holt-Winters exponential smoothing models did well. For horizons three, four, five, and six deseasonalized Brown, Holt, Holt-Winters, and Parzen performed best. For seven through eighteen periods ahead, Lewandowski did the best.
2. Composite Method A, an average of six methods, performed very well overall and better than the individual methods included in the average.
3. Composite Method B, a weighted average of the methods combined in A, also did well, but not as well as Composite A.
4. Combining the predictions of several different methods can reduce forecasting errors.

| | | Realization Percentage vs. | |
	Average MAPE	NF1	NF1(D)
NF1	20.0	0	
NF1D	13.7	31	0
*D ARR Exp	12.3	38	10
*D Sing Exp	12.6	37	8
*D Holt Exp	14.8	26	x
D Brown Exp	16.0	20	x
*D Mov Avg	16.6	17	x
D Regression	18.1	9	x
D Quad Exp	20.4	x	x
Bayesian	12.6	37	8
Parzen	12.6	37	8
Box-Jenkins	13.8	31	x
*Auto AEP	14.2	29	x
*Winters	14.6	27	x
Lewandowski	14.9	25	x
Composite B*	13.0	35	5
Composite A*	13.1	34	4

Notes:
D = Deseasonalized
* = Six Models for Composites A and B
x = Model performed worse that NF1

EXHIBIT 4.12 Summary table of forecast errors in Big Mak competition (adapted from R. L. McLaughlin, "Forecasting Models: Sophisticated or Naive?")

One of the measures conspicuous by its absence in the Big Mak competition is the percentage or proportion of change successfully predicted in each of the data series forecast. McLaughlin wrote a short follow-up article to address this fact and included a striking table illustrating the importance of the naive model, NF1.

Remember that NF1 is a no-change forecast. When NF1 is used as a forecasting model, the actual change in the data series is also the error. So, if NF1 produces an average error of 10 percent, and our error using a different forecasting model averages 8 percent, the non-NF1 model forecast 20 percent of the total change.

Exhibit 4.12 illustrates three measures of forecast error for a sample of the forecasting models used in the Big Mak competition. The various models are listed in the first column. The second column is the average *mean absolute percent error* (MAPE) for each of the models and becomes the base for computing the percentage of total change successfully predicted. The third column illustrates the percent of change successfully predicted. The fourth column represents the percentage of change successfully predicted after seasonal change has been removed. The conclusion is that the models did well against NF1 only by forecasting seasonality. Once the seasonality was removed, most of the models did worse than NF1!

Understanding seasonality is the topic of the next chapter.

5

Seasonal Adjustment

FUNDAMENTAL TO ACCURATE FORECASTING, yet often overlooked or ignored, is the concept of seasonal adjustment. Seasonal adjustment is a process in which the underlying month-to-month or quarter-to-quarter swings in the raw data of a time series are removed statistically. For many forecasters, seasonally adjusting a data series is a complex and daunting task because seasonality includes many factors that are often hidden in the series. These are the hidden patterns we must coax from the data before we can produce valid and reliable forecasts.

WHY SEASONALLY ADJUST?

Why worry about seasonal factors? Won't smoothing the raw data balance out the sharp peaks and valleys? Yes, smoothing will do that, but as we saw in the previous chapter, smoothing lags increasing or decreasing trends and can distort important timing patterns. Smoothing, whether by moving averages or by one of the exponential models, is not sufficient for our purposes. We want to understand more about the patterns in the underlying data series. Once again, it is the hidden patterns that we want to detect, understand, and then apply in our forecasting efforts. For example, with seasonally adjusted data, month-to-month or quarter-to-quarter increases or decreases in a data series can be interpreted in the context of prevailing economic conditions.

Without seasonally adjusted data, we can't know whether an increase in a data series is reflecting an underlying increase in economic conditions or whether it is just due to some seasonal factor. The same logic holds for a decreasing series.

Seasonal factors refer to shifts in month-to-month or quarter-to-quarter intrayear patterns. In the broader context, they also refer to the entire range of seasonal factors, such as long-term trend, cycle, seasonal, calendar, and irregular components contained in a data series. This broader view of seasonal adjustment better fits our interests and is a precursor to really understanding the patterns in the data series. Once they are understood, we can employ these patterns in the development of accurate and reliable forecasts. Before proceeding, however, you should understand the concept of centering.

THE CONCEPT OF CENTERING

When you're graphing a moving average, each point should be plotted in the middle of the periods being averaged. For example, the average for January, February, and March would be located, or *centered*, in the middle of the three-month span: February. Note that when you do this, data points are lost at the beginning and the end of the series.

Why center averages? We center averages because we want the smoothed data to represent accurately the timing of pattern changes in the data. If the averages are not centered, the smoothed average is offset, in time, with respect to the pattern in the underlying series. The steeper the change in a data series, either up or down, the greater the pattern shift between the uncentered smoothed average and the underlying data series. Exhibit 5.1 is an example of a time series that has been smoothed by a twelve-month moving average. Both uncentered and centered averages are shown. Note that in the uncentered averages, the smoothed average is *current*—that is, up-to-date—but it is offset with regard to the cyclical pattern, or peaks and troughs, in the data series.

In the centered average, on the other hand, the pattern of the smoothed series reflects the pattern in the underlying series, but there are missing data points at the beginning and end of the series. This "missing data points" issue is particularly troublesome when the number of months used in the moving average is large. The preferred solution to the issue of smoothness-versus-currency is to first seasonally adjust your data series and then, if you must smooth the data, use a shorter moving average. With this approach, fewer data points are lost at the beginning and end of the data series.

Centered

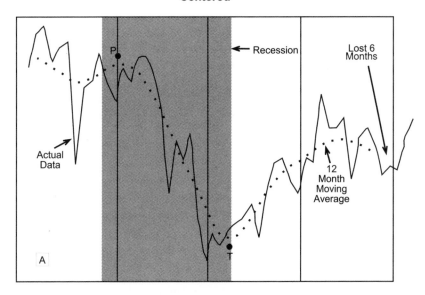

Uncentered

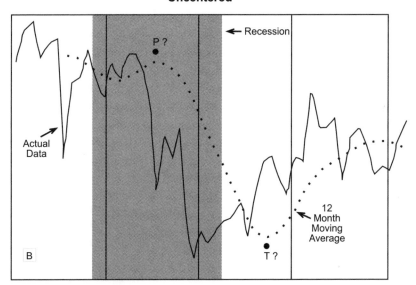

EXHIBIT 5.1 Comparison of twelve-month moving average graphs illustrating centered and noncentered series

FIVE FACTORS OF CHANGE

The large number of factors that influence any given time series, from one
period to the next, makes it impossible to account for each and every one of
them. What is helpful, in such cases, is to adopt the discipline that seeks to
subdivide the primary factors believed to account for change into five basic
categories: *trend*, *cycle*, *seasonal*, *calendar*, and *irregular*. These five factors of
change, each of which accounts for a different element of change, are useful
in understanding the dynamics of time series.

Trend (T)

The first factor is the long-term secular trend in a series that is attributable
to such forces as growth or decline in population, industrialization, productivity, and major shifts in technology. Most macroeconomic series in the
United States exhibit a strong upward trend, although there are exceptions.
For example, manufacturing employment has been declining, while the number of service workers has been increasing. These two examples serve to illustrate the consequences of the broader trend defined as the shift from an
industry-dominated society to a service and information society. The period
of time considered by the trend factor is defined as a period longer than one
business cycle: in other words, change that goes beyond the monthly or quarterly change normally encountered in short-term forecasting. An example
of a long-term trend is the increase in total number of people in the civilian
workforce. The greater the population, the greater the number of people in
the workforce.

Cycle (C)

As the longer-term trend is either increasing or decreasing, the cycle, or cyclical factor, moves above and below the trend line in a wavelike manner. This
cyclicality is related to changes in the business cycle, but various time series
may behave in concert with the general business cycle or opposite to it. In the
U.S. economy, millions of people make millions of economic decisions daily.
This creates an ebb and flow to the economic transactions when they're viewed
in the aggregate. Cycles tend to recur, but not at any specific frequency. We
know that cycles occur, but we do not know, in advance, when one will end
and the next will begin. In other words, they are recurrent but not periodic.
As an example, consider how the average length of the workweek varies, or
cycles, above and below forty hours. In economic recoveries, the workweek

cycles above forty hours as companies work overtime to keep up with demand. As the recovery peaks and eventually turns into recession, the average length of the workweek drops below forty hours as companies cut workers' hours rather than subject them to layoff. Later we will explore more the dynamics of the business cycle and how we can monitor changes in it.

Seasonal (S)

A third factor accounting for month-to-month or quarter-to-quarter change in a time series is the seasonal factor. Unlike cyclicality, seasonality is both *recurrent* and *periodic*. This means that seasonal factors are fairly predictable from one year to the next. However, there are occasions when the seasonal factors change; this situation is known as *moving seasonality*. A major contributor to seasonality is the weather. For example, in the fall and winter, sales of jackets and coats increase relative to the level of sales during the summer months. Special holidays also influence seasonal factors. The Christmas season, for instance, is another time of the year when sales surge to levels much greater than at other times. Seasonal factors would also be defined in repetitive calendar variations such as the greater number of shopping days in March (31) versus February (28). Leap-year differences in February would be picked up as calendar factors, however, because leap year is not an annual event.

Calendar (H)

A very big day for retailers of all sorts is Easter. Sometimes Easter falls in March, and sometimes it falls in April. Another example of a calendar factor is the number of Saturdays in a month. Once again, Saturdays are big sales days for many retailers; whether there are four or five Saturdays in a month makes a difference of 25 percent! A third example is a company that rotates its vacation shutdown from year to year. These different shutdown periods would be treated as calendar factors.

Irregular (I)

The final factor covers the residuals or random shocks that cannot be classified into one or more of the prior factors. These are also referred to as irregular factors. For retail merchants an irregular factor could be the unexpected break in a water main in front of a store, or the city's deciding to paint the curbs, or any number of other seemingly random events.

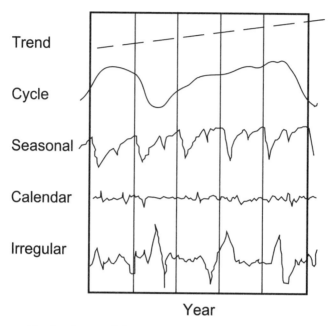

EXHIBIT 5.2 The five factors of change in graphic form

Exhibit 5.2 illustrates the five factors of change in graphic form.
Seasonal adjustment through classical decomposition is the process of identifying the five factors of change. Once the factors are identified, we can use them to create more accurate and more reliable forecasts.

CENSUS METHOD I

The adjustment of time series for seasonal variations uses a ratio-to-moving-average approach. This early approach, called Census Method I, was computed manually. In the context of the ratio-to-moving-average approach, it is assumed that there are really only three factors of change: the *trend-cycle*, *seasonal-calendar* effects, and all of the other factors of change lumped together in a factor called *irregular*. In Census Method I, the adjusted factors of a time series are estimated by computing a twelve-month moving average of the original data. This twelve-month moving average represents the *trend-cycle* factor. These estimates are then divided into the original data to create an adjusted series that reflects the *seasonal and irregular* components. The average of these ratios for a given month generates a *seasonal fac-*

tor for that month. The seasonally adjusted series is created by dividing the original data by the seasonal factors. An example of this early manual approach is provided in Exhibit 5.3. The steps in the calculations follow:

A. Raw Data. Get the last five years of raw data, and enter them in Section A. Missing data must be estimated.

B. Twelve-Month Moving Total (Uncentered). Add up the first twelve figures in Section A, and enter the total in the first box in the first row of Section B. Next, drop January from this total, and add in the

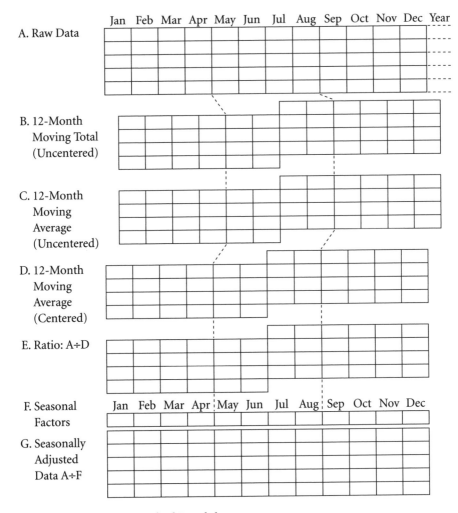

EXHIBIT 5.3 Census Method I worksheet

second January. This number is entered in the second box in Section B. Continue this routine until all boxes in Section B are filled.

C. Twelve-Month Moving Average (Uncentered). Divide each figure in Table B by 12. The answers are entered in Table C.

D. Twelve-Month Moving Average (Centered). Recall from our prior discussions that an even-numbered moving average requires some additional calculations to center. We simply compute a two-month moving average of the numbers in Table C and enter them in Table D.

E. Ratio: A/D. Beginning with the July number in the top row of Table A, divide this number by the centered twelve-month moving average value for July in the top row of Table D. Continue dividing each number in Table A by its companion number in Table D.

F. Seasonal Factors. Seasonal factors are defined by averaging the four values in each column of Table E and entering the average in Table F.

G. Seasonally Adjusted Data. Finally, divide each January in Table A by the January Seasonal Factor in Table F and enter the answers in Table G. Continue for all numbers in Table A.

For quarterly data, use the middle four columns. First, make a four-quarter moving total, and put the answers in B. Next, divide by four, and put the answers in C. Center in the same way as the monthly data, using a two-month moving average, and enter the answer in D. The rest is the same.

The simple approach of Census Method I is not without shortcomings. For example, because of the need to center the twelve-month moving average, six data points are lost at the beginning and end of the data series. The length of the moving average also blunts or attenuates the sharp peaks and troughs reflected in the rapid growth or decline of the series. Blunting the sharp rise and fall periods also distorts the slope of the moving average line and distorts rates of change. Finally, the combined shift in slope and the blunting of the peaks and troughs shifts the timing of turning points.

Julius Shishkin, commissioner of labor statistics and chief statistician at the Census Bureau, along with his staff, recognized these issues and proceeded to develop a modified approach to seasonal adjustment that addressed the shortcomings of Method I, as explained in the following section.

CENSUS METHOD II, X-11 VARIANT

In 1954 the Census Bureau created the first computer program for adjusting seasonal and irregular time series based on software developed by Shishkin and his colleagues during the 1954 recession. In 1955 the Census Bureau replaced Census Method I, a manual procedure, with a revised procedure called Census Method II, which employed the new software. Over the years, the Census Bureau has continued to improve the software, and each experimental variant of it carries an "X" prefix followed by a sequence number. The first variant available to the public was X-3 in 1960.

The more precise name of the software in use today is *Census Method II, X-11 Variant*. The current variant is X-11.2, for monthly data, and X-11.2 Q, for quarterly data. These latest versions have been available since 1988. X-11 is used in virtually all developed countries and is the de facto standard for seasonally adjusting economic time series. The Census Bureau is working on a new version, X-12 ARIMA, which follows from the work of Estela Bee Dagum of Statistics Canada. It is in beta test and is planned for release sometime in the 1999 time frame. As of this writing, it is available for review but is, as yet, not officially released. The final section of this chapter previews the software.

Census Method II and the X-11 variant added precision to seasonal adjustment efforts; however, the increased precision is often lost in industrial forecasting activities. See Exhibit 5.4 for a pattern comparison of seasonally adjusted housing starts data over a three-year period.

As we proceed, we will refer to the current software as simply X-11. For acceptable accuracy, X-11 requires a minimum of six years of monthly or quarterly data. Our recommendation is to compute as many years of data that are available as will allow you to determine the behavioral characteristics of your company's sales and orders series before, during, and after each of the prior recessions. For example, do your company's figures lead or lag peaks and troughs in the national economy? You can answer this question only by the use of seasonally adjusted data. Analyzing raw data only will not answer the question!

The output of the X-11 program is divided into seven major parts:

1. Prior adjustments, if any
2. Preliminary estimates of irregular component weights and regression trading-day factors
3. Final estimates of the foregoing
4. Final estimates of seasonal, trend-cycle, and irregular components
5. Analytical tables
6. Summary measures
7. Sliding spans diagnostics, if requested

Output tables and documentation offered in the X-11 version of the software available from the government are useful but cryptic.

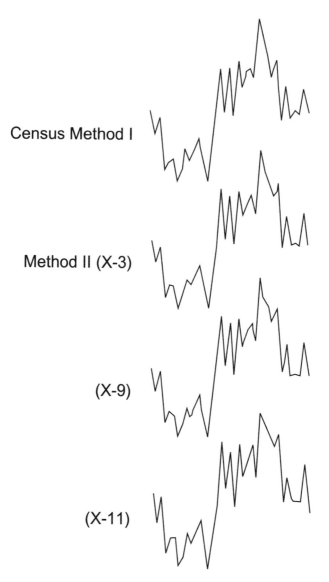

Census Method I

Method II (X-3)

(X-9)

(X-11)

EXHIBIT 5.4 Comparison of Census Method I, Method II, and X-11 variant

Following the entry of raw data into the computer, X-11 extracts the underlying cyclical pattern in the series, using a series of complex moving average computations. This cyclical pattern is called the *trend-cycle*, or simply the cycle. No attempt is made to separate the trend from the cycle, as its impact is usually minimal in the near term. With the basic trend-cycle pattern computed, differences between actual and seasonally adjusted numbers, for a given month, are believed to be due to seasonal trading-day and irregular factors, or *seasonal-irregular* factors. For example, if the trend-cycle figure for a certain month's sales is 11,055 units, and the month's actual sales are 11,560 units, then dividing the trend-cycle factor into the actual sales yields an indexed ratio of 104.6. This seasonal-irregular ratio is 4.6 percent greater than the trend-cycle value.

If the difference between the trend-cycle and raw data is 4.6 percent and is attributed to the seasonal trading days and irregular factors, how do we separate the contributions of the seasonal trading days and irregular factors? To do this, X-11 analyzes each month separately. For example, all of the Januarys are analyzed, and then all of the Februarys, and so on. When moving averages of all of the January values are computed, the seasonal day factors can be isolated. The remainder consists of the irregular values.

With all of the power and sophistication of X-11, it is important to recognize that only the seasonal and trading-day patterns are forecast. It does not forecast the trend-cycle pattern for your data series. This, you must do yourself!

One of the greatest benefits from using X-11 to analyze time series is to understand the relationship between your company's orders/sales and your industry's data, all in the context of the national economy. To do this, you need lots of data—data that span as many of the prior recessions and recoveries as possible. The greater the number of business cycles included in the raw data, the greater the value of the analyses. However, if your company has been around since before World War II, you probably do not want to include data from the war years, as that period was dominated by the all-out war effort and would distort the averages. Our recommendation is to begin with January 1948 and progress to the present. This period would include the cold-war shocks, Korea, the Cuban Missile Crisis, Vietnam, Grenada, and Desert Storm. Remember that the seasonal factors are developed using six or eight years of data. The greater number of years is useful in developing the trend-cycle components.

In deciding which data series to analyze, we recognize that company forecasters' roles and responsibilities are to forecast company sales, not industry sales or the national economy. The problem is that a company's sales do not occur in a vacuum. The company, industry, and economy are all inextricably linked. Effective forecasters know what is going on in the economy, the industry, the company, and the major product lines within the company.

By understanding the national economy and the relationship between various sectors of the economy and our company, we can access vast amounts of data and information to help us in our forecasting efforts. For example, if a company series has a high correlation with a national economic index, then it would be advantageous to use the economic index, especially if industry data are not available. Such a series could be used as a *proxy* series for industry data or for tracking certain trends. A caution is that any national index is almost guaranteed to be more stable, as it comprises a great deal more data than an index computed using company data only. Another clear advantage to using economic data is that they are almost always reported as seasonally adjusted data. The data are adjusted using the same X-11 program described here.

Industry data can provide a rich source of data usually more detailed than the aggregate economic data described previously. Although the data are usually more specific, they are oftentimes not seasonally adjusted, or if they are, the adjustment is limited to a simple three-month moving average. In this case the data would be smoothed but not seasonally adjusted. If at all possible, obtain actual units and dollars, and adjust the data using X-11. Better yet, ask the trade association to run the data through X-11 and then supply all raw and adjusted data to the association members.

Economic and industry series can be helpful in forecasting company sales, but which company series should be computed? The obvious answer is orders, sales or shipments, production rates, backlog, inventories, and major product lines. These areas are outlined in detail later in the book.

Until X-12 ARIMA is released, we can explore the contribution of X-11 ARIMA software recently published by SPSS, Inc., in their release 7.0 for Windows.

X-11 ARIMA

The Census Bureau's version of X-11 is available only for text-based operating systems such as DOS or Unix. SPSS, Inc., recently released a Windows-compatible statistics software package that contains a module called *SPSS Trends 6.1*. It consists of a broad range of analytical techniques, such as:

- *Plots* for producing a variety of technical graphs
- *Smoothing* models for creating a variety of one-period-ahead forecasts
- *Decomposition* models for extracting trend, cycle, and irregular components
- *Regression* models for ordinary least-squares and curve fitting
- *ARIMA* modeling using the three-step model of identification, estimation, and diagnosis

- *Spectral analysis* for defining time series as a combination of periodic cycles
- *X-11 ARIMA* for estimating seasonal factors for monthly and quarterly series

These elements of *SPSS Trends* make this module a powerful addition to the forecaster's tool kit. X-11 ARIMA offers substantial gains in accuracy over the conventional ratio-to-moving-average approach. As noted, the conventional approach loses data points at the beginning and end of the data series, and this loss of data points negatively impacts the accuracy of seasonal factors. We want accurate and reliable seasonal factors so that we can be assured that month-to-month or quarter-to-quarter changes in a data series are the result of changing economic conditions and not of some unidentified seasonal factor. Dagum, in an early article, reported that incorporating ARIMA into the X-11 approach resulted in reductions of about 30 percent in bias and 20 percent in the absolute values of total error when tested across several hundred Canadian and American data series.

To really understand the assumptions behind the ARIMA model and how to select the appropriate values for the model using the three-step approach, you should read Box and Jenkins or McCleary and Hay (see references in Chapter 4). The good news is that the X-11 ARIMA program in *SPSS Trends* provides a choice called "best automatic model," which enables the forecaster less experienced with ARIMA modeling a chance to apply it and learn from the experience.

To provide a comparison, we used a common data set in both the Census Method I and SPSS X-11 ARIMA analysis. Any differences observed, therefore, are due to methodological differences (see Exhibits 5.4 and 5.5).

Briefly, the features of the *SPSS Trends* X-11 ARIMA software offer either a multiplicative, additive, or logarithmic model. Variables can be adjusted using the ARIMA procedure, and extreme values can be modified to attenuate volatile series. Trading-day regression estimates can be computed and weighted equally, differentially, or not at all. Different moving averages can be selected, or the user can let the software select them automatically. Finally, a broad selection of output can be defined for tables and plots.

Tables offers four options: None, Brief Set, Analysis Set, and Standard Set. *None* is obvious. The brief set option includes three to thirteen tables, depending on the options selected. The analysis set includes seven to twenty-nine tables, and the standard set includes nineteen to forty tables. The A-through-F prefix notation for the tables maps closely to the table structure in the Census Bureau's Technical Paper No. 15—the manual for Census Method II, X-11 Variant—so the interested reader can compare the tables.

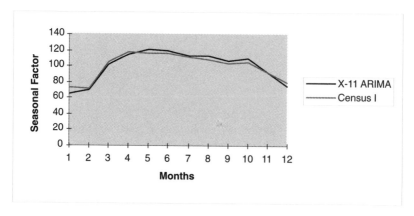

EXHIBIT 5.5 Comparison: Seasonal adjustment factors

Plots offers three options: None, Standard Set, and All Plots. The *stan-dard set* automatically generates and displays a plot of the original series, original series with ARIMA extrapolated values, original series modified for extremes, final seasonal factors, final unmodified seasonal-irregular ratios, final ratios modified for extremes, and extrapolated seasonal factors for each month or quarter. *All plots* includes all of the standard set plus final irregular series, final modified irregular series, a list of the values, and a cumulative periodogram bound by 95 percent confidence limits from the Kolmogorov-Smirov significance test of the final irregulars. All of the plots or graphs can be edited using the SPSS Chart Editor.

6

The Average Recession
Recovery Model (ARRM)

IN PREVIOUS CHAPTERS, we reviewed the many differ-
ent time series methods applied to forecasting as well as the results of the
monumental study by Makridakis and his colleagues in their quest for the
"best" forecasting methodology. This chapter on the Average Recession
Recovery Model (ARRM) and a special form of the ARRM, the Average Experience Model (AEM), is in a sense a transition chapter. The models are somewhat technical in nature, yet basic in the sense that they serve as fundamental
tools in our approach to forecasting. They are also different in that they are
a marked departure from the more conventional way of employing time
series.

A SPECIAL CASE OF TIME SERIES

The Average Recession Recovery Model is a special case of time series that
not only responds to conventional analysis and charting but also, because
of its structure, permits all manner of additional discovery. Economic time
series are generally continuous and include many different segments, such
as growth-and-decline cycles, long-term trends, and turning points. (See
Exhibit 6.1.) This means that persons interested in understanding how a particular variable is performing in the current recession or recovery when compared with its performance in prior recessions or recoveries face a difficult

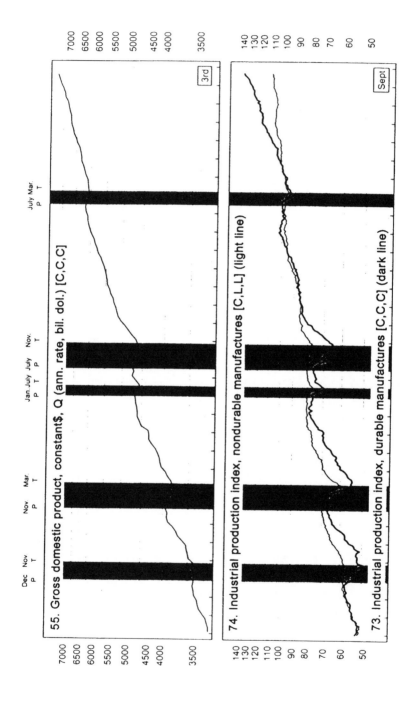

55. Gross domestic product, constant$, Q (ann. rate, bil. dol.) [C,C,C]

74. Industrial production index, nondurable manufactures [C,L,L] (light line)

73. Industrial production index, durable manufactures [C,C,C] (dark line)

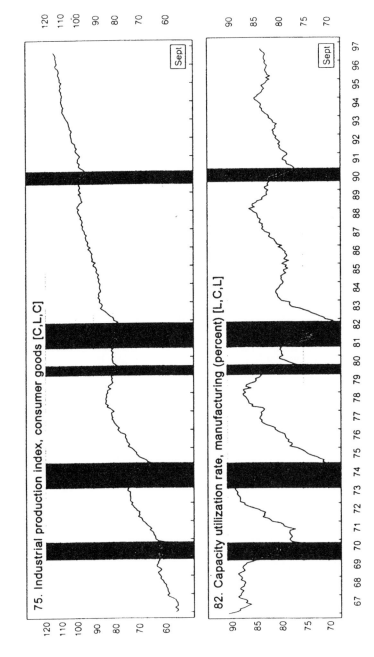

EXHIBIT 6.1 Sample of continuous time series (reproduced from the Conference Board's *Business Cycle Indicators*)

task. ARRMs, on the other hand, consist of the very same data as are contained in the continuous series, only the data are parsed into segments corresponding to official U.S. economic recessions and recoveries. (See Exhibit 6.2.) This parsing magnifies the important level and duration of changes critical to the phase of the economic cycle of interest and provides a quantitative measure of the similarities and differences.

For example, if you are interested in how a particular variable, such as housing starts, increases in the early stages of an economic recovery, the ARRM can provide that information. Conversely, if you think that a recession is approaching and you want to know how much housing starts have decreased during a recession, the ARRM can also provide that insight. By parsing continuous economic series into periods of expansion (recovery) and contraction (recession) and indexing these periods to common peak or trough dates, we can construct an average recession recovery model for any series. This "bounded model" places all prior recessions or recoveries in context and serves as a practical delimiter of what might be expected in future recessions or recoveries.

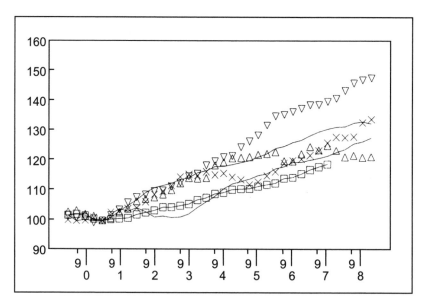

EXHIBIT 6.2 Real GDP time series shown in Exhibit 6.1 parsed into recession and recovery periods

CONCEPTS

We have shown that the economy, and hence the various economic time series that make up the economy, consists of *cycles, trends, and turning points*. Cycles are the increasing and decreasing oscillations along the long-term trend, and turning points are the data points that mark a high or a low point in the series. A data series that levels off or plateaus in its path, does not change direction, and then resumes its path is said to have moved through an *inflection point*.

In a continuous time series, turning points are difficult to forecast, as there is no additional information that places the behavior of the series in the context of prior behavior. With knowledge of prior behavior, we have a bounded model to employ in our forecasts which, in turn, serves to increase the probability that the forecasts are accurate. For example, we know that consumer attitudes and consumer spending patterns change depending on whether the broader economy is in recession or recovery. We also know that the number of people employed increases during recoveries and decreases during recessions. Most economic time series behave differently depending on whether the general economy is in recovery or in recession. In fact, it is the changes in the economic time series themselves that are used to define whether the U.S. economy is in recession or recovery. It is these changes on which we wish to capitalize.

Fundamental to the ARRM is its reliance on the National Bureau of Economic Research (NBER) official peak and trough dates for the U.S. economy. These peak and trough dates define recessions and recoveries through a complex analytical process. The dates serve as universal reference dates for *all* U.S. economic time series. Periods of expansion (recovery) are measured from "trough to peak," and periods of contraction (recession) are measured from "peak to trough." In the NBER dating process, a business cycle is defined as the number of months from "trough to previous trough" or "peak to previous peak." Although the United States has experienced thirty-one business cycles since 1854, the most meaningful history is the period following World War II. See Exhibit 6.3 for a listing of business cycle reference dates and the duration of expansions, contractions, and business cycles.

There are two types of ARRMs: trough models and peak models. A trough model (ARRMt) indexes prior recoveries to a common trough date and is used in forecasting the behavior of a variable during recoveries. A peak model (ARRMp) indexes prior recessions to a common peak date and is used in forecasting a variable during recessions. Depending on the type of ARRM, peak or trough, the appropriate dates are set equal to 100,

Business cycle reference dates	
Trough	**Peak**
December 1854	June 1857
December 1858	October 1860
June 1861	April 1865
December 1867	June 1869
December 1870	October 1873
March 1879	March 1882
May 1885	March 1887
April 1888	July 1890
May 1891	January 1893
June 1894	December 1895
June 1897	June 1899
December 1900	September 1902
August 1904	May 1907
June 1908	January 1910
January 1912	January 1913
December 1914	August 1918
March 1919	January 1920
July 1921	May 1923
July 1924	October 1926
November 1927	August 1929
March 1933	May 1937
June 1938	February 1945
October 1945	November 1948 ars
October 1949	July 1953
May 1954	August 1957
April 1958	April 1960
February 1961	December 1969
November 1970	November 1973
March 1975	January 1980
July 1980	July 1981
November 1982	July 1990
March 1991	

Average, all cycles:
 1854–1991 (31 cycles)
 1854–1919 (16 cycles)
 1919–1945 (6 cycles)
 1945–1991 (9 cycles)

Average, peacetime cycles:
 1854–1991 (26 cycles)
 1854–1919 (14 cycles)
 1919–1945 (5 cycles)
 1945–1991 (7 cycles)

1. 30 cycles
2. 15 cycles
3. 25 cycles
4. 13 cycles

EXHIBIT 6.3 Business cycle reference dates (reproduced from the April 1995 issue of the *Survey of Current Business*)

Contraction (trough from previous peak)	Expansion (trough to peak)	Cycle	
		Trough from previous trough	Peak from previous peak
....	30	....	....
18	22	48	40
8	46	30	54
32	18	78	50
18	34	36	52
65	36	99	101
38	22	74	60
13	27	35	40
10	20	37	30
17	18	37	35
18	24	36	42
18	21	42	39
23	33	44	56
13	19	46	32
24	12	43	36
23	44	35	67
7	10	51	17
18	22	28	40
14	27	36	41
13	21	40	34
43	50	64	93
13	80	63	93
8	37	88	45
11	45	48	56
10	39	55	49
8	24	47	32
10	106	34	116
11	36	117	47
16	58	52	74
6	12	64	18
16	92	28	108
8	....	100	....
18	35	53	[1] 53
22	27	48	[2] 49
18	35	53	53
11	50	61	61
19	29	48	[3] 48
22	24	46	[4] 47
20	26	46	45
11	43	53	53

Duration in months

NOTE-Figures printed in bold italic are the wartime expansions (Civil War, World W I and II, Korean War and Vietnam War), the postwar contractions, and the full cycles that include the wartime expansions.

Source: National Bureau of Economic Research, Inc., 1050 Massachusetts Avenue, Cambridge, MA 02138

EXHIBIT 6.3 (continued)

and the data preceding and subsequent to the turning point are also indexed. Exhibit 6.4 illustrates the two types of ARRMs. Later we will explain the computations involved in constructing an ARRM.

The range and variability of the data are also factored by the AARM. For example, when we average a reasonably small number of data points, the variance can be large and the mean or arithmetic average shifted by high or low values. To the extent that there are large differences between recoveries or recessions, the mean will be shifted toward the extreme values, and the variance increased accordingly. Therefore, the ARRM defines the mean

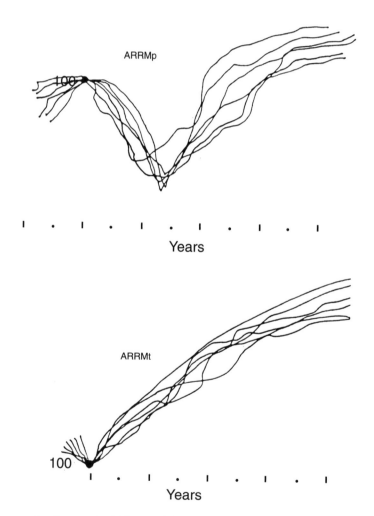

EXHIBIT 6.4 Patterns in ARRM peak (ARRMp) and trough (ARRMt) models

of all prior recessions or recoveries in the sample, including plus and minus one standard deviation. In a normal distribution, 68 percent of the distribution falls within plus or minus one standard deviation. We take some poetic license and refer to the plus and minus one standard deviation as the *2-in-3 probability band*. In other words, it is within this band that roughly two-thirds of prior recession or recovery data have fallen. See Exhibit 6.5.

The final concept of which you should be aware relates to the use of a visual reference to demark the recessionary period. Conventional economic time series use a shaded area to define the recessionary period. As an alternative, simple vertical lines that correspond to official peak and trough dates can also be used. An example is shown in Exhibit 6.6.

STRUCTURE OF AN ARRM

When encountering a new tool or a new concept, such as this model, it is important to have some sort of shared vocabulary through which to communicate the concept. An ARRM, whether peak or trough, consists of the following elements:

- Appropriate peak and trough reference dates
- An area delineating the recessionary period
- A baseline where the recovery or recession is set equal to 100

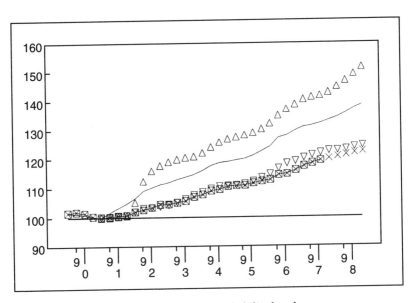

EXHIBIT 6.5 ARRM illustrating the 2-in-3 probability band

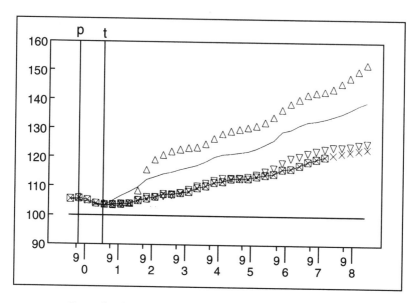

EXHIBIT 6.6 Example of an ARRM with vertical lines marking peak and trough dates

- The ARRM line or the average of the variable of interest across the prior post–World War II recoveries or recessions
- A 2-in-3 probability band
- Actual data for the current recovery or recession
- A forecast for the current recovery or recession
- A y-axis as an indexed scale (left)
- An x-axis showing the month or quarter and year

An example, with legends for the key components, is shown in Exhibit 6.7.

A second part of the anatomy of an ARRM is the general layout of the different data sets used in the structure. There are five broad categories: *raw data set, general statistics, annual data sets by quarter, forecasts,* and *graphics.* The raw data set can be maintained either within the spreadsheet or in a separate external file. For the S&P 500, for example, we maintain monthly data and convert them to quarterly data for use in the ARRM.

The general statistics category is the key to the ARRM. In Exhibit 6.8, which shows the general statistics for the S&P 500 ARRM, are B19 and S&P 500. The B19 refers to the series number published originally by the U.S. Department of Commerce and now published by The Conference Board in its monthly publication, *Business Cycle Indicators.* Also the top three rows

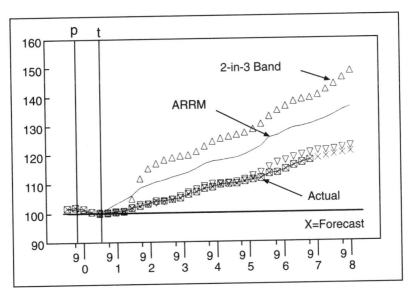

EXHIBIT 6.7   Complete ARRMt with key features labeled

show the peak and trough quarters for each of the nine prior recessions—
1949, 1954, 1958, 1961, 1970, 1975, 1980, 1982, and 1991. The peak and trough
dates are in quarters; for example, a peak of 48.4 means that the economy
peaked (or the recession began) in fourth quarter 1948 and the recession
ended in fourth quarter 1949.

Proceeding down the left-hand side of the table, note that the first year
is 1990. As a general rule when constructing an ARRM, we begin with the
year prior to the peak or trough date to show the behavior of the variable as
it approached a turning point. The four numbers adjacent to the years and
in the column under each of the prior recessions are indexed numbers. The
index is set equal to 100 in the first quarter of 1991, the trough date of the
latest recession, and all prior and subsequent data are indexed as well. As
this example is a trough model (ARRMt) for the current recovery, the common index point is the trough date of the 1991 recession. For each of the
prior recessions, the respective trough data are set equal to 100, and all data
in each respective series are indexed to that trough date. The indexed series
are then arranged as if each prior recession's trough occurred in first quarter 1991. This has the effect of generating a family of climb-out curves which
are then averaged, and the standard deviations are computed to generate the
ARRM line and 2-in-3 probability band as shown previously in Exhibit 6.7.

Year:	1949	1954	1958	1961	1970	1975	1980	1982	1991
Peak:	48.4	53.3	57.3	60.2	69.4	73.4	80.1	81.3	90.3
Trough:	49.4	54.2	58.2	61.1	70.4	75.1	80.3	82.4	91.1
1990	105.7	100.0	106.8	104.4	120.0	147.3	90.1	110.4	95.1
	102.5	94.2	112.0	101.7	119.7	137.8	91.7	107.3	98.9
	98.9	92.2	111.1	101.3	112.7	130.6	96.3	100.3	94.9
	95.8	93.9	97.9	100.7	100.6	109.0	95.5	100.3	89.7
1991	100.0	100.0	100.0	100.0	100.0	100.0	100.0	100.0	100.0
	106.6	109.3	105.1	112.1	109.5	113.5	98.3	120.1	107.1
	113.0	118.3	114.6	119.2	122.0	128.3	111.8	129.7	109.1
	120.8	128.9	126.1	120.8	128.9	126.2	120.7	143.0	109.5
1992	120.5	139.5	133.8	127.0	125.2	128.4	119.2	145.4	116.5
	130.5	147.5	138.6	126.3	122.4	143.4	120.4	145.6	116.0
	142.4	165.9	141.5	112.5	133.9	146.4	113.9	140.9	118.0
	143.6	169.7	139.2	104.5	137.4	150.3	110.8	136.8	119.8
1993	150.0	174.3	135.6	107.7	138.7	147.8	103.5	141.0	125.1
	152.6	180.5	135.1	118.5	144.8	146.6	103.5	145.1	126.0
	157.6	184.6	134.3	125.9	146.1	142.7	103.2	155.8	128.3
	157.8	177.4	133.3	128.3	136.4	141.3	123.9	162.4	131.3
1994	164.8	170.3	149.4	132.4	133.5	135.3	133.9	165.4	132.8
	165.4	178.6	159.0	140.1	129.8	128.7	147.5	173.0	127.6
	171.3	177.2	161.0	145.1	121.5	138.2	150.1	219.9	130.4
	161.4	156.2	169.3	149.8	115.1	146.4	150.3	211.4	130.1
1995	158.0	159.5	168.4	153.2	96.1	139.9	145.4	211.9	135.8
	161.0	167.6	149.9	156.4	88.2	143.1	141.2	214.1	148.1
	171.4	182.8	139.4	158.0	100.1	145.8	145.5	245.4	159.9
	187.4	201.1	143.7	157.1	113.1	153.0	149.8	257.7	169.1
1996	202.7	213.4	158.0	165.8	111.3	151.7	160.7	280.6	180.2
	220.9	221.0	167.9	165.6	113.2	158.9	167.5	224.4	186.4
	239.1	225.7	171.0	159.3	126.4	156.2	170.7	226.8	186.9
	252.8	222.0	176.6	147.2	129.1	177.6	178.6	231.2	205.6
1997	284.3	216.3	186.9	144.2	132.5	191.7	226.9	234.5	222.2
	290.8	215.5	193.5	157.4	130.3	189.5	218.1	241.6	233.2
	298.8	214.2	199.7	165.7	129.3	191.3	218.6	255.4	263.1
	309.3	212.7	204.2	170.7	125.8	181.0	220.9	275.3	269.0
1998	316.4	238.3	208.6	170.9	124.5	176.0	253.2	300.4	288.9
	304.0	253.6	210.7	165.6	119.3	164.5	265.9	303.5	318.4
	291.9	256.9	209.5	177.2	113.5	164.4	289.5	295.5	319.0
	306.1	270.1	221.1	180.6	121.8	164.0	231.5	307.2	320.2
1999	303.8	268.5	220.8	190.1	129.1	196.9	234.0	294.7	322.1
	267.7	239.2	212.4	182.4	123.4	212.7	238.6	278.6	324.6
	273.4	222.3	196.2	183.7	126.2	234.4	242.0	310.6	327.8
	287.2	229.1	192.3	170.7	128.5	238.4	249.3	332.7	331.6

EXHIBIT 6.8 General statistics for the S&P 500 ARRMt

The forecasts are generated using the table shown in Exhibit 6.9. Each year consists of three sets of quarterly data plus additional statistics. Look at the year 1991. The number 353.50 is the value of the S&P 500 for the first quarter of 1991. The 100 indicates the baseline, and the 54.5 is the quarterly change on an annualized basis. The second S&P 500 number, 378.65, is the second quarter's result, which is a 7.1 percent increase, as reflected in the index value of 107.1. This translates into a quarterly change on an annualized basis of 31.6 percent. The 12.4 just under the 1991 is the year-over-year change. Finally, the 376 below the 12.4 is the year average for the S&P 500.

Let's move to the year marked 1996 to illustrate how the forecast is generated. For reference purposes, the third quarter's actual numbers for 1996 (reading left to right) were: 186.9, 1.0, 671, and 660.54. The forecast number

100.0	54.5	1991	353.50
107.1	31.6	12.4	378.65
109.1	7.6	376	385.61
109.5	1.6		387.10
116.5	28.3	1992	412.00
116.0	−1.8	10.5	410.16
118.0	7.0	416	417.15
119.8	6.4		423.66
125.1	18.9	1993	442.36
126.0	2.8	8.6	445.46
128.3	7.5	451	453.55
131.3	9.8		464.25
132.8	4.6	1994	469.46
127.6	−14.8	2.0	450.99
130.4	9.1	460	460.87
130.1	−0.7		460.00
135.8	18.7	1995	480.11
148.1	41.6	17.7	523.69
159.9	35.6	542	565.08
169.1	25.1		597.67
180.2	29.0	1996	637.01
186.4	14.5	23.9	658.97
186.9	1.0	671	660.54
205.6	46.6		726.79

EXHIBIT 6.9 Forecasting table for the S&P 500 ARRMt

was 205.6 which is a sharp increase over third quarter (46.6 percent annualized) to yield an S&P 500 value of 726.79 for the fourth quarter.

SCOPE OF APPLICATIONS

The ARRM is appropriate for a variety of macroeconomic and microeconomic applications. For example, in our monthly forecasting letter, *Turning Points,* we use the Average Recession Recovery Models exclusively to forecast the U.S. economy, including fifteen key variables that make up the overall economy. (See Exhibit 6.10.)

	1997 Actuals				1998 Forecasts			
	1ST	2ND	3RD	4TH	1ST	2ND	3RD	4TH
A. GDP (Current$)	7933.6	8034.3	8124.3	8218.8	8307.9	8396.5	8484.6	8572.1
*B. GDP Deflator	111.0	112.2	112.6	113.3	113.9	114.5	115.2	115.8
C. Real GDP	7101.6	7159.6	7214.0	7256.4	7293.8	7330.3	7366.0	7400.7
D. % Growth	4.9	3.3	3.1	2.4	2.1	2.0	2.0	1.9
*E. Production	118.3	119.4	121.6	122.7	123.7	124.6	125.3	126.0
F. % Growth	4.4	3.8	7.6	3.7	3.3	2.8	2.4	2.0
G. Personal Con.	4819.5	4829.4	4896.2	4939.6	4981.5	5023.5	5065.4	5107.3
*H. Durables	637.8	629.0	656.1	664.1	672.0	680.0	687.9	695.9
*I. Total Motor Veh.	15.9	14.8	15.8	15.8	15.8	15.8	15.8	15.8
*J. Nondurables	1457.8	1450.0	1465.5	1473.6	1481.7	1489.7	1497.8	1505.9
*K. Services	2723.9	2749.8	2776.1	2802.0	2827.9	2853.8	2879.6	2905.5
L. Gross Investment	1149.5	1197.1	1204.6	1221.1	1230.1	1238.4	1245.7	1252.2
M. Fixed	1085.8	111.4	1149.3	1174.1	1185.1	1195.4	1204.7	1213.2
*N. Residential	273.3	278.2	280.1	283.9	286.9	288.9	290.1	290.5
*O. Housing Starts	1432.0	1430.0	1451.7	1458.3	1464.9	1470.8	1476.0	1480.3
P. Nonresidential	812.5	837.0	874.5	890.1	898.3	906.4	914.6	922.7
*Q. Structures	195.9	193.5	196.7	197.0	197.3	197.6	197.9	198.2
*R. Equipment	616.6	649.3	685.3	693.1	701.0	708.8	716.7	724.5
*S. Inventory Chg	63.7	77.6	47.5	47.0	45.0	43.0	41.0	39.0
T. Net Exports	−126.2	−136.6	−164.1	−180.0	−196.0	−211.9	−227.8	−243.8
*U. Exports	922.7	962.5	973.0	980.3	987.7	995.0	1002.4	1009.7
*V. Imports	1048.9	1099.1	1137.1	1160.4	1183.7	1207.0	1230.2	1253.5
W. Government	1260.5	1270.2	1273.4	1275.8	1278.1	1280.4	1282.7	1285.0
*X. Federal	452.8	460.1	458.8	457.3	455.7	454.2	452.7	451.1
*Y. State/Local	807.7	810.1	814.7	818.5	822.4	826.2	830.0	833.9

Figures are in billions of chain-weighted (1992) dollars, unless otherwise noted.
Asterisks (*) cite 15 independent variables.

EXHIBIT 6.10 ARRMt-generated forecast of the U.S. economy

The Macro-ARRM Model of the U.S. Economy, shown in Exhibit 6.10, reflects the structure of the U.S. economy and is a critical starting point in any forecasting activity. This table is constructed from the National Income and Product Accounts (NIPA), and the contents are reported in the *Survey of Current Business,* a monthly publication by the Bureau of Economic Analysis of the U.S. Department of Commerce. For users who are computer literate, the *Survey* is available in electronic form from STAT-USA, a fee-based electronic service offered by the government. In Chapter 7 we explore NIPA and the structure of the economy in some detail.

	1999 Forecasts			Annual Summaries — Volume				% Change			
1ST	2ND	3RD	4TH	1996	1997	1998	1999	1997	1998	1999	
8659.1	8745.4	8831.2	8916.4	7636.0	8077.7	8788.0	8831.0	5.8	8.8	0.5	GDPS
116.5	117.1	117.8	118.4	109.7	112.3	113.0	113.6	2.4	0.7	0.5	DEF
7434.6	7467.6	7499.8	7531.1	6928.4	7182.9	7347.7	7382.9	3.7	2.3	0.5	GDP
1.8	1.8	1.7	1.7								
126.4	126.8	127.1	127.2	125.8	120.5	121.9	123.2	−4.2	1.1	1.1	IPI
1.6	1.2	0.8	0.4								
5149.2	5191.1	5233.1	5275.0	4714.1	4871.2	4911.7	4960.2	3.3	0.8	1.0	PER
703.8	711.8	719.7	727.7	611.1	646.7	655.3	668.0	5.8	1.3	1.9	DUR
15.7	15.7	15.7	15.7	15.4	15.6	15.5	15.8	0.7	−0.1	1.6	CAR
1514.0	1522.1	1530.1	1538.2	1432.3	1461.7	1467.7	1477.6	2.1	0.4	0.7	NON
2931.4	2957.3	2983.2	3009.1	2671.0	2762.9	2788.9	2814.9	3.4	0.9	0.9	SER
1257.8	1262.5	1266.4	1269.4	1069.1	1193.1	1213.2	1223.5	11.6	1.7	0.9	DOM
1220.8	1227.5	1233.4	1238.4	1041.7	1130.1	1155.0	1176.0	8.5	2.2	1.8	FIX
289.9	288.5	286.3	283.1	272.1	278.9	282.3	285.0	2.5	1.2	1.0	RES
1484.0	1486.9	1489.1	1490.5	1464.5	1443.0	1451.4	1461.4	−1.5	0.6	0.7	HS
930.9	939.0	947.2	955.3	771.7	853.5	875.0	892.3	10.6	2.5	2.0	NON
198.5	198.8	199.1	199.4	188.7	195.8	196.1	197.2	3.8	0.2	0.5	STR
732.3	740.2	748.0	755.9	586.0	661.1	682.2	697.1	12.8	3.2	2.2	EQT
37.0	35.0	33.0	31.0	25.0	59.0	54.3	45.6	135.8	−7.9	−15.9	INV
−259.7	−275.7	−291.6	−307.5	−114.5	−151.7	−169.2	−188.0	32.5	11.5	11.1	EXIM
1017.1	1024.4	1031.8	1039.1	857.0	959.6	975.9	984.0	12.0	1.7	0.8	EXP
1276.8	1300.1	1323.4	1346.7	971.5	1111.4	1145.1	1172.0	−12.6	3.0	2.4	IMP
1287.3	1289.6	1291.9	1294.2	1257.9	1270.0	1287.3	1284.1	−1.0	1.4	−0.2	GOV
449.6	448.1	446.6	445.0	464.2	457.2	449.6	451.0	1.5	−1.7	0.3	FED
837.7	841.5	845.4	849.2	793.7	812.8	837.7	833.0	−2.3	3.1	−0.6	S&L

The micro-ARRMs are updated and published quarterly. Presenting all allows the reader to quickly determine which elements of the economy are expanding or contracting the most. This information can then be linked to specific industries and companies.

AVERAGE EXPERIENCE MODEL (AEM)

The Average Experience Model (AEM) is a special case of the ARRM. The underlying concepts and structure are the same as for the ARRM, but the AEM lends itself to unique applications often not thought of in the context of economic forecasting. For example, the AEM is ideally suited for averaging *experiences* such as advertising promotions, S-curves for new-product demand, seasonality, inventory patterns, and performance of new salespeople.

For S-curve experiences, data for a specific product line can be used directly, or a composite data set can be constructed from different product lines to produce a hybrid experience believed to more accurately reflect the new product. These raw data are then seasonally adjusted to control for variability due to the different introductory periods. The seasonally adjusted data are indexed to a common introductory date. The average of the family of curves generated becomes the Average Experience Model for the new product. Initial planning volume is determined from the AEM. Regular comparisons of actual versus AEM are used to adjust current and near-term volume based on the fit of the actual data versus the AEM. Similar approaches can be used with promotions, inventory patterns, and new salesperson performance. See Exhibit 6.11 for examples of AEMs.

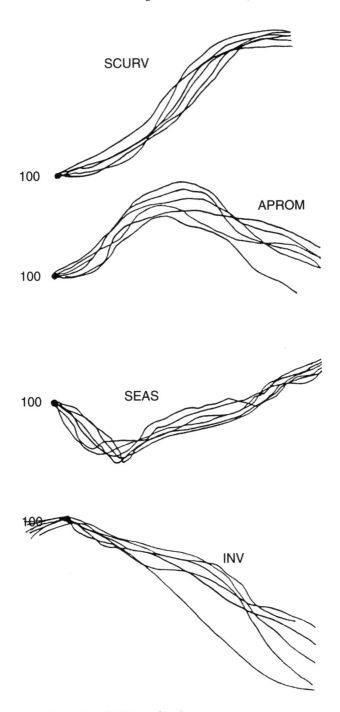

EXHIBIT 6.11 Examples of AEM applications

PART III

Forecasting and
Strategic Marketing

7

Economics, Business Cycles, and Strategic Planning

IN PARTS I AND II, we focused on developing a general understanding of different conceptual approaches, briefly outlined the various forecasting tools available, and introduced our Average Recession Recovery Model (ARRM) and Average Experience Model (AEM) as specific tools. In Part III, we shift the discussion to forecasting in the context of strategic planning.

Recall from our previous discussions that strategic marketing is responsible for the longer look ahead and for providing the leadership for creating and updating the company's business plan, whether it spans a period of two, three, or five years. Central to the process of effective business planning is a basic understanding of the economy.

ORIGINS OF CONTEMPORARY ECONOMICS

"Economies" have existed in one form or another for as long as there has been trade. Many early philosophers wrote extensively about subjective theories of value, labor value, and money, but Adam Smith, in his 1776 book *An Inquiry into the Nature and Causes of the Wealth of Nations,* provided us with a vision of political economy driven by self-interest within the context of ethics, law, politics, and economics. Smith's early vision of today's economic system as a "notion of natural, effective self-adjusting mechanism as being usually at work throughout competitive economies or markets" continues with us to this day. Following Adam Smith, the next hundred years or so were dominated essentially by competing treatises on growth, prices, wages, value, profits, distribution, and equilibrium theory.

By the turn of the century, early investigators were exploring the boom and bust of various trade cycles, using newly developed statistical techniques. Theories explaining trade cycles ranged from price fluctuation, to savings and capital employment, to overconsumption, to internal shocks such as strikes, to external shocks and "acts of God." The most important person to emerge was Wesley Clair Mitchell. Mitchell's early work on contemporary business-cycle research held that business cycles were an integral part of business life and were not limited to one or two major sectors, as was hypothesized, but permeated virtually *all* economic activity. His work emphasized description and understanding, rather than the search for a single set of causal factors. Mitchell's emphasis on empiricism led to his being criticized by his academic colleagues as advocating measurement without theory— a charge that has since been found to be without merit.

As a comment on the utility of Mitchell's early emphasis on empiricism, it is interesting to note that as we enter the new millennium, there is still no single economic theory that accounts for the business cycle!

If there is no single theory of business cycles, then it makes sense for us as practical businesspeople to understand the structure of the economy and to track on those key parameters that are meaningful to us as we seek to chart our course through alternating calm and troubled economic waters. We are interested in changes in the business cycle and how those changes impact our business. Mitchell's statistical work on business cycles contributed directly to the development of leading economic indicators, estimates of national income, and the development of our system of national accounts.

STRUCTURE OF THE U.S. ECONOMY

The National Income and Product Accounts (NIPA) form the structure of the U.S. economy and provide a rich cognitive map of economic functioning. Prior to 1996, NIPA data were presented in nominal or current dollars and constant dollars. Constant dollars were benchmarked using a common year to control for the effects of inflation. In 1996 the NIPA data were restructured to chain-weighted dollars to improve the accuracy of inflation-adjusted data. The basic structure of the accounts, however, remains the same.

The NIPAs are presented in tabular format and are organized into nine categories:

1. National Product and Income
2. Personal Income and Outlays
3. Government Receipts and Expenditures
4. Foreign Transactions
5. Saving and Investment
6. Income, Employment, and Product by Industry
7. Quantity and Price Indexes
8. Supplementary Tables
9. Seasonally Unadjusted Estimates

An example of the structure for five of the nine tables is reproduced in Exhibit 7.1.

Each month, selected NIPA tables are reproduced in the *Survey of Current Business (SCB)* and contain current economic data plus data for the recent two to four years. The *SCB* is published by the Bureau of Economic Analysis (BEA) of the U.S. Department of Commerce. A one-year subscription via first-class mail is $90.

The NIPAs are revised each July as additional data become available. About every five years, comprehensive revisions to the NIPAs are usually made to incorporate major definitional and classification changes, statistical changes, and any presentational changes that could make the tables more informative. Additionally, historical data are published in a two-volume set following each major revision. These volumes are also available from the BEA.

Probably the most familiar item of economic data is Gross Domestic Product. GDP is the sum of *personal consumption expenditures, gross private domestic investment* (including changes in business inventories and before deduction of charges for consumption of fixed capital), *net exports of goods and services* (exports less imports), and *government purchases.* In brief form, $GDP = PCE + GPDI + NE + GP.$ Note from the structure (Exhibit 7.1) that these data are from the production side of the NIPA ledger. Economic data in this format are found in NIPA Table 1.1 for current dollars and Table 1.2 for constant dollars. Compare the two tables in Exhibit 7.2.

GDP is the market value of goods and services produced by labor and property *within* the United States and is a change from previously reported *Gross National Product (GNP),* which refers to goods and services produced by labor and property *supplied* by United States residents.

Personal Consumption Expenses, or PCE, refers to goods and services purchased by persons resident in the U.S. PCE is further broken down into

	1995	1996	Seasonally adjusted at annual rates					
			1996			1997		
			II	III	IV	I	II	III
Gross domestic product	7,265.4	7,636.0	7,607.7	7,676.0	7,792.9	7,933.6	8,034.3	8,128.8
Personal consumption expenditures	4,957.7	5,207.6	5,189.1	5,227.4	5,308.1	5,405.7	5,432.1	5,530.7
Durable goods	608.5	634.5	638.6	634.5	638.2	658.4	644.5	667.1
Nondurable goods	1,475.8	1,534.7	1,532.3	1,538.3	1,560.1	1,587.4	1,578.9	1,601.2
Services	2,873.4	3,038.4	3,018.2	3,054.6	3,109.8	3,159.9	3,208.7	3,262.3
Gross private domestic investment	1,038.2	1,116.5	1,105.4	1,149.2	1,151.1	1,193.6	1,242.0	1,249.8
Fixed investment	1,008.1	1,090.7	1,082.0	1,112.0	1,119.2	1,127.5	1,160.8	1,198.9
Nonresidential	723.0	781.4	769.3	798.6	807.2	811.3	836.3	869.6
Structures	200.6	215.2	210.6	217.7	227.0	227.4	226.8	230.6
Producers' durable equipment	522.4	566.2	558.7	580.9	580.2	583.9	609.5	639.0
Residential	285.1	309.2	312.7	313.5	312.0	316.2	324.6	329.3
Change in business inventories	30.1	25.9	23.4	37.1	31.9	66.1	81.1	50.9
Net exports of goods and services	−86.0	−94.8	−93.8	−114.0	−88.6	−98.8	−88.7	−110.2
Exports	818.4	870.9	865.0	863.7	904.6	922.2	960.3	965.9
Goods	583.9	617.5	613.9	609.7	640.5	656.2	690.0	691.6
Services	234.6	253.3	251.1	254.0	264.2	266.0	270.3	274.3
Imports	904.5	965.7	958.7	977.6	993.2	1,021.0	1,049.0	1,076.1
Goods	757.5	809.0	802.9	820.2	834.6	855.8	880.1	904.5
Services	146.9	156.7	155.8	157.5	158.6	165.2	168.9	171.6
Government consumption expenditures and gross investment	1,355.5	1,406.7	1,407.0	1,413.5	1,422.3	1,433.1	1,449.0	1,458.6
Federal	509.6	520.0	524.6	521.6	517.6	516.1	526.1	525.8
National defense	344.6	352.8	357.3	354.8	350.6	343.3	350.6	352.2
Nondefense	165.0	167.3	167.3	166.8	167.0	172.8	175.5	173.6
State and local	846.0	886.7	882.4	891.9	904.7	917.0	923.0	932.7

EXHIBIT 7.1 National Income and Product Accounts (NIPA) structure (in billions of dollars)

durable goods, nondurable goods, and services. Durable goods consist of products that can be stored or inventoried and have an average life of three years or more. Nondurable goods are all other goods that can be stored or inventoried. Services, by definition, cannot be stored and are consumed at the time of purchase. PCE accounts for a little over two-thirds of GDP.

Gross Private Domestic Investment (GPDI) consists of fixed investment and change in business inventories. It covers all investment by business,

Table at left — current dollars (billions of dollars)

	1995	1996	Seasonally adjusted at annual rates					
			1996 II	1996 III	1996 IV	1997 I	1997 II	1997 III
Gross domestic product	7,265.4	7,636.0	7,807.7	7,676.0	7,792.9	7,933.8	8,034.3	8,128.8
Personal consumption expenditures	4,957.7	5,207.6	5,189.1	5,227.4	5,308.1	5,405.7	5,432.1	5,530.7
Durable goods	608.5	634.5	638.6	634.5	638.2	658.4	644.5	667.1
Nondurable goods	1,475.8	1,534.7	1,532.3	1,538.3	1,560.1	1,587.4	1,578.9	1,601.2
Services	2,873.4	3,038.4	3,018.2	3,054.6	3,109.8	3,159.9	3,208.7	3,262.3
Gross private domestic investment	1,038.2	1,116.5	1,105.4	1,149.2	1,151.1	1,193.6	1,242.0	1,249.8
Fixed investment	1,008.1	1,090.7	1,082.0	1,112.0	1,119.2	1,127.5	1,160.8	1,198.9
Nonresidential	723.0	781.4	769.3	798.6	807.2	811.3	836.3	869.6
Structures	200.6	215.2	210.6	217.7	227.0	227.4	226.8	230.6
Producers' durable equipment	522.4	566.2	558.7	580.9	580.2	583.9	609.5	639.0
Residential	285.1	309.2	312.7	313.5	312.0	316.2	324.6	329.3
Change in business inventories	30.1	25.9	23.4	37.1	31.9	66.1	81.1	50.9
Net exports of goods and services	-86.0	-94.8	-93.8	-114.0	-88.6	-98.8	-88.7	-110.2
Exports	818.4	870.9	865.0	863.7	904.6	922.2	960.3	965.9
Goods	583.9	617.5	613.9	609.7	640.5	656.2	690.0	691.6
Services	234.6	253.3	251.1	254.0	264.2	266.0	270.3	274.3
Imports	904.5	965.7	958.7	977.6	993.2	1,021.0	1,049.0	1,076.1
Goods	757.5	809.0	802.9	820.2	834.6	855.8	860.1	904.5
Services	146.9	156.7	155.8	157.5	158.6	165.2	168.9	171.6
Government consumption expenditures and gross investment	1,355.5	1,406.7	1,407.0	1,413.5	1,422.3	1,433.1	1,449.0	1,458.6
Federal	509.6	520.0	524.6	521.6	517.6	516.1	526.1	525.8
National defense	344.6	352.8	357.3	354.8	350.6	343.3	350.6	352.2
Nondefense	165.0	167.3	167.3	166.8	167.0	172.8	175.5	173.6
State and local	846.0	886.7	882.4	891.9	904.7	917.0	923.0	932.7

Table at right — constant dollars (billions of dollars)

	1995	1996	Seasonally adjusted at annual rates					
			1996 II	1996 III	1996 IV	1997 I	1997 II	1997 III
Gross domestic product	6,742.1	6,928.4	6,926.0	6,943.8	7,017.4	7,101.6	7,159.6	7,217.6
Personal consumption expenditures	4,595.3	4,714.1	4,712.2	4,718.2	4,756.4	4,818.1	4,829.4	4,897.9
Durable goods	583.6	611.1	614.8	611.9	617.1	637.8	629.0	655.9
Nondurable goods	1,412.6	1,432.3	1,431.6	1,433.9	1,441.2	1,457.8	1,450.0	1,465.9
Services	2,599.6	2,671.0	2,666.5	2,672.8	2,698.2	2,723.9	2,749.8	2,777.5
Gross private domestic investment	991.5	1,069.1	1,059.2	1,100.3	1,104.8	1,149.2	1,197.1	1,205.5
Fixed investment	962.1	1,041.8	1,035.7	1,060.9	1,068.7	1,079.0	1,111.4	1,148.2
Nonresidential	706.5	771.7	759.7	789.3	800.8	808.9	837.0	872.5
Structures	179.9	188.7	185.6	190.0	196.9	195.9	193.5	195.1
Producers' durable equipment	528.3	586.0	577.1	602.9	606.7	616.6	649.3	685.3
Residential	257.0	272.1	277.2	274.1	271.1	273.3	278.2	280.8
Change in business inventories	27.3	25.0	21.3	37.9	32.9	63.7	77.6	49.5
Net exports of goods and services	-98.8	-114.4	-112.6	-138.9	-105.6	-126.3	-136.6	-162.9
Exports	791.2	857.0	847.4	851.4	901.1	922.7	962.5	972.7
Goods	573.9	628.4	619.2	623.0	666.2	686.2	725.8	732.5
Services	218.0	229.9	229.3	229.4	236.8	238.9	240.8	242.2
Imports	890.1	971.5	960.0	990.2	1,006.6	1,048.9	1,099.1	1,135.7
Goods	749.2	823.1	811.7	841.7	857.5	891.3	938.4	971.5
Services	141.2	149.0	148.8	149.0	150.0	158.4	161.8	165.6
Government consumption expenditures and gross investment	1,251.9	1,257.9	1,265.1	1,261.5	1,261.8	1,260.5	1,270.1	1,273.6
Federal	470.3	464.2	470.7	465.7	459.6	452.8	460.1	458.9
National defense	322.6	317.8	323.2	319.4	313.6	309.9	309.4	310.4
Nondefense	147.5	146.1	147.2	146.0	145.7	148.5	150.2	148.2
State and local	781.6	793.7	794.4	795.9	802.3	807.7	810.1	814.7
Residual	.6	-1.6	-.9	-2.4	-3.8	-2.9	-3.9	-5.3

NOTE.—Percent changes from preceding period for selected items in this table are shown in table 8.1.

EXHIBIT 7.2 Example of production data in NIPA table format (table at left, current dollars; table at right, constant dollars—in billions of dollars)

whether foreign owned or not. Fixed investment, in turn, consists of non-residential and residential. Nonresidential is made up of structures and producers' durable equipment. Structures refers to new construction of hotels, motels, mining exploration, and wells. Producers' durable equipment refers to private business purchases of new machinery, equipment, furniture, and vehicles. Residential consists of structures and residential producers' durable equipment—equipment owned by landlords and rented to tenants. The last component of GPDI, change in business inventories, is the actual change in inventory held by businesses and valued at the average price of the period.

Net exports is exports minus imports. A negative number means a trade deficit, and a positive number means a trade surplus.

Finally, government consumption expenditures, or government purchases, covers purchases from business and compensation of government employees.

The NIPA tables provide a wealth of information.

INDUSTRIES

Gathering, analyzing, and reporting industry data must be conducted in an organized manner if the data and subsequent analyses are to be meaningful. The structure employed most frequently in classifying industrial data is the Standard Industrial Classification system. This classification system is used in the NIPA tables, consumer price index, and producer price index and serves as the government's standard classification system. Perhaps it is best explained in the *Standard Industrial Classification Manual* produced by the Office of Management and Budget:

> The Standard Industrial Classification (SIC) is the statistical classification standard underlying all establishment-based Federal economic statistics classified by industry. The SIC is used to promote the comparability of establishment data describing various facets of the U.S. Economy. The classification covers the entire field of economic activities and defines industries in accordance with the composition and structure of the economy. (page 3)

The structure of the SIC system thus permits the tabulation, analysis, and publication of establishment data on a division, two-digit major group, three-digit industry group, or four-digit industry code, or greater level of detail, depending on the need. In line with the foregoing description, it is helpful to define, within the context of this system, what constitutes an "establishment."

An establishment is an economic unit that is generally at a single physical location and where business is conducted or where services (including industrial operations) are performed. An establishment may or may not be synonymous with the company. For example, in the case of a company that has several plants in different locations, each plant is defined as an establishment. For a trucking company that provides physically dispersed services, the establishment is defined by branch offices, terminals, or stations. In some cases, the establishment may be defined as the main office. An establishment is classified according to its primary activity. The SIC system provides a comprehensive indexing and cross-reference as an aid in identifying the SIC code, given the description of primary activity, or identifying the description of primary activity, given the SIC code.

The structure of the SIC system consists of eleven major divisions, eighty-three major groups, and hundreds of more detailed classifications. A table of major divisions and two-digit industry codes is shown in Exhibit 7.3.

A combined list of major divisions, two-digit, three-digit, and four-digit industry groups can be found in Appendix A. For more details, please refer to the *SIC Manual*.

Division A   Agriculture, forestry, and fishing
       Major Group 01 Agriculture production—crops
       Major Group 02 Agriculture production—livestock and animal specialties
       Major Group 07 Agriculture services
       Major Group 08 Forestry
       Major Group 09 Fishing, hunting, and trapping
Division B   Mining
       Major Group 10 Metal Mining
       Major Group 12 Coal Mining
       Major Group 13 Oil and gas extraction
       Major Group 14 Mining and quarrying of nonmetallic minerals, except fuels
Division C   Construction
       Major Group 15 Building construction—general contractors and operative builders
       Major Group 16 Heavy construction other than building construction—contractors
       Major Group 17 Construction—special trade contractors

EXHIBIT 7.3 Structure of the Standard Industrial Classification (SIC) System

Division D   Manufacturing
            Major Group 20   Food and kindred products
            Major Group 21   Tobacco products
            Major Group 22   Textile mill products
            Major Group 23   Apparel and other finished products made from
                             fabrics and similar materials
            Major Group 24   Lumber and wood products
            Major Group 25   Furniture and fixtures
            Major Group 26   Paper and allied products
            Major Group 27   Printing, publishing, and allied industries
            Major Group 28   Chemicals and allied products
            Major Group 29   Petroleum refining and related industries
            Major Group 30   Rubber and miscellaneous plastic products
            Major Group 31   Leather and leather products
            Major Group 32   Stone, clay, glass, and concrete products
            Major Group 33   Primary metals industries
            Major Group 34   Fabricated metal products, except machinery and
                             transportation equipment
            Major Group 35   Industrial and commercial machinery and
                             computer equipment
            Major Group 36   Electronic and other electrical equipment and com-
                             ponents, except computer equipment
            Major Group 37   Transportation equipment
            Major Group 38   Measuring, analyzing, and controlling instruments;
                             photographic, medical and optical goods; watches
                             and clocks
            Major Group 39   Miscellaneous manufacturing industries
Division E   Transportation, communication, electric, gas, and sanitary services

Divsion K   Nonclassifiable establishments

EXHIBIT 7.3 (continued)

MARKETS AND PRODUCTS

Markets, much like *economies, industries,* or *organizations,* is an abstract term
that has been invented to describe aggregate activity for classification or cat-
egorization purposes. Markets do not exist apart from their organizational
structure, so identifying markets for strategic planning purposes is largely
an idiosyncratic event. There are, however, some caveats. In general, when
defining markets, it is very helpful to begin by utilizing the SIC cross-reference data to gain insight into how the economic data are organized before

setting off to invent your own market structure. For example, let's say that your company is interested in designing and manufacturing automatic controls for regulating residential and commercial environments, and your company's history has been in the design and manufacturing of air-conditioning equipment. Conceptually, the two markets appear similar, but the detailed data are available and found under different SIC classifications.

In this example, *air conditioning units, complete: domestic and industrial* carries an SIC code of 3585. This indicates that this product is part of major group 35: Industrial and commercial machinery and computer equipment, which is part of major division D: Manufacturing. The new product, *refrigeration pressure controls,* has an SIC code of 3822. This product is part of major group 38: Measuring, analyzing, and controlling instruments; photographic, medical and optical goods; watches and clocks, which is also part of major division D: Manufacturing.

Now you can search a commercially available database using the SIC code and generate a list of all U.S. companies that report activity in that standard industrial classification. This list can also provide information on the size of each company in terms of employees and sales, locations, affiliation, whether they are public or private, and the names of the key executives. Other databases can provide similar information for European and Asian companies.

INDUSTRIAL PRODUCTION AND CAPACITY UTILIZATION

The same structure continues for capacity and capacity utilization. The responsible organization changes, however, from the Commerce Department to the Federal Reserve. Each month, the Federal Reserve publishes a statistical release labeled *G.17, Industrial Production and Capacity Utilization.* The report contains a summary and detailed data tables of industrial production and capacity utilization by major market groups and by major industry groups. See Exhibits 7.4 and 7.5.

The G.17 report also contains a second set of tables that present industrial production and capacity utilization data for industry groups plus a reference to relevant SIC codes. See Exhibits 7.6 and 7.7.

THE CYCLE OF BUSINESS

Business cycles differ from normal economic fluctuations in that business cycles are more pronounced and more pervasive than period-to-period fluctuation in economic activity. A working definition of business cycles was

Index, 1992 = 100 / Percent change

Industrial Production	1997 July^r	Aug.^r	Sept.^r	Oct.^p	Percent change 1997 July^r	Aug.^r	Sept.^r	Oct.^p	Oct. 96 to Oct. 97
Total Index	120.8	121.5	122.1	122.7	.8	.6	.5	.5	5.6
Previous estimates	120.9	121.5	122.4		.8	.5	.7		
Major market groups:									
Products, total	116.4	117.4	117.6	118.2	.3	.8	.2	.5	4.8
Consumer goods	112.5	113.3	113.5	114.2	.2	.7	.2	.7	3.1
Business equipment	139.2	142.1	142.0	143.2	1.3	2.1	-.1	.8	11.2
Construction supplies	119.8	121.1	121.0	120.7	-.7	1.1	-.1	-.2	2.6
Materials	127.9	128.2	129.3	129.9	1.5	.2	.9	.5	6.7
Major industry groups:									
Manufacturing	122.6	123.5	123.8	124.6	.8	.8	.2	.6	5.9
Durable	135.4	137.5	137.8	138.7	1.0	1.5	.2	.7	9.1
Nondurable	109.1	108.8	109.2	109.7	.6	-.2	.3	.5	2.1
Mining	107.4	106.7	105.9	104.8	-.3	-.7	-.7	-1.1	1.4
Utilities	113.2	112.6	116.5	116.8	1.3	-.5	3.5	.3	4.4

Percent of capacity

Capacity Utilization	Average 1967–96	1982 Low	1988–89 High	1996 Oct.	Percent of capacity 1997 July^r	Aug.^r	Sept.^r	Oct.^p	Capacity growth Oct. 96 to Oct. 97
Total industry	82.1	71.1	85.3	83.0	83.9	84.1	84.2	84.3	3.9
Previous estimates					83.9	84.1	84.4		
Manufacturing	81.2	69.0	85.7	82.0	82.9	83.2	83.1	83.3	4.3
Advanced processing	80.6	70.4	84.2	79.9	81.0	81.5	81.3	81.6	5.2
Primary processing	82.3	66.2	88.9	86.7	87.2	87.1	87.1	87.2	2.3
Mining	87.5	80.3	86.8	91.0	93.7	92.9	92.2	91.1	1.3
Utilities	87.2	75.9	92.6	89.0	88.9	88.3	91.3	91.4	1.6

^r Numbers have been revised. ^p Numbers are preliminary.

EXHIBIT 7.4 Summary tables from the Federal Reserve's *Industrial Production and Capacity Utilization Report* (seasonally adjusted)

first advanced by Wesley Clair Mitchell in his book *Business Cycles: The Problem and Its Setting* and, while lengthy, convoluted, and vague, continues as *the* definition of business cycles to this day. Mitchell writes:

> *Business cycles are a type of fluctuation found in the aggregate economic activity of nations that organize their work mainly in business enterprises: a cycle consists of expansions occurring at about the same time in many economic activities, followed by similarly general recessions, contractions, and revivals which merge into the expansion phase of the next cycle; this sequence of changes is recurrent but not periodic; in duration business cycles vary from more than one year to ten or twelve years; they are not divisible into shorter cycles of similar character with amplitudes approximating their own. (p. 468)*

Business *cycles,* by definition, increase to a high point, peak, decline to a low point, trough, and once again increase to a high point, only to once again decrease to a low point. This cyclical movement occurs along longer-term secular *trends.* The month and year in which these high and low points occur are very important, as they serve as business-cycle peak and trough reference dates. These reference dates define economic *turning points* and provide an economic reference that is useful in comparing one business cycle with another.

It may come as a surprise that the official business cycle peak and trough dates are not defined by the government! They are defined by a private non-profit corporation, the National Bureau of Economic Research (NBER), using a complex methodology that has not changed much from Mitchell's original approach. For a detailed explanation of the dating methodology, refer to *Measuring Business Cycles,* by Arthur F. Burns and Wesley C. Mitchell (New York: NBER, 1946).

From 1854 to 1991, there have been thirty-one business cycles in the United States. The average expansion duration is 35 months, with the longest being 106 months (February 1961 to December 1969) and the shortest, 10 months (March 1919 to January 1920). The average contraction duration is eighteen months, with the longest being sixty-five months (March 1879 to March 1882). The implementation of national income accounting and the corresponding NIPA structure in the early 1940s resulted in a more structured economy. Therefore, the more relevant economic history for our purposes becomes the period following the end of World War II, since the almost total dedication of the U.S. economy to war production renders the war years unusable as economic reference points.

Since World War II, the United States has experienced nine business cycles. The average expansion duration is fifty months, with the longest

Index, 1992=100

Item	1996 IP Proportion[1]	Seasonally adjusted 1997 May	June	July[r]	Aug[r]	Sept[r]	Oct[p]	Not seasonally adjusted 1997 May	June	July	Aug[r]	Sept[r]	Oct[p]
Total index	100.0	119.5	119.9	120.8	121.5	122.1	122.7	118.0	121.9	119.4	124.6	125.4	124.2
Products, total	59.92	115.9	116.0	116.4	117.4	117.6	118.2	113.6	118.1	116.2	121.5	122.2	120.4
Final products	45.14	117.1	117.4	117.8	119.1	119.1	119.9	114.9	119.1	116.4	122.7	123.4	124.9
Consumer goods	28.15	112.6	112.3	112.5	113.3	113.5	114.2	109.3	113.7	111.6	117.7	117.9	116.0
Durable	5.89	128.4	130.6	128.5	133.0	132.2	133.0	130.4	134.4	115.9	132.9	135.9	140.6
Automotive products	2.40	126.4	128.4	123.1	133.3	134.4	135.3	133.2	135.1	100.9	133.4	138.0	146.3
Autos and trucks	1.38	130.0	132.6	123.5	140.5	143.4	143.9	143.7	143.5	83.4	139.7	146.5	161.2
Autos	.67	117.7	114.9	118.0	124.5	125.1	122.1	128.8	122.8	79.0	122.4	121.0	133.5
Trucks	.71	150.5	159.5	135.8	165.8	171.7	176.1	161.2	167.8	88.5	159.9	176.2	193.6
Auto parts and allied goods	1.02	118.8	120.1	119.2	121.5	120.6	121.8	117.3	121.6	116.8	122.3	124.3	125.4
Other durable goods	3.48	129.7	132.0	132.1	132.6	130.5	131.2	128.4	133.8	126.2	132.4	134.3	136.5
Appliances and electronics	1.19	181.1	187.3	189.9	195.3	186.9	189.4	179.7	193.0	186.2	191.4	195.3	199.8
Appliances and air cond.	.55	126.1	134.5	132.0	137.1	120.5	120.7	127.9	138.7	120.4	120.7	121.9	130.8
Home electronics	.65	249.8	252.2	263.0	268.3	274.3	280.3	243.3	259.3	272.2	284.9	292.6	289.6
Carpeting and furniture	.78	111.7	114.2	108.3	110.1	110.7	111.9	107.4	116.2	104.3	114.6	115.3	116.8
Miscellaneous	1.51	109.6	109.7	111.9	109.5	109.0	108.6	109.9	109.5	104.1	108.3	109.9	111.3
Nondurable	22.26	108.6	107.8	108.5	108.4	108.9	109.6	104.2	108.6	110.1	113.8	113.4	110.0
Nonenergy	18.77	107.8	107.4	108.0	107.8	107.8	108.6	106.0	111.1	110.7	115.3	115.5	112.3
Foods and tobacco	9.72	107.6	106.9	108.1	108.1	107.7	108.3	105.4	110.8	109.3	116.4	116.0	114.1
Clothing	1.89	94.8	94.1	94.5	94.2	94.6	94.2	95.7	98.8	94.1	98.8	99.0	96.9
Chemical products	4.40	118.0	117.3	116.3	116.5	117.3	118.3	114.3	123.0	127.0	128.0	130.1	121.3
Paper products	2.76	103.4	104.5	105.4	104.2	104.3	105.9	103.1	103.7	104.3	105.0	104.6	104.0
Energy products	3.49	113.5	110.4	111.9	112.4	115.2	115.8	94.0	94.4	106.3	105.0	102.0	97.4
Fuels	1.06	111.9	111.8	108.9	111.3	111.6	113.0	112.6	113.5	109.8	111.6	113.9	113.1
Utilities	2.43	114.0	109.5	113.0	112.6	116.5	116.9	85.3	85.4	104.7	102.0	96.4	90.1
Equipment, total	17.00	124.9	126.2	126.9	129.1	128.8	129.5	124.5	128.5	124.6	131.4	132.9	132.2
Business equipment	13.81	136.1	137.4	139.2	142.1	142.0	143.2	136.2	141.0	136.7	145.0	146.9	145.8
Information processing & related	5.68	156.5	159.9	162.4	164.8	166.7	169.0	153.9	161.1	169.1	170.5	173.4	170.2
Computer and office	1.55	366.5	378.4	394.7	410.5	422.4	433.0	359.5	393.2	428.2	429.5	440.7	434.8
Industrial	4.49	129.3	129.2	131.9	134.3	132.4	133.2	128.7	132.4	129.4	136.6	138.5	135.0
Transit	2.30	112.1	112.1	112.3	117.8	118.4	118.0	118.2	117.5	98.3	116.5	117.9	123.3
Autos and trucks	1.13	117.7	110.1	108.8	117.9	118.0	116.9	123.0	119.1	77.9	118.8	119.0	129.7
Other	1.33	128.2	129.2	129.6	130.1	128.0	129.5	128.1	132.1	120.3	133.5	133.9	134.0
Defense and space equipment	2.31	75.6	76.1	75.0	75.8	75.5	75.7	75.1	75.6	73.7	74.7	75.6	75.7
Oil and gas well drilling	.64	154.2	161.4	149.8	147.3	141.7	136.8	143.6	150.4	148.9	151.3	152.2	148.5
Manufactured homes	.23	166.4	163.1	166.3	164.4	161.2	166.0	170.2	176.5	150.8	179.2	170.9	184.6

	IP proportion¹												
Intermediate products	14.78	112.2	112.0	112.0	112.2	113.0	113.2	109.6	114.8	115.4	117.9	118.4	115.9
Consumption supplies	5.72	120.6	120.6	119.8	121.1	121.0	120.7	121.5	126.9	122.3	126.4	127.7	127.1
Business supplies	9.06	107.3	106.9	107.5	107.0	108.4	108.7	102.7	107.8	111.4	112.9	112.9	109.3
Materials	40.08	125.2	126.0	127.9	128.2	129.3	129.9	125.0	128.1	124.6	129.4	133.3	133.3
Durable	23.04	141.7	143.3	145.8	147.2	148.1	149.2	142.4	146.4	139.8	148.4	150.8	151.2
Consumer parts	4.34	127.2	130.1	134.5	135.7	135.9	136.0	133.1	138.5	110.6	138.0	137.8	142.3
Equipment parts	8.63	180.4	183.2	187.3	190.2	192.4	195.9	178.8	184.5	185.1	189.2	194.2	195.3
Other	10.08	121.0	121.2	122.0	122.5	122.8	122.9	120.9	123.3	120.8	124.6	126.5	124.6
Basic metals	3.33	118.4	118.7	118.0	119.0	118.8	118.9	118.8	119.2	114.6	117.0	120.5	118.2
Nondurable	8.92	109.8	109.9	111.3	110.0	110.8	111.1	109.9	111.4	109.3	110.7	111.6	113.4
Textile	.96	105.4	107.8	112.8	108.4	111.2	111.5	110.0	110.0	104.2	110.9	111.1	113.8
Paper	1.61	114.8	111.7	116.3	115.8	113.9	115.9	113.6	113.5	114.3	116.8	114.0	116.1
Chemical	4.39	109.7	109.4	110.4	109.3	109.9	109.9	110.3	110.6	109.7	109.2	111.2	109.8
Other	1.96	107.4	109.7	108.0	107.1	109.3	109.0	105.3	111.3	105.9	108.4	110.0	117.1
Energy	8.12	104.1	103.9	105.0	104.4	106.3	106.1	101.7	104.3	106.1	106.1	103.9	101.5
Primary	5.22	102.5	101.9	103.1	103.0	104.2	103.8	101.4	103.3	102.5	103.0	101.8	98.9
Converted fuel	2.90	107.0	107.6	108.6	107.0	110.2	110.5	102.2	106.4	112.6	111.9	107.7	106.3
SPECIAL AGGREGATES													
Total excluding:													
Autos and trucks	97.48	119.4	119.8	120.9	121.3	121.8	122.4	117.5	121.6	120.3	124.4	125.1	123.6
Motor vehicles and parts	95.20	119.3	119.5	120.5	120.9	121.4	122.0	117.2	121.1	120.7	123.9	124.7	123.0
Computers	97.55	116.5	116.8	117.6	118.2	118.6	119.1	115.1	118.7	115.9	121.0	121.7	120.6
Computers and semiconductors	93.68	112.4	112.6	113.2	113.7	114.0	114.4	111.0	114.5	111.6	116.6	117.1	115.9
Consumer goods excluding:													
Autos and trucks	26.76	111.5	111.1	111.8	111.8	111.9	112.7	107.6	112.1	112.4	116.4	116.4	113.8
Energy	24.65	112.4	112.6	112.6	113.4	113.2	114.0	111.4	116.3	112.2	119.3	120.1	118.5
Business equipment excluding:													
Autos and trucks	12.67	138.5	140.1	142.3	144.6	144.5	145.8	137.5	143.2	142.6	147.6	149.7	147.4
Computer and office equipment	12.25	121.7	122.4	123.6	125.9	125.3	126.0	122.1	125.4	119.5	127.8	129.3	128.5
Materials excluding:													
Energy	31.96	131.8	132.8	135.0	135.5	136.3	137.2	132.2	135.4	139.3	136.5	138.8	133.1

¹ The IP proportion data are estimates of the industries' relative contributions to overall IP growth in the following year.
ʳ Numbers have been revised.

EXHIBIT 7.5 Detailed table showing the Federal Reserve's Industrial Production and Capacity—Market Groups

Index, 1992=100

Item	SIC	1996 IP Proportion[1]	Seasonally adjusted						Not seasonally adjusted					
			1997 Apr.[r]	May[r]	June	Jul.[r]	Aug.[r]	Sept.[r]	1997 Apr.[r]	May[r]	June	July[r]	Aug.[r]	Sept.[r]
Metal mining	**10**	.42	103.5	104.2	107.4	103.4	104.5	102.9	102.7	104.8	110.6	104.4	105.7	105.2
Iron ore	101	.06	109.0	108.9	110.7	102.0	114.5	113.7	103.0	114.0	115.8	107.6	119.9	120.2
Nonferrous ores	102–4,8,9	.36	102.9	103.6	107.1	103.8	103.1	101.4	102.9	103.7	110.1	104.2	103.7	103.1
Copper	102	.12	106.4	108.4	119.8	109.9	109.4	105.5	107.3	105.9	123.6	112.5	112.0	107.2
Coal mining	**12**	.87	104.1	115.9	107.4	114.1	109.8	109.3	103.9	109.9	106.9	104.3	111.6	112.5
Oil and gas extraction	**13**	3.71	104.5	105.0	105.8	104.8	103.9	103.3	103.3	103.5	103.9	103.4	103.3	104.0
Crude oil and natural gas	131	2.84	96.1	96.4	96.0	97.0	96.4	96.8	96.6	96.4	95.6	95.3	94.6	95.3
Crude oil, total		1.52	88.7	87.2	86.8	87.9	86.9	87.8	88.7	87.5	86.7	86.4	85.8	89.9
Natural gas		1.32	106.3	109.1	108.7	109.5	109.5		107.6	108.6	107.9	107.4	106.7	
Natural gas liquids	132	.22	108.7	107.8	109.1	109.9	99.9	109.8	109.9	108.6	109.5	110.4	110.2	110.8
Oil and gas well drilling	138	.64	152.5	154.2	161.4	149.8	147.3	141.7	140.8	143.6	150.4	148.9	151.3	152.2
Stone and earth minerals	**14**	.60	122.3	121.3	123.7	119.8	123.3	122.1	121.2	133.1	141.0	137.2	144.3	142.9
Foods	**20**	9.37	108.3	108.1	107.9	108.8	108.4	108.1	104.6	106.0	110.2	111.1	115.4	116.4
Meat products	201	1.26	112.6	113.9	112.4	114.3	114.5	110.8	113.8	112.6	116.1	110.7	117.0	113.7
Beef		.48	111.4	113.1	108.8	112.0	112.8	106.0	109.5	112.1	116.3	113.2	118.6	111.1
Pork		.27	96.1	95.1	100.5	102.9	100.6	103.5	101.0	91.2	95.6	90.7	96.4	104.0
Poultry		.49	126.6	128.9	125.7	126.0	127.5	122.3	128.0	128.5	130.7	122.4	130.2	123.7
Miscellaneous meats		.02	92.5	93.9	93.1	91.8	89.9	92.5	92.7	89.0	91.3	83.4	85.5	90.8
Dairy products	202	.81	100.2	100.6	102.2	103.0	102.5	102.9	107.9	109.4	110.9	104.7	99.4	97.0
Butter	2021	.01	80.8	76.0	76.4	80.6	77.1	78.6	94.1	80.8	68.3	62.9	57.4	63.2
Cheese	2022	.19	108.7	109.5	111.8	113.3	112.0	111.3	109.9	113.2	114.6	108.7	106.2	111.7
Concentrated milk	2023	.14	91.5	93.1	95.7	100.8	98.9	100.8	109.6	112.0	107.5	97.8	84.5	79.7
Frozen desserts	2024	.12	98.7	97.8	99.0	94.4	94.1	96.3	108.1	110.9	126.7	117.7	110.2	95.9
Milk and misc. dairy products	2026	.34	101.6	101.6	102.7	103.0	103.6	102.9	106.6	106.8	106.2	102.7	100.8	99.8
Canned and frozen food	203	1.30	106.8	105.5	106.7	108.0	105.9	104.2	96.4	99.0	104.3	110.4	124.0	128.5
Grain mill products	204	1.30	108.5	108.7	108.0	109.8	107.0	108.6	105.7	106.2	106.6	108.4	109.2	112.8
Bakery products	205	1.03	102.6	102.3	102.1	104.8	103.9	103.3	96.4	99.7	107.0	114.2	115.5	115.8

	SIC	IP prop.												
Sugar and confectionery	206	.64	114.4	112.7	111.2	107.1	110.5	112.8	98.8	96.9	99.5	95.5	107.9	120.3
Fats and oils	207	.24	98.1	96.9	97.0	95.9	96.4	96.8	98.9	93.5	93.5	87.8	91.9	94.6
Beverages	208	1.74	112.1	111.4	111.4	111.0	112.4	112.6	111.6	113.8	120.4	120.6	123.7	120.7
Beer and ale	2082,3	.54	105.8	105.5	109.8	105.7			115.9	117.7	122.7	116.5		
Soft drinks	2086.7	.98	116.8	116.2	113.6	115.6	116.6	118.6	109.6	113.9	121.5	130.0	133.5	136.8
Coffee and miscellaneous	209	1.05	110.2	110.8	109.8	111.4	110.8	111.4	102.0	106.0	111.7	118.1	120.1	121.5
Roasted coffee	2095	.17	103.4	104.8	95.7	99.0	100.2		93.0	97.2	85.7	90.5	96.0	
Tobacco products	21	1.16	105.5	104.2	101.8	103.3	104.8	104.7	108.6	100.3	113.4	88.5	115.6	107.8
Textile mill products	22	1.57	108.6	107.3	108.9	111.3	110.2	111.3	113.3	110.7	115.5	107.2	114.1	114.0
Fabrics	221–4	.39	111.3	103.4	105.3	112.4	105.1	109.0	115.9	109.3	106.9	101.4	107.2	106.5
Cotton and synthetic	221,2	.32	113.4	103.1	105.3	113.0	105.7		117.2	108.6	105.7	100.8	107.7	
Narrow fabrics	224	.04	116.7	115.4	113.4	115.4	114.0	113.8	115.7	116.5	118.0	109.0	116.1	116.6
Knit goods	225	.44	111.9	113.8	111.9	114.5	113.6	114.1	112.1	118.7	126.3	116.2	122.2	123.4
Knit garments	2253,4,7–9	.32	113.6	116.5	114.7	118.3	117.2	118.1	108.0	119.9	127.0	123.4	134.3	132.9
Fabric finishing	226	.15	99.1	92.7	96.8	103.0	94.0	96.0	104.0	98.3	96.5	93.4	98.0	95.2
Carpeting	227	.18	96.2	102.6	108.0	96.1	111.9	105.4	114.7	95.4	118.6	101.7	111.8	107.3
Yarns and miscellaneous	228,9	.41	112.1	112.4	114.7	117.2	117.5	119.4	115.1	115.4	118.4	111.3	119.6	121.9
Cotton and synthetic yarns	2281,2,4	.19	102.5	102.3	106.4	110.4	109.2	114.0	108.6	108.7	110.8	102.0	113.0	116.0
Apparel products	23	1.80	96.1	96.4	96.4	96.5	95.7	96.0	94.5	96.3	98.5	94.6	98.9	99.3
Lumber and products	24	2.06	113.6	114.0	114.6	113.4	113.1	112.9	114.0	112.6	118.2	111.8	117.1	117.6
Logging and lumber	241,2	.79	103.2	103.1	104.8	101.8	103.1	103.4	102.0	99.6	108.6	101.3	107.3	109.5
Logging	241	.28	95.3	94.2	93.1	93.0	91.4	92.7	86.4	90.0	95.7	97.7	101.1	101.9
Lumber products	243–5,9	1.27	121.5	122.1	121.9	122.2	120.5	120.1	123.0	122.2	125.4	119.6	124.6	123.7
Millwork and plywood	243	.65	114.4	114.3	114.8	115.3	112.6	113.8	113.5	115.4	117.8	115.9	117.0	117.4
Plywood	2435,6	.15	101.1	101.1	103.3	102.0	96.9	98.8	102.0	103.0	105.3	98.8	100.4	102.5
Manufactured homes	245	.23	168.0	166.4	163.1	166.3	164.4	161.2	176.2	170.2	176.5	150.8	179.2	170.9

[1] The IP proportion data are estimates of the industries' relative contributions to overall IP growth in the following year.
[r] Numbers have been revised.

EXHIBIT 7.6 Summary table of the Federal Reserve's *Industrial Production and Capacity Report* showing industry groups and relevant SIC codes

		1996 IP Proportion[1]	Seasonally adjusted						Not seasonally adjusted					
			1997 May	June	July[r]	Aug.[r]	Sept.[r]	Oct.[p]	1997 May	June	July[r]	Aug.[r]	Sept.[r]	Oct.[p]
Item	SIC													
Total index		100.0	119.5	119.9	120.8	121.5	122.1	122.7	118.0	121.9	119.4	124.6	125.4	124.2
Manufacturing		86.34	121.0	121.6	122.6	123.5	123.8	124.6	120.6	124.7	120.9	126.9	128.3	127.5
Primary processing		27.72	115.8	115.7	116.3	116.4	116.8	117.0	115.8	118.1	114.5	118.1	119.4	119.3
Advanced processing		58.62	123.6	124.5	125.7	127.0	127.3	128.3	123.0	128.0	124.0	131.3	132.7	131.5
Durable		46.79	132.7	134.1	135.4	137.5	137.8	138.7	133.2	137.3	130.5	139.1	141.4	141.6
Lumber and products	24	2.06	114.0	114.6	113.4	113.1	112.6	112.4	112.6	112.4	111.8	117.1	117.6	118.9
Furniture and fixtures	25	1.30	113.9	114.5	112.4	110.6	112.5	112.6	110.7	115.4	110.9	118.6	118.9	113.8
Stone, clay, and glass products	32	2.12	112.8	113.5	114.0	113.7	113.7	114.1	114.0	117.5	115.0	118.3	117.7	118.7
Primary metals	33	3.52	123.4	123.1	123.4	123.7	124.8	124.8	124.2	123.6	117.7	121.1	126.6	124.8
Iron and steel	331.2	1.88	123.6	120.3	120.9	119.6	122.9	122.6	124.1	121.4	116.4	116.2	125.0	122.1
Raw steel		.09	115.8	115.1	115.4	116.3	119.0	118.3	115.7	115.1	110.6	112.2	118.1	117.9
Nonferrous	333–6.9	1.64	123.1	126.2	126.2	128.5	126.9	127.3	124.2	126.1	119.2	126.7	128.3	127.9
Fabricated metal products	34	5.28	121.1	120.8	121.1	121.7	121.9	121.9	119.8	122.9	120.1	124.9	126.7	124.1
Industrial machinery & equip.	35	9.51	170.5	172.2	176.6	181.2	180.4	182.4	170.3	178.0	176.7	183.7	187.6	184.7
Computer and office equip.	357	2.45	371.8	383.9	400.4	416.4	428.4	439.2	364.7	398.9	434.3	435.6	447.1	441.0
Electrical machinery	36	8.58	178.1	181.7	185.9	188.2	188.7	191.6	176.4	183.1	182.8	188.4	193.1	193.8
Semiconductors	3672–9	3.87	312.8	321.2	333.3	340.9	345.4	354.4	310.8	323.1	326.9	337.3	347.6	352.5
Transportation equipment	37	8.41	110.2	112.4	112.6	116.9	118.2	118.6	115.8	118.0	94.6	117.0	118.2	124.0
Motor vehicles and parts	371	4.80	123.7	127.1	126.7	134.6	136.6	136.4	134.8	138.2	90.1	136.7	137.0	148.6
Autos and light trucks		2.29	121.6	123.1	116.9	131.0	133.3	133.0	134.8	133.5	79.1	130.5	135.3	149.0
Aerospace and misc.	372–6.9	3.62	96.4	97.4	98.3	99.1	99.9	100.7	96.9	98.0	96.6	97.4	99.3	100.0
Instruments	38	4.72	105.2	105.9	105.9	107.0	106.1	107.2	103.6	107.3	107.3	109.2	109.4	107.5
Miscellaneous	39	1.29	117.0	117.5	118.9	118.4	117.8	118.1	116.3	117.8	113.7	118.8	120.6	121.7
Nondurable		39.55	108.7	108.4	109.1	108.8	109.2	109.7	107.3	111.4	110.5	114.0	114.4	112.7
Foods	20	9.37	108.1	107.9	108.8	108.4	108.1	108.6	106.0	110.2	111.2	115.4	116.4	114.1
Tobacco products	21	1.16	104.2	101.8	103.3	104.8	104.7	106.3	100.3	113.4	88.5	115.6	107.8	117.8
Textile mill products	22	1.57	107.3	108.9	111.3	110.2	111.3	111.6	110.7	115.5	107.2	114.1	114.0	117.3
Apparel products	23	1.80	96.4	96.4	96.5	95.7	96.0	96.1	96.3	98.5	94.6	98.9	99.3	97.5
Paper and products	26	3.29	112.8	111.7	114.8	114.0	113.5	114.8	110.8	113.2	112.7	115.2	113.5	117.3

Index, 1992=100

	SIC	IP prop.												
Printing and publishing	27	6.44	99.8	99.7	100.2	99.5	100.1	100.7	96.8	101.6	104.7	106.3	106.2	101.9
Chemicals and products	28	10.17	112.7	112.3	112.4	111.9	112.9	113.3	111.7	115.7	116.7	117.0	118.9	114.9
Petroleum products	29	1.75	112.1	111.3	108.7	110.1	110.8	112.0	113.6	116.0	113.5	114.6	116.0	113.2
Rubber and plastics products	30	3.78	123.4	124.0	124.2	126.5	126.3	126.5	123.2	126.2	120.4	127.6	127.8	128.5
Leather and products	31	.20	77.0	75.6	75.3	73.2	72.8	72.0	77.0	77.7	71.3	74.7	74.7	73.4
Mining														
Metal mining	10	.42	108.1	107.8	107.4	106.7	105.9	104.8	107.3	108.3	106.7	108.5	109.0	108.2
Coal mining	12	.87	104.2	107.4	103.4	104.5	102.9	101.5	104.8	110.6	104.4	105.7	105.2	100.1
Oil and gas mining	13	3.71	115.9	107.4	114.1	109.8	109.3	108.5	109.9	106.9	104.3	111.6	112.5	111.9
Stone and earth minerals	14	.60	121.3	123.7	119.8	123.3	122.1	122.2	133.1	141.0	137.2	144.3	142.9	145.0
Utilities		8.07	112.4	111.7	113.2	112.6	116.5	116.8	99.1	103.7	113.9	112.0	107.3	102.5
Electric	491.3pt	6.26	110.5	111.1	113.4	112.6	117.8	118.1	102.6	114.7	128.1	126.1	120.4	108.9
Gas	492.3pt	1.81	119.0	113.5	112.5	112.4	112.0	112.1	86.6	65.1	64.1	62.6	61.4	79.6
SPECIAL AGGREGATES														
Manufacturing excluding:														
Motor vehicles and parts		81.54	120.8	121.2	122.3	122.8	123.1	123.9	119.8	123.9	122.4	126.3	127.7	126.3
Computer and office equipment		83.89	117.6	118.0	118.8	119.6	119.8	120.4	117.2	120.9	116.8	122.8	124.1	123.3
Computers and semiconductors		80.02	112.8	113.1	113.7	114.3	114.4	114.9	112.5	116.0	111.7	117.7	118.7	117.9
Memo: Motor vehicle assemblies[2]														
Total			11.6	11.7	11.0	12.4	12.6	12.6	12.7	12.0	7.8	11.7	12.7	14.6
Autos			5.8	5.7	5.8	6.1	6.1	6.0	6.5	5.9	4.1	5.8	6.0	6.9
Trucks			5.8	6.0	5.2	6.3	6.5	6.6	6.2	6.2	3.7	5.9	6.7	7.7
Light			5.4	5.8	4.9	6.0	6.2	6.3	5.9	5.9	3.4	5.6	6.4	7.4
Heavy and medium			0.3	0.3	0.3	0.3	0.3	0.3	0.3	0.3	0.3	0.3	0.3	0.3

1. The IP proportion data are estimates of the industries' relative contributions to overall IP growth in the following year.
2. Millions of units at an annual rate.

Note—*Primary processing manufacturing* includes textile mill products, paper and products, industrial chemicals, synthetic materials, and fertilizers, petroleum products, rubber and plastic products, lumber and products, primary metals, fabricated metals, and stone, clay, and glass products.
Advanced processing manufacturing includes foods, tobacco products, apparel products, printing and publishing, chemical products and other agricultural chemicals, leather and products, furniture and fixtures, industrial machinery and equipment, electrical machinery, transportation equipment, instruments and miscellaneous manufactures.
r Numbers have been revised.
p Numbers are preliminary.

EXHIBIT 7.7 Detailed table of the Federal Reserve's *Industrial Production and Capacity Report* showing industry groups and SIC codes

duration from February 1961 to December 1969 as indicated previously. The shortest duration was twelve months (July 1980 to July 1981). The average contraction duration is eleven months, with the longest sixteen months (November 1973 to March 1975 and July 1981 to November 1982).

Now, given that business cycles are recurring but not periodic, we can employ the concepts of expansion and contraction (or recovery and recession) as a useful backdrop and simplified economic model. In the context of these models, we are in either a recovery or a recession within the in-between points defined as turning points. Because business cycles are nonperiodic, we cannot say with any certainty that the recovery or, conversely, the recession will last a given number of months. What we can say is that the current recovery is the longest post–World War II recovery and, by looking more closely at the pattern of the various economic time series, whether the recovery is likely or not to continue. These are topics we will explore in greater detail in subsequent chapters.

8

Linking Economic and Company Data

WITH A BACKDROP OF THE MACROECONOMY and a mental model of recoveries and recessions, the discussion now turns to exploring relationships between general economic factors and what is happening or not happening within your own company. Remember that the business cycle is defined across a broad number of economic variables, rather than a few data series. This is an important point, as your company is active in one or more economic sectors defined in the prior chapter. The task is to now link the trends in the broader economy to your company's performance.

What are the major economic factors that influence your company, your suppliers, and your customers? How can information about these factors assist internal planning and forecasting activities? The diagram in Exhibit 8.1 illustrates conceptually a number of broad economic relationships.

EXPLORING RELATIONSHIPS

By *relationships,* we mean specifically the relationship or nature of change of one variable compared with another. The relationship could be positive in the sense that as one variable increases, the other variable also increases, or it could be negative in that as one variable increases the other decreases. Furthermore, the relationships could be either linear or nonlinear. For example, if one variable increases one unit and the other variable increases a like unit,

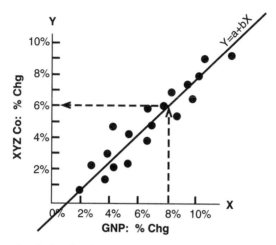

EXHIBIT 8.1 Simple relationship between GNP growth and company growth

then the relationship is said to be linear. Also, if one variable increases one unit and the other variable increase three units, then the relationship is said to be linear; that is, there is a disproportionate increase in the second variable for each unit increase in the primary variable, although the relationship is linear. Finally, key relationships between data series can involve single variables or multivariables. While single relationships are less complex than multivariate relationships, they are no less meaningful. First, seek to develop accurate relationships between single variables, and move to multivariate analyses when stronger correlations are desired.

REGRESSION AND CORRELATION

The change in one variable that accompanies a specific change in another variable is referred to as a *functional relation;* that is, the change in the *dependent variable* (the one being observed) is a function of the change in the *independent variable* (the one selected or manipulated by the experimenter). Such a relation may be represented algebraically by an equation or presented graphically in the form of a curve. Functional relations are often studied experimentally, by which the experimenter manipulates the independent variable and observes changes in the dependent variable. In the context of forecasting, however, experimental methods are less practical, so the methods of regression and correlation analyses are preferred.

Regression and correlation are the two principal methodological approaches employed in the exploration of relationships. There are four broad categories of regression analyses: *simple linear, simple curvilinear, multiple linear,* and *multiple curvilinear.* Simple and multiple linear regression analyses involve straight-line relationships between single variables and multivariables. The most frequent method of describing the relationship algebraically between two variables in a simple linear regression is the equation of a straight line, $Y = a + bX$, where Y refers to the value of the dependent variable, b refers to the slope of the line, X refers to the value of the independent variable, and a refers to the y-intercept. The slope, b, is also the *coefficient of regression.*

$Y = a + bX$ is also known as the *linear regression equation* that describes the *linear regression line.* The linear regression line is often referred to as the *line of best fit* or the *least-squares line.* These last two terms refer to the methodology used to construct the regression line and indicate that the linear line through the various data points fits the best, or, in other words, minimizes the squared error terms. See Exhibit 8.2 for a general orientation to the types of linear relationships described.

Multiple curvilinear regression analyses, on the other hand, include nonlinear relationships described, for example, by parabolic, exponential, or other types of curves or algebraic equations. In these cases the curves are referred to as *regression curves,* and the specific equations are referred to as simply *regression equations.* See Exhibit 8.3 for a sample of nonlinear curves and their respective equations.

Regression analysis is used to estimate the values of one variable when the values of another variable are either given or known. This type of analysis can provide valuable information regarding the average difference or change in the values of the estimated variable for each corresponding difference or change in the known variable, but forecasters often want additional information. For example:

- How accurately can the dependent variable be estimated from the independent variable?
- How important is the relationship between the dependent and independent variables?
- Given that the relationships are computed using sample data, how likely are the relations to depart from the universe from which the sample was drawn?

These three questions are addressed by special statistical measures termed the *standard error of estimate, correlation coefficient,* and *index of correlation.*

The Straight Line Equation

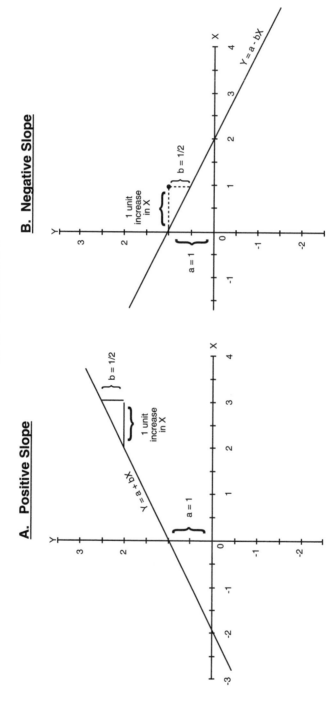

A. Positive Slope

B. Negative Slope

EXHIBIT 8.2 Types of linear relationships

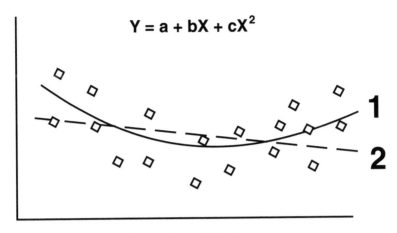

$$Y = a + bX + cX^2$$

EXHIBIT 8.3 A nonlinear relationship (solid line)

The last question is beyond the scope of this book and is addressed by knowledge of the distributions of these coefficients, the standard errors, and the type of sampling employed.

The *accuracy* question refers to the variations in the dependent variable that are unrelated to changes in the independent variable. These differences are called residuals, and the *standard error of estimate* is the standard deviation of the residuals. The unit of measure for the standard error is the same as for the variable measured. So, if percent change is the unit of measure, the standard error will be expressed in percent change. The standard error of estimate is the statistical measure used to determine the closeness with which the dependent variable may be estimated, given specific values for the independent variable.

The relative *importance of the relationship* is measured by the *correlation coefficient* for linear regression and by the *index of correlation* for curvilinear regression. Whereas the standard error of estimate measures the size of the residuals without regard to the degree of variation, the *coefficient of determination* measures what proportion of the original variation has been accounted for. The square root of this term is the correlation coefficient. For linear regression, the symbol for the correlation coefficient is r. The values of r can range from plus 1 to minus 1. A correlation coefficient of plus 1 indicates a perfect positive correlation, while a minus 1 indicates a perfect negative correlation. For curvilinear regression, the values range from 0.0 to 1.0.

Note that two regression lines can be fitted to any set of data. For example, we can fit the equation $Y = a + bX$ and also the equation $X = a + bY$. While there are two possible regression lines, there is only one correlation coefficient

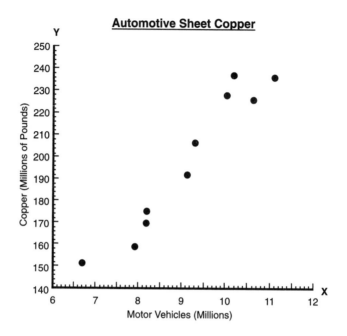

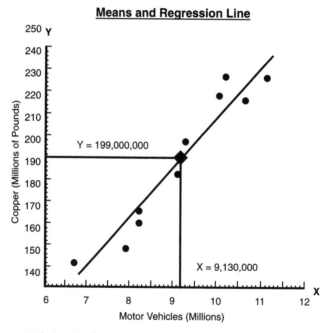

EXHIBIT 8.4 Relationship between quantity of sheet copper for automotive use and number of automobiles produced

for any set of data. The correlation coefficient indicates how closely the two regression lines approach one another. The higher the correlation coefficient, the closer the two lines. When the correlation coefficient equals 1.00, the two lines coincide. When there is no correlation and the coefficient is 0.0, the two lines are orthogonal. This indicates that the two lines can be used to estimate graphically the degree of correlation between the two variables.

Keep in mind that regression and correlation do *not* imply causation. The analytical tools are useful for estimating values of the dependent variable from known values of the independent variable. The *coefficient of determination* (the square of the correlation coefficient) simply indicates the proportion of the dependent variable accounted for, given the nature and values of the independent variable. The changes in the independent variable do not cause the changes in the dependent variable; they simply co-relate or co-vary.

A real-world example drawn from the automotive field is shown in Exhibit 8.4. In this example, we are interested in estimating or forecasting the number of pounds of copper consumed, given the number of automobiles manufactured.

ECONOMIC INDICATORS

We have discussed briefly the relationship of one variable to another and how that relationship can be quantified and assessed, employing regression and correlation, to help forecast company variables of interest, or dependent variables. One potentially valuable source of independent variables is found in the category of business cycle indicators.

Business cycle indicators are classified into three categories: *leading, coinciding,* and *lagging,* depending on the timing of their movements. Leading indicators are those data series that tend to move in advance of the general business cycle. The coinciding indicators move in conjunction with the broader business cycle, and the lagging indicators move following movement in the general business cycle. The specific data series in each category were carefully selected based on the following criteria:

- *Conformity* to the general business cycle
- *Consistent timing* as a leading, coinciding, or lagging indicator
- *Economic significance* based on generally accepted business cycle theory
- *Statistical adequacy* by way of a reliable data gathering process
- *Smoothness* in the month-to-month movements
- *Currency* or timely availability through a prompt publication schedule

The business cycle indicators were published previously in the monthly *Survey of Current Business Conditions* by the U.S. Department of Commerce, Bureau of Economic Analysis. Effective December 1996, the business cycle indicators (BCI) are now published by the Conference Board, a New York City–based nonprofit private corporation.

Each BCI category consists of a composite index and a number of component series. The composite indexes are typically reported in the financial and trade press. For our purposes, we want to present, for each category, both the composite and the component series. Each of these become candidate data series with which to regress and correlate your company-specific data.

The leading indicators and their respective series numbers are as follows:

BCI No. 910   Composite leading index
BCI No. 1   Average weekly hours, manufacturing
BCI No. 5   Initial claims for unemployment insurance, thousands
BCI No. 8   Manufacturers' new orders, consumer goods and materials
BCI No. 32   Vendor performance, slower deliveries diffusion index
BCI No. 27   Manufacturers' new orders, nondefense capital goods
BCI No. 29   Building permits, new private housing units
BCI No. 19   Stock prices, S&P 500 common stocks
BCI No. 106   Money supply, M2
BCI No. 129   Interest rate spread, 10-year Treasury bonds less federal funds
BCI No. 83   Index of consumer expectations (University of Michigan)

The coinciding indicators and their component data series are as follows:

BCI No. 920   Composite coincident index
BCI No. 41   Employees on nonagricultural payrolls
BCI No. 51   Personal income less transfer payments
BCI No. 47   Industrial production
BCI No. 57   Manufacturing and trade sales

The lagging indicators and component series are as follows:

BCI No. 930   Composite lagging index
BCI No. 91   Average duration of unemployment, weeks
BCI No. 77   Ratio, manufacturing and trade inventories to sales
BCI No. 62   Change in labor cost per unit of output, manufacturing
BCI No. 109   Average prime rate charged by banks

BCI No. 101   Commercial and industrial loans outstanding

BCI No. 95   Ratio, consumer installment credit outstanding to personal income

BCI No. 120   Change in Consumer Price Index for services

All of the indicators listed are published monthly in The Conference Board's *Business Cycle Indicators.* The BCI also contain a large number of data series that are not part of either the leading, coinciding, or lagging indicators but can be useful in forecasting. These indicators carry a three-letter designation following the title. For example, series number 21, *average weekly overtime hours, manufacturing,* carries the three-letter suffix (L,C,L). The first letter indicates that the series *leads* at business cycle peaks; the second letter indicates the series *coincides* with business cycle troughs; and the last letter signifies that the series *leads* the business cycle overall. These three-letter indications can be helpful in narrowing the search for indicators that lead your company's sales. In addition to specific numerical data, each series is graphed. Current and historical data are also available at the BCI website at http://www.tcb-indicators.org. A sample of the graphs published each month is shown in Exhibit 8.5.

ECONOMIC INDICATORS AND COMPANY DATA

Exploring relationships is all about looking for those indicators that meet the six key criteria of conformity, consistent timing, economic significance, statistical adequacy, smoothness, and currency or timeliness, and then exploring how each or a combination of them relates to your company's bookings and billings.

Bookings relate to the value of the orders taken by your company's sales force and usually lead company sales by one or more periods. *Billings* relate to the value of shipments which, in turn, translate into sales or revenue. For many companies, there is an intervening variable called the *backlog,* which we will revisit in our discussions of the paired index in Chapter 15. Given that bookings can be shifted by special pricing or promotions, the most important company data series to use as a dependent variable is billings or sales.

The first thing to do is to seasonally adjust your company's sales and then construct a series of scatter plots, using single variables initially, and then move to multiple variables when and if single variables fail your correlation-coefficient requirements. Continue to search for those indicators that correlate highly with your company's sales.

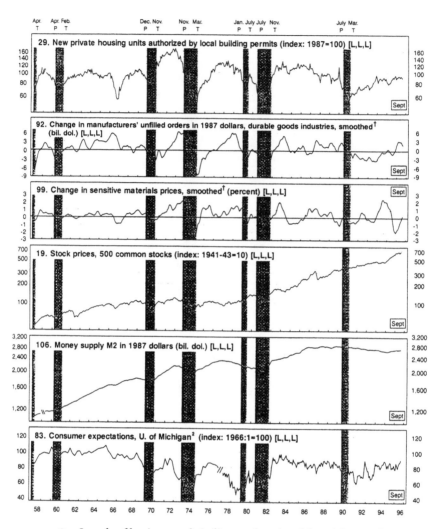

EXHIBIT 8.5 Sample of business cycle indicators (reprinted from The Conference Board with permission)

But what is a "good enough" correlation coefficient? The answer is that it depends on the purpose of your forecast. For example, if this is your only forecast, and factory staff and resources depend heavily on minimal forecast error, then you will require a correlation coefficient above 0.95, which would still give you, on average, about a 10 percent error. If, on the other hand, your forecast is supplemented with accurate sales-activity numbers, then the correlation coefficient could be as low as 0.75.

The final graph, Exhibit 8.6, is also from the BCI and illustrates the relationship between the composite index of leading indicators (six-month growth rate annualized) and the official recessionary periods as defined by the National Bureau of Economic Research. Note that the indicators are not infallible. Occasionally they signal an impending recession that failed to materialize. In fact, the last two recessions they failed to lead at all! The short horizontal dashed lines provide additional information. These indicate the time periods in which more than one-half of the component series were falling. On balance, the indicators lead major changes in the economy and should be used as a guide and not as an absolute.

Table 2 Timing of the Revised Composite Indexes at Cyclical Turning Points					
	Composite Leading Index		Composite Coincident Index		Composite Lagging Index	
Leads (-) or lags (+) at business cycle peaks (months)						
Apr 1960	-11		0	-3*	+3	
Dec 1969	-8	-11*	-2		+3	
Nov 1973	-9		0		+13	
Jan 1980	-15		0		+3	
Jul 1981	-3	-8*	+1		+2	+3*
Jul 1990	-6**	-18*	-1		-9	-8*
Leads (-) or lags (+) at business cycle troughs (months)						
Feb 1961	-3	-2*	0		+9	+6*
Nov 1970	-7	-1*	0		+15	
Mar 1975	-1		0		+18	+21*
Jul 1980	-3	-2*	0		+3	
Nov 1982	-8	-10*	+1		+6	+7*
Mar 1991	-2		0		+21	+36*

* Timing of current version when different from the Department of Commerce peak/trough designations
** -25 for absolute peak in cycle

EXHIBIT 8.6 Table from *Business Cycle Indicators* showing lead times of the leading indicators

9

The Economic Pentad

MONITORING AND REPORTING on upcoming changes in the economy and how those changes impact specific industries and groups of companies is an extremely valuable function. It is critical that the executive staff of your organization have some ongoing sense of how the economy is changing, or not changing, over time so that they can incorporate this economic insight into their review of capacity expansion and new-product-development plans. The Economic Pentad, or five-phase system, provides an integrated approach to this longer look ahead.

In the previous chapter, we explored the leading, coinciding, and lagging indicators and how they can be used to anticipate turning points in the broader economy. The process really begins much earlier with the implementation of the government's fiscal and monetary policy. It is helpful to view changes in fiscal and monetary policy as first-order perturbations to the economic system, with changes in either fiscal or monetary policy impacting other economic indicators as the first-order changes ripple through the economy.

THE FIVE-PHASE SYSTEM

The Economic Pentad was developed by my friend and colleague Robert L. McLaughlin as an additional tool for forecasters interested in a longer look ahead. The underlying concept is basic and straightforward. It holds that

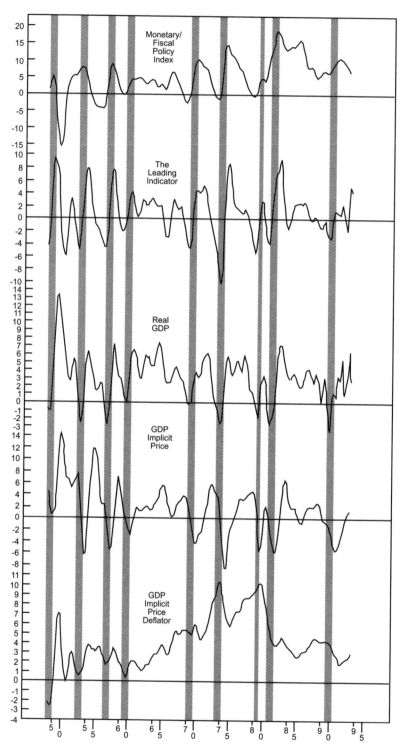

EXHIBIT 9.1 The Economic Pentad

knowledge about the government's monetary and fiscal policies can be used intrinsically as a longer-term leading indicator. The five phases, as presented in Exhibit 9.1, are: the Monetary/Fiscal Policy Index (MFP), the Leading Indicator (LI), Real Gross Domestic Product (GDP), the Lagging Indicator (LgI), and the Gross Domestic Product Implicit Price Deflator (IPD). The graph shown was first presented in the June 1994 issue of *Micrometrics*. The black dots illustrate the time-phased effects of a neutral to slightly restrictive monetary policy coupled with a constraining fiscal policy. The stack graph shows how the resultant MFP index flowed through to GDP and finally to a measure of inflation, the IPD.

MONETARY/FISCAL POLICY INDEX

The key to the five-phase system is the top series, the monetary/fiscal policy index. The index is an equally weighted average of two key series, monetary policy and fiscal policy, and is shown in Exhibit 9.2. *Monetary policy* is defined by the M2 money supply in billions of constant 1987 dollars (BCI series number 106). A positive or increasing value conveys monetary *stimulation,* while a negative or decreasing value signals monetary *restraint.* The series consists of quarter-to-quarter changes at an annual rate and may be graphed as shown or smoothed using a three-quarter moving average of a three-quarter moving average—a 3 × 3 moving average. The MFP series in Exhibit 9.1 contains the smoothed series.

Fiscal policy is also a percentage change series that is derived by dividing total *federal government expenditures* by total *federal government receipts* (see Exhibit 9.3 for the relevant NIPA tables). When spending (expenditures)

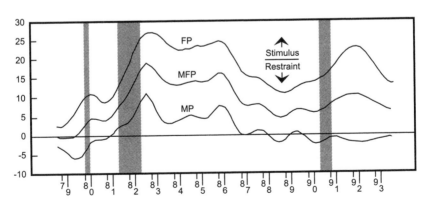

EXHIBIT 9.2 The monetary/fiscal policy (MFP) index

Table 3.2.—Federal Government Receipts and Current Expenditures

[Billions of dollars]

| | 1995 | 1996 | Seasonally adjusted at annual rates | | | | | |
| | | | 1996 | | | 1997 | | |
			II	III	IV	I	II	III
Receipts	1,463.2	1,587.6	1,583.8	1,598.6	1,641.6	1,675.3	1,709.3	1,740.2
Personal tax and nontax receipts	605.8	686.7	688.8	695.7	717.5	746.9	767.9	781.1
Income taxes	588.7	666.8	668.6	674.8	697.2	725.0	744.1	757.7
Estate and gift taxes	14.9	17.5	17.8	18.4	17.7	19.3	21.1	20.7
Nontaxes	2.2	2.5	2.4	2.5	2.6	2.6	2.6	2.7
Corporate profits tax accruals	182.1	194.5	197.2	196.7	192.0	204.9	207.7	218.6
Federal Reserve banks	23.4	20.1	20.0	20.1	20.4	20.9	21.2	21.7
Other	158.7	174.4	177.2	176.6	171.7	184.0	186.5	197.0
Indirect business tax and nontax accruals	93.5	95.8	90.0	91.5	110.2	88.2	92.2	92.4
Excise taxes	58.1	56.4	54.9	55.7	59.6	56.5	59.0	59.0
Customs duties	19.4	19.2	19.5	20.2	16.8	18.6	20.5	20.9
Nontaxes	16.1	20.2	15.6	15.5	33.7	13.2	12.7	12.6
Contributions for social insurance	581.8	610.5	607.8	614.8	622.0	635.3	641.5	648.1
Current expenditures	1,637.6	1,698.1	1,695.4	1,698.2	1,718.8	1,730.8	1,746.0	1,752.7
Consumption expenditures	443.5	451.5	453.7	454.0	453.6	458.0	464.2	465.0
Transfer payments (net)	720.9	763.5	757.5	761.5	777.3	785.9	791.4	794.6
To persons	709.4	747.2	746.3	749.7	754.4	775.5	780.5	784.7
To the rest of the world (net)	11.5	16.3	11.2	11.9	22.9	10.5	10.8	9.9
Grants-in-aid to State and local governments	211.9	218.3	223.2	218.7	217.5	219.6	222.5	224.2
Net interest paid	224.8	227.1	223.5	226.6	231.8	228.9	229.8	230.9
Interest paid	250.0	253.1	250.1	253.4	256.1	253.2	254.4	255.1
To persons and business	188.7	181.8	182.7	179.5	176.7	168.7	163.3	162.3
To the rest of the world	61.3	71.3	67.3	74.0	79.4	84.6	91.2	92.8
Less: Interest received by government	25.2	26.0	26.6	26.9	24.3	24.4	24.6	24.2
Subsidies less current surplus of government enterprises	36.4	37.7	37.5	37.4	38.5	38.4	38.1	38.0
Subsidies	33.7	33.1	33.0	33.1	33.4	33.8	34.3	34.3
Less: Current surplus of government enterprises	-2.7	-4.6	-4.5	-4.2	-5.1	-4.7	-3.9	-3.6
Less: Wage accruals less disbursements	0	0	0	0	0	0	0	0
Current surplus or deficit (-), national income and product accounts	-174.4	-110.5	-111.6	-99.5	-77.1	-55.5	-36.8	-12.5
Social insurance funds	54.1	55.3	53.3	58.2	60.6	58.7	60.4	64.1
Other	-228.6	-165.8	-165.0	-157.8	-137.7	-114.2	-97.2	-76.6

EXHIBIT 9.3 Relevant NIPA tables as sources for federal government expenditures and total federal government receipts

is larger than receipts (taxes), the government is operating in deficit—that is, stimulative. Fiscal policy includes active or discretionary policy as well as passive or nondiscretionary policy.

Active policy requires legislative changes in budget programs and is used to stimulate the economy during recessions or periods of slow growth, as

Table 3.3.—State and Local Government Receipts and Current Expenditures

[Billions of dollars]

	1995	1996	1996			1997		
			II	III	IV	I	II	III
Receipts	999.0	1,043.4	1,046.9	1,046.7	1,054.9	1,070.9	1,080.0	1,099.1
Personal tax and nontax receipts	189.4	200.2	198.9	201.7	205.1	208.7	211.3	215.9
Income taxes	140.3	149.1	148.2	150.3	153.1	155.7	157.4	161.1
Nontaxes	26.7	28.8	28.5	29.1	29.6	30.1	30.7	31.3
Other	22.4	22.3	22.2	22.3	22.5	22.9	23.3	23.5
Corporate profits tax accruals	31.1	34.5	35.0	34.9	34.0	36.4	36.8	38.6
Indirect business tax and nontax accruals	489.3	508.9	508.9	509.4	515.1	522.0	524.0	533.4
Sales taxes	239.4	249.8	250.4	249.6	251.9	256.2	255.6	258.6
Property taxes	197.4	202.3	201.5	203.0	204.7	206.2	207.8	209.3
Other	52.5	56.8	57.1	56.8	58.5	59.6	60.6	65.4
Contributions for social insurance	77.3	81.4	80.9	82.0	83.1	84.2	85.4	86.8
Federal grants-in-aid	211.9	218.3	223.2	218.7	217.5	219.6	222.5	224.2
Current expenditures	895.9	938.0	932.5	944.2	954.5	966.1	975.1	987.9
Consumption expenditures	698.6	730.9	727.0	735.9	743.3	751.7	757.4	766.6
Transfer payments to persons ...	280.6	294.8	292.7	296.6	300.6	305.1	309.5	314.0
Net interest paid	−59.6	−61.7	−61.2	−62.2	−63.0	−64.0	−64.9	−65.9
Interest paid	64.1	64.6	64.6	64.6	64.7	64.6	64.6	64.6
Less: Interest received by government	123.7	126.3	125.7	126.8	127.7	128.6	129.5	130.5
Less: Dividends received by government	12.5	13.6	13.6	13.7	14.0	14.3	14.7	14.7
Subsidies less current surplus of government enterprises	−11.2	−12.3	−12.3	−12.4	−12.5	−12.3	−12.2	−12.1
Subsidies	.3	.3	.3	.3	.3	.3	.3	.3
Less: Current surplus of government enterprises	11.5	12.7	12.7	12.8	12.8	12.7	12.5	12.5
Less: Wage accruals less disbursements	0	0	0	0	0	0	0	0
Current surplus or deficit (−), national income and product accounts	103.1	105.3	114.4	102.6	100.4	104.7	104.9	111.3
Social insurance funds	70.5	71.3	71.3	71.5	71.4	71.3	71.6	71.4
Other	32.5	34.1	43.1	31.1	28.9	33.5	33.3	39.9

EXHIBIT 9.3 (continued)

well as to restrain the economy during inflationary periods. Stimulation may take the form of increased spending on special programs or may manifest itself in lower taxes.

Passive policy includes the so-called automatic stabilizers that do not require legislative involvement. For example, during periods of slow growth or recessions, spending is increased through larger payments for unemployment insurance and welfare. During periods of strong economic growth, spending decreases as more and more people find employment and reduce the demand for unemployment insurance and welfare support.

Return to Exhibit 9.1, the Economic Pentad, and examine the MFP index. Note that any turning point in the MFP—peak and a downturn or a trough and an upturn—has important consequences for the four subsequent series. As forecasters, marketing researchers, planners, or corporate economists, we are interested in advance information regarding the timing and magnitude of economic changes. Changes that are negative and unexpected can have disastrous consequences for our various businesses. Conversely, changes that are positive and expected can facilitate stunning successes. The MFP provides a much longer look ahead than the conventional leading indicators.

THE LEADING INDICATOR

The leading indicator is the same composite leading index (BCI series number 910) described in the previous chapter. The leading indicator is a composite of ten individual series and is often changed in an attempt to improve the length and reliability of its lead around critical economic turning points. As is often the case with individual time series, it is difficult to interpolate the time-phased relationship of a key measure of the economy without some sort of contextual anchor. The Economic Pentad provides the contextual anchor as well as the opportunity for comparisons across prior economic recessions and recoveries. Note that the MFP leads the composite leading indicator which results in a longer look ahead.

REAL GDP

With real GDP being the sum total of output for the U.S. economy, it is interesting as well as productive to see how GDP has responded in prior recession and recovery periods to changes in monetary and fiscal policy.

THE LAGGING INDICATOR

The lagger is used to confirm the changes in the economy. As is the case with the composite leading indicator, the lagging indicator is a composite index comprising seven component indexes (see Chapter 8 for a review). The component series are all used to confirm that a turning point has occurred.

OTHER TYPES OF DATA

The five-phase economic system presented here can also be modified to fit your specific needs. For example, it would be productive to monitor monetary and fiscal policy changes via the MFP index and then relate changes in the index to changes in revenue, capital spending, and price changes for your industry, company, or product lines. More creative individuals could expand the system by incorporating series reflecting their company's overall sales or sales for certain key product lines. One suggestion is to incorporate company-specific series in a panel just below the GDP panel. In this manner, key executives could also see the relationship of your company's sales to overall GDP and both in the context of changes in the MFP index.

10

Patterns of Change

FORECASTING, AS WE HAVE NOTED PREVIOUSLY, is about change. If there is no change, then tomorrow will be the same as today and today will be the same as yesterday, and forecasting would be a breeze! Because there is change, it is difficult to know beforehand the direction, range, and magnitude of the variables in which we are interested. Therefore, to help reduce or minimize forecast errors, we look for patterns of change in the data. Knowing the patterns, we can restrict the scope of potential errors.

How we do this involves, first of all, the concept of indexing.

THE CONCEPT OF INDEXING

Indexing is a fundamental tool in many of our analyses. It is a major component of our Average Recession Recovery Models (ARRMs) and Average Experience Models (AEMs). Indexing is useful as a summary measure and is perhaps most frequently associated with measures of industrial production and consumer prices, in which the level of the variable is expressed relative to a base period. For example, the total industrial production index for January 1997 is 117.689, with 1992 equalling 100. The index number of 117.689 can be read directly as a 17.689 percent increase in total industrial production since 1992.

Indexing always involves a base period or a base point at which the base value is usually set equal to 100. A base period could also be constructed from an average of a number of years, like the Standard & Poor's Composite Index of 500 Stocks (S&P 500), for which the base period is a three-year period (1941–1943) and the base is set equal to 10. Typically, however, the base period is set equal to 100.

It is also useful to index an indexed series. This is illustrated in Exhibit 10.1, a graph of the Average Recession Recovery Model for the S&P 500. (Return to Chapter 6 for a review of the ARRM.) We can see at a glance that the S&P 500 has increased more than 200 percent since the first quarter of 1991, the trough of the last recession. Furthermore, because the ARRM9 line is the trend of the variable of interest averaged across the nine prior recoveries (the average of an indexed series), we can see what the average increase has been across all nine prior recoveries. The many different types of index numbers used in various price and value index construction range from calculating prices indexes for a single item, to unweighted indexes and weighted indexes. Indexes familiar to most economists are the Laspeyre, Paasche, Fisher Ideal, and Value index. For examples of these specialty indexes and how to calculate them, refer to Paul Newbold, *Statistics for Business and Economics,* 2nd ed. (Prentice Hall, 1988).

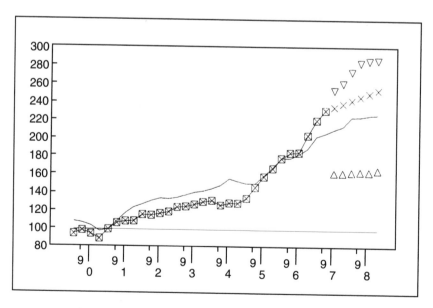

EXHIBIT 10.1 Average Recession Recovery Model (ARRMt) for the S&P 500 Stock Index

BUSINESS CYCLES

Whether rising or falling, business activity seldom moves in a straight line for any period of time. It increases for a period and then either moves laterally or decreases for a period. When the length of time that a series increases exceeds the length of time that it decreases, we have an upward trend. And, conversely, we have a downward trend when the opposite occurs. This rising and falling of business activity is reflected in a number of key indicators that are useful in tracking economic activity. When an upward trend in a number of major indicators peaks and turns downward, we have a peak turning point, and we have a trough turning point when a decreasing trend bottoms out and turns upward. These peak and trough dates, also called reference dates, are central to the analysis and understanding of cycle patterns.

CYCLE PATTERNS

In the context of this book, cycle patterns describe the pattern of change in a data series as it approaches, passes through, and follows a peak or trough reference date in the business cycle. The Consumer Price Index percent change graph shown in Exhibit 10.2 is provided as a point of reference for

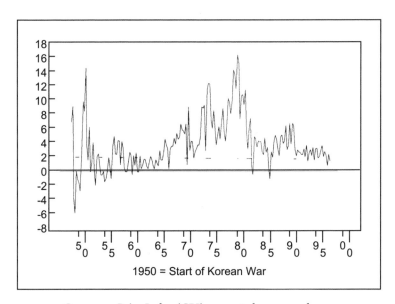

EXHIBIT 10.2 Consumer Price Index (CPI) percent change graph

discussion purposes. The graph displays the annual percent change in the CPI from 1948 to 1997. The small horizontal lines just above the solid horizontal line describe each of the recessions from 1949 to 1991. From this graph, it is very difficult to extract any sort of meaningful pattern of change, so we construct a series of index numbers to help us detect the cycle pattern.

Exhibit 10.3 contains inflation data indexed to a common trough year for each of the nine prior post–World War II recessions. For example, for the first row (1949), the trough value of 100 was determined by dividing the annual percent change in the CPI (1949 over 1948) by itself and set equal to 100. Moving left from the trough column, the 1949 data for the column labeled –1 was determined by dividing the percent change of 1948 over 1947 and dividing that by the 1949 percent change (101). Each column's value is computed in a similar manner until the desired number of years preceding and succeeding the trough year have been indexed.

The mean cycle pattern was determined by computing the average of the nine recession indexes. To see how the mean was affected by extreme values, we recomputed the mean after removing the highest and lowest values. The last row, % Change, indicates the average annual percent change of the index numbers. For example, in trough years, the CPI increased an average 4.5 percent over the year prior. The year prior to the trough year increased an average of 6.0 percent over the prior year. A graph of the cycle pattern for the CPI is shown in Exhibit 10.4. The cycle pattern illustrated is a *trough* cycle pattern. Peak cycle patterns are computed in a similar manner.

Trough					Cycle Pattern: Z1CPI–1. Consumer Price Index (CPI)					
Year	–4	–3	–2	–1	Trough	+1	+2	+3	+4	+5
1949	67	84	94	101	100	101	109	112	112	113
1954	90	97	99	100	100	100	101	105	107	109
1958	93	93	94	97	100	101	102	104	105	106
1961	94	97	98	99	100	101	102	104	105	109
1970	84	86	90	95	100	105	108	115	127	139
1975	75	78	83	92	100	106	113	121	135	153
1980	69	74	79	88	100	110	117	121	126	131
1982	68	75	85	94	100	103	108	111	114	118
1991	83	87	91	96	100	103	106	109	112	115
Mean	80	85	90	96	100	103	107	111	116	121
–HiLo	80	86	91	96	100	103	107	111	115	119
%Chg	NA	6.5	5.6	6.0	4.5	3.3	3.9	3.5	4.3	4.6

EXHIBIT 10.3 CPI data indexed to a common trough year

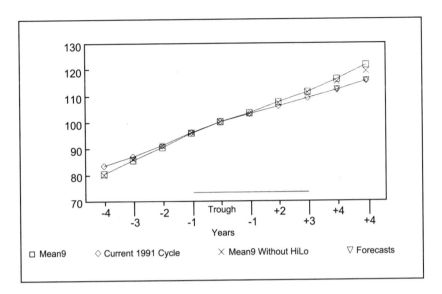

EXHIBIT 10.4 Cycle pattern for the CPI

TRENDS

Short-term trend patterns are derived from the Average Recession Recovery Models (ARRMs) for both peak and trough models. Recall from Chapter 6 that a trough ARRM has as its focus the recovery, while a peak ARRM addresses recessions. The actual values of the variable (CPI, PPI, or some other variable of interest) are used to construct the ARRM. In the case of a trough model, the ARRM9 line is shown in addition to the emerging trend in the current recovery. This provides a "bounded" range within which the forecaster can operate. This bounded range is another way of reducing possible forecast errors by reducing the domain of potential forecast values.

TURNING POINTS

Detecting turning points is one of the most challenging tasks for a forecaster. While the ARRM and cycle pattern analyses are useful tools in detecting turning points, they are insufficient. In the next chapters we explore a number of additional tools and techniques that, when used in conjunction with the cycle pattern analyses, can be quite helpful in anticipating economic turning points.

Exhibits 10.5 and 10.6 illustrate a trio of graphs for the CPI and PPI, respectively. The top graph in each exhibit is the Average Recession Recovery

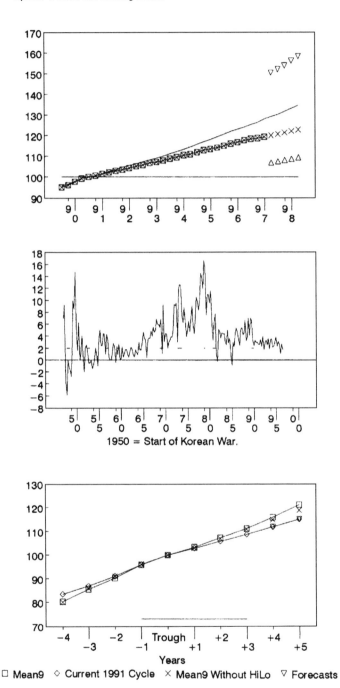

EXHIBIT 10.5 ARRMt (top), percent change (middle), and cycle pattern (bottom) for the CPI

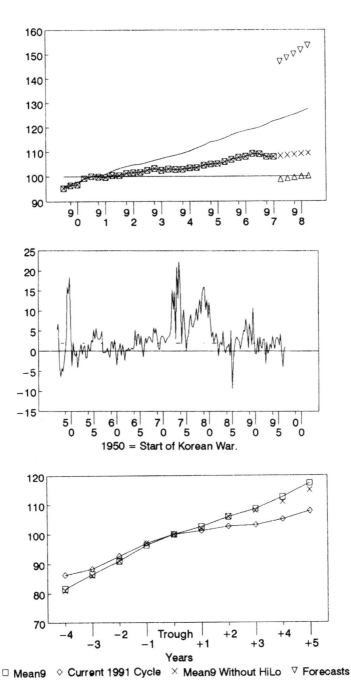

EXHIBIT 10.6 ARRMt (top), percent change (middle), and cycle pattern (bottom) for the Producer Price Index (PPI)

Model (ARRM). The ARRM is itself an indexed graph, with the index computed as discussed in Chapter 6. The middle graph shows the annual percent change across all nine prior post–World War II recessions. The last graph shows the cycle pattern emerging from the indexed values of all prior recession trough years indexed to a common year. The result is a powerful set of graphs that can be very useful to forecasters as they seek to forecast annual percent change.

11

The ARRMlong

MARKETING PROFESSIONALS are often asked to provide longer-term forecasts for industries, companies, divisions, and major product lines. For companies in the forest products business, for example, such forecasts may span a fifty-year period. For companies whose business is closely linked with age-group demographics, the time period may be twenty to thirty years. For land developers, fifteen-year forecasts may be more commonplace. The forecast horizon for the majority of manufacturing companies is along the lines of five to ten years. A continual challenge faced by the long-term forecaster is deciding whether to just extend recent trends into the future or to include some assumptions about cyclicality. And if we were to include a factor for cyclicality, what factor would we use? The *Average Recession Recovery Model*, long-term (ARRMlong), a special case of the ARRM presented in Chapter 6, provides one approach to this dilemma.

KEY CONCEPTS

The ARRMlong uses historical information from each of the major sectors of the U.S. economy to construct a data-based approach to long-term forecasting. We use the entire U.S. economy as a frame of reference and utilize the National Income and Product Accounts (NIPA) structure as shown in Exhibit 11.1. Persons interested in developing ARRMlongs specific to a

| | 1995 | 1996 | Seasonally adjusted at annual rates | | | | | |
| | | | 1996 | | | 1997 | | |
			II	III	IV	I	II	III
Gross domestic product	6,742.1	6,928.4	6,926.0	6,943.8	7,017.4	7,101.6	7,159.6	7,217.6
Personal consumption expenditures	4,595.3	4,714.1	4,712.2	4,718.2	4,756.4	4,818.1	4,829.4	4,897.9
Durable goods	583.6	611.1	614.8	611.9	617.1	637.8	629.0	655.9
Nondurable goods	1,412.6	1,432.3	1,431.6	1,433.9	1,441.2	1,457.8	1,450.0	1,465.9
Services	2,599.6	2,671.0	2,666.5	2,672.8	2,698.2	2,723.9	2,749.8	2,777.5
Gross private domestic investment	991.5	1,069.1	1,059.2	1,100.3	1,104.8	1,149.2	1,197.1	1,205.5
Fixed investment	962.1	1,041.7	1,035.7	1,060.9	1,068.7	1,079.0	1,111.4	1,148.2
Nonresidential	706.5	771.7	759.7	789.3	800.8	808.9	837.0	872.5
Structures	179.9	188.7	185.6	190.0	196.9	195.9	193.5	195.1
Producers' durable equipment	528.3	586.0	577.1	602.9	606.7	616.6	649.3	685.3
Residential	257.0	272.1	277.2	274.1	271.1	273.3	278.2	280.8
Change in business inventories	27.3	25.0	21.3	37.9	32.9	63.7	77.6	49.5

	-98.8	-114.4	-112.6	-138.9	-105.6	-126.3	-136.6	-162.9
Net exports of goods and services								
Exports	791.2	857.0	847.4	851.4	901.1	922.7	962.5	972.7
Goods	573.9	628.4	619.2	623.0	666.2	686.2	725.8	732.5
Services	218.0	229.9	229.3	229.4	236.8	238.9	240.8	244.2
Imports	890.1	971.5	960.0	990.2	1,006.6	1,048.9	1,099.1	1,135.7
Goods	749.2	823.1	811.7	841.7	857.5	891.3	938.4	971.5
Services	141.2	149.0	148.8	149.3	150.0	158.4	161.8	165.6
Government consumption expenditures and gross investment	1,251.9	1,257.9	1,265.1	1,261.5	1,261.8	1,260.5	1,270.1	1,273.6
Federal	470.3	464.2	470.7	465.7	459.6	452.8	460.1	458.9
National defense	322.6	317.8	323.2	319.4	313.6	303.9	309.4	310.4
Nondefense	147.5	146.1	147.2	146.0	145.7	148.5	150.2	148.2
State and local	781.6	793.7	794.4	795.9	802.3	807.7	810.1	814.7
Residual	.6	-1.6	-.9	-2.4	-3.8	-2.9	-3.9	-5.3

NOTE. - Chained (1992) dollar series are calculated as the product of the chain-type quantity index and the 1992 current-dollar value of the corresponding series, divided by 100. Because the formula for the chain-type quantity indexes uses weights of more than one period, the corresponding chained-dollar estimates are usually not additive. The residual line is the difference between the first line and the sum of the most detailed lines.

Percent changes from preceding period for selected items in this table are shown in table 8.1 contributions to the percent change in real gross domestic product are shown in table 8.2.

EXHIBIT 11.1 National Income and Product Accounts (NIPA) data showing the structure and content for real Gross Domestic Product (in billions of chained 1992 dollars)

company or industry can simply determine the relationship of their variables of interest to the U.S. economic structure. The three key concepts employed in the ARRMlong are *reference growth periods, reference growth rates,* and *long-term trends.*

Reference growth periods refer to periods of time or stretches in a time series history in which growth was more-or-less uniform and consistent and you, as the forecaster, believe that growth period is representative of the expected growth period to be covered by the long-term forecast. The growth rate is the rate of growth described in the reference growth period. See Exhibit 11.2 for an illustration of different growth periods and different growth rates for GDP.

Each sector of the economy also grows at different rates. Determining which periods to adopt as reference periods involves some judgment on the part of the forecaster. For example, if a variable has been growing at a consistent rate of 3.5 percent per year, is it likely to continue to grow at that rate, or is it likely to increase or decrease? This is the most difficult portion of constructing an ARRMlong.

To gain insight into the relevant history of each variable, we begin with quarterly data as reported by the Department of Commerce Bureau of Economic Analysis and then compute logarithms for the entire data set. For illustration purposes only, a subset of the quarterly data for GDP is shown in Exhibit 11.3 with a graph of the logarithms of GDP for 1948 to the present.

Note the line that has been fitted visually to the graph from 1948 to 1973. Notice also that if we were to extend that line beyond 1973, it would seriously overstate the projected growth trend for GDP. Instead, we fit a second line to the series beginning with 1973 and include the data through 1996. You can see that the slope of this second line is much less than the slope of the first line. The growth rate for the period 1948 to 1973 is estimated at 3.7 percent, and the growth rate for the period 1973 to 1996 is estimated at 2.5 percent. Given that there are 26 years in the most recent sample, we would use the 2.5 number as an updated trend.

These data were presented to illustrate the general concepts. We construct the ARRMlong forecast by developing separate ARRMlong forecasts for each of the major sectors shown in Exhibit 11.1. These sectors are then "rolled up" to generate the overall ARRMlong.

Let's look more closely at Industrial Production.

GROWTH PERIOD

The Industrial Production Index (IPI) measures the output of our mines, factories, and utilities and is often used as a proxy series for GDP. A graph

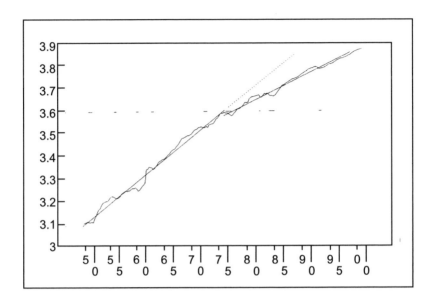

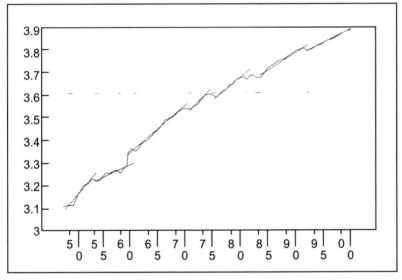

EXHIBIT 11.2 Examples of different growth periods and growth rates for real GDP

of the logarithms of the IPI is shown in Exhibit 11.4. Note how similar the series is to GDP in Exhibit 11.3. One of the criteria for selecting a representative growth period is that you want the period to span several business cycles. As a reference, the small horizontal lines opposite y = 1.8 on the graph identify the nine prior post–World War II recessions. If we select the period from 1967 to 1984, we observe that the period spans four recessions, and so we conclude that the trend line is fairly representative.

GROWTH RATE

The growth rate for the selected period is calculated using the present value, future value, and interest rate formula used in loan calculations. Using an IPI present value of 57.5 (the estimated value of the IPI in 1967), a future value of 91 (an interpolated value of the IPI for early 1984), and a time period of seventeen years, we estimate the annual growth rate at 2.74 percent. This value is the value we use in estimating the longer-term trend.

With a long-term growth rate determined that we believe will be representative of the next several years, we then turn to the identification of the cyclical patterns.

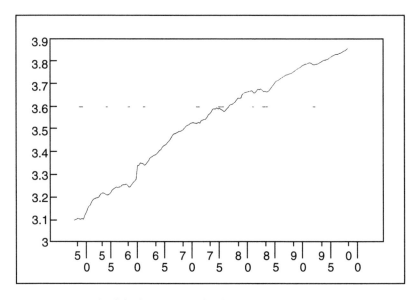

EXHIBIT 11.3 Graph of the logarithms of real GDP growth rates

TRENDS

The trend figures are derived from the growth rates. For the IPI example, the trend used in the ARRMlong is 1.027, which interpreted means that the IPI is expected to increase, on average, 2.7 percent per year. To illustrate, the trend table in Exhibit 11.8 shows a value for the IPI in 1985 of 95.3. The next year's value is 2.7 percent greater: 95.3 + 2.57 = 97.87, or 97.9.

The values in this table represent only the trend component of the ARRMlong. To see the effects of any cyclicality, we must compute the cyclical patterns and multiply the trend values for each year by their respective cyclical factors.

CYCLICAL PATTERNS

The cyclical patterns are computed in exactly the same manner as was presented in Chapter 10. For continuity with the IPI example, we reproduce the IPI cyclical pattern table in Exhibit 11.5. The cells are labeled Final Pattern and Hi/Lo Pattern. The final pattern numbers are the cyclical factors computed by averaging all nine prior recoveries. The hi/lo pattern numbers are

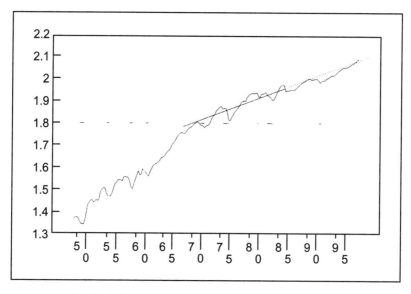

EXHIBIT 11.4 Graph of the logarithms of the Industrial Production Index (IPI)

Trough					Cycle Pattern: *E−6. IPI Industrial Production Index						Means	
Year	−4	−3	−2	−1	Trough	+1	+2	+3	+4	+5		
1949	67	84	94	106	100	116	126	130	141	133		
1954	87	94	98	106	100	113	118	119	112	125		
1958	90	101	105	107	100	112	115	115	125	132		
1961	93	87	97	99	100	108	115	123	135	147		
1970	92	94	99	103	100	101	111	120	118	108		
1975	94	103	111	110	100	109	118	125	129	127		
1980	86	93	98	102	100	102	97	101	110	105	Means	
1982	101	105	103	105	100	104	113	107	109	114	All	Five
1991	96	100	102	102	100	103	107	112	116	119	106	105
Mean	89	96	101	104	100	108	113	117	122	123	107	108
−HiLo	81	86	91	96	100	104	108	112	116	121	102	104
%Chg	NA	6.9	5.4	3.6	−4.2	7.5	5.3	3.3	4.0	1.3	3.7	3.1
		Final Pattern:		0.963	0.922	0.992	1.044	1.079				
		Hi/Lo Pattern		0.923	0.962	1.000	1.038	1.077				

EXHIBIT 11.5   Industrial Production Index (IPI) cyclical factors

the cyclical factors computed across seven prior recessions—dropping the highest and lowest mean values. By dropping the two extreme values, we have a greater probability of computing a more representative average cyclical factor.

For planning purposes, we guesstimate that there will be a recession, on average, every five years, and so we apply the cyclical factors with the trough year aligned at five-year increments. The trend components are then multiplied by the cyclical factors to generate a trend-cycle ARRMlong forecast. The cyclical factors are shown in Exhibit 11. 6.

APPLICATIONS

The product of the trend and cyclical factors forms the ARRMlong as shown in Exhibit 11.7. In addition to the trend-cycle forecast provided by the ARRMlong methodology, we have another check and balance on the long-term forecast assumptions. Each month, we forecast a three-year horizon by quarter and place this forecast in the context of the ARRMlong. If there are serious departures from our trend or cyclical factor analyses, then these differences become obvious, and we modify our ARRMlong trend or cyclical factors, or both.

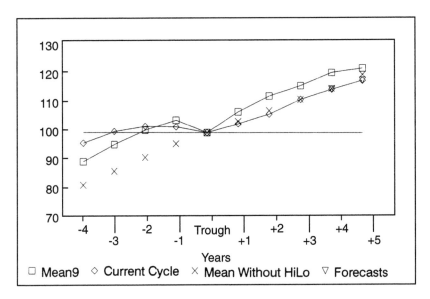

EXHIBIT 11.6 Industrial Production Index (IPI) cyclical pattern

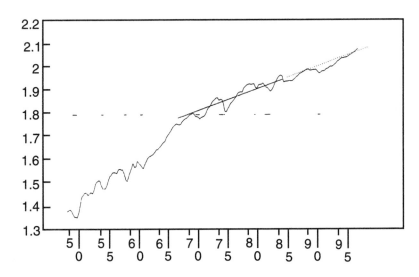

EXHIBIT 11.7 The ARRMlong

The ARRMlong is intended to serve as a planning aid and not as a point forecast. It is most useful in scenario planning when the vice president of strategic marketing or the chief financial officer is interested in conducting a series of "what-if" analyses assuming that a recession or recessionary period will occur somewhere in the next five-year planning cycle. Similar ARRMlong applications for industries, companies, divisions, and product lines can be constructed based on the methodology of the economic model presented here.

MICROMETRICS®

A *Turning Points* Supplement for the Micro-Forecaster

Volume 19, Number 3

March 21, 1997

The ARRMlong

The ARRMlong, is our attempt to provide you and your planning colleagues with a longer-term forecast that goes much beyond our regular three-year horizon. The ARRMlong is presented twice annually in the March and October issues respectively. From our experience, these two months seem to match-up fairly well with the majority of corporate planning calendars. The preferred use of the ARRMlong, from our perspective, is in scenario planning.

Our ARRMlong is in annual numbers and covers the period of time from the present to the year 2010. It includes our long-term forecast for many of the key microsectors of the economy.

The graph of logarithms on the right shows the long-term cycle pattern for Real GDP. We know that the average recovery period following World War II has lasted about four and one-half years. We also know that the average recession has lasted a little less than one year. To construct the ARRMlong, we compute trends and create cycle patterns for each of the major series and then combine them to form the ARRMlong.

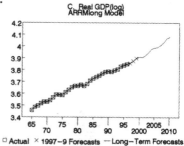

C. Real GDP(log)
ARRMlong Model

□ Actual ✕ 1997–9 Forecasts ─ Long-Term Forecasts

Knowing the average durations, the growth trends, and the cyclical patterns enables us to develop our long look ahead. As you might expect, the most difficult task in building the ARRMlong, is choosing the growth rates and cycle patterns for each of the time series involved. For example, we know that the economy goes through a process of growth and expansion followed by a process of slowdown and decline. What we don't know, however, is the exact timing of those events. So, for our planning purposes we make some assumptions and develop a series of multiple scenarios about what might happen. By using the ARRMlong and planning in this way, we can prepare for almost any eventuality. Stated simply, the ARRMlong offers a view of the future that can serve as a point of discussion, not a point of prediction! When developing multiple scenarios for the future, the average of prior events is often an effective starting point for what might happen. Let's look at the ARRMlong in detail.

Micrometrics Press, Box 32970, Phoenix, AZ 85016 (602) 957-1445

EXHIBIT 11.8 Turning Points

Index Numbers (1985=100)					ARRMLONG	Volume (Billions of chained 1992 Dollars)					Long-Term Growth Rates	Base Year				
1965	1975	1985	1995	2005		1965	1975	1985	1995	2005	% Period	1985	1986	1987	1988	1989
54	73	100	127	178	C. Real GDP (Billions of chained 1992$)	2874.9	3865.1	5329.5	6742.9	9462.0	2.5 1968–81	5329.5	5489.9	5648.4	5863.0	6060.3
55	70	100	125	176	*E. Industrial Production	51.7	66.3	94.4	118.1	166.3	2.7 1967–84	94.4	95.3	100.0	104.5	106.1
50	72	100	126	167	G. Personal Consumption	1796.5	2574.7	3567.0	4577.8	5971.7	3.0	3567.0	3705.7	3821.1	3970.3	4062.1
37	56	100	141	217	*H. Consumer Durables	152.6	238.1	411.4	579.8	891.7	4.5 1966–84	411.4	448.4	454.9	483.5	496.2
83	124	100	162	160	*I. Total Motor Vehicles	7.7	11.4	9.2	14.9	14.7		9.2	10.4	11.0	11.5	10.3
62	80	100	125	149	*J. Consumer Nondurables	729.3	938.3	1178.4	1421.9	1755.7	2.2 1968–78	1178.4	1215.9	1239.2	1274.4	1303.5
46	71	100	130	168	*K. Consumer Services	914.6	1396.3	1977.3	2577.0	3324.3	3.1 1978–87	1977.3	2041.4	2126.9	2212.4	2282.4
52	56	100	122	157	L. Domestic Investment	426.7	482.1	826.2	1010.2	1303.1	2.0	826.2	819.4	828.2	830.2	866.3
59	59	100	122	163	M. Fixed Investment	396.6	473.6	799.7	975.9	1304.5	2.0	799.7	806.2	800.4	818.6	832.1
67	67	100	115	125	*N. Residential Investment	153.8	153.5	229.5	262.8	286.4	0.5 1971–83	229.5	257.0	257.6	252.5	243.3
84	67	100	78	109	*O. Housing Starts	1469.5	1159.8	1741.5	1357.3	1750.0		1741.5	1812.0	1633.5	1495.0	1389.0
43	56	100	125	179	P. Business Investment	242.9	320.1	570.2	714.3	1018.1	2.5	570.2	549.2	542.8	566.1	588.9
56	60	100	80	99	*Q. Structures	127.0	136.2	227.6	181.1	225.2	0.8 1970–78	227.6	203.3	195.9	196.8	201.2
34	54	100	156	232	*R. Equipment	115.9	183.9	342.5	534.5	792.9	3.5 1965–91	342.5	345.9	346.9	369.2	387.7
		100	116	–5	*S. Inventories	30.1	–11.5	26.5	27.8	–1.5		26.5	13.3	27.8	11.6	34.2
					T. Net Exports	–27.3	–7.2	–145.3	–107.6	39.4		–145.3	–163.9	–156.2	–114.5	–82.8
34	68	100	230	433	*U. Exports	115.6	226.2	337.4	775.4	1459.2	5.0 1968–86	337.4	362.2	402.0	465.8	520.2
29	49	100	182	293	*V. Imports	143.0	235.4	485.2	883.0	1419.8	6.0 1969–76	485.2	526.1	558.2	580.2	603.0
70	82	100	155	264	W. Government	567.0	663.5	813.4	1260.2	2147.9	1.5 1967–87	813.4	855.4	861.5	886.9	904.5
												1985	1986	1987	1988	1989

The ARRMlong

This issue of the ARRMlong uses the new chain-weighted measures from the revised National Income and Product Accounts (NIPA) published by the Department of Commerce, Bureau of Economic Analysis.

The three tables on pages 2 and 3 describe three different elements of the Average Recession Recovery Model (Long term)--ARRMlong. Reading from the top down, the three tables are; the final model, the long term trends and the cyclical factors. Let's begin with the cyclical factors in the table at the bottom.

Cyclical Factors. Each of the microsectors of the economy (durables, services, nondurables, and so on) were analyzed over the nine post World War II recessions to determine their specific patterns of behavior. From these analyses, an average cyclical pattern was developed for each sector. These are shown in the table at the bottom. Each average pattern was used to forecast the cyclical component for future years.

Trends. A Long-term trend was computed for each of the microsectors using a period of time of two or more business cycles. In actuality, most of the analyses covered periods from four to nine business cycles, unless there was evidence of a structural change in one or more of the cycles. Long-term trends or growth rates do not change much, if at all, from one business cycle to the next. From time to time, however, rates may be altered somewhat. These long-term growth rates are shown in the middle table.

T. Long-Term Trends

Sector	Growth	1985	1986	1987	1988	1989
E. Production	1.027	95.3	97.9	100.5	103.2	106.0
H. Durables	1.045	357.5	373.6	390.4	408.0	426.4
I. Total Motor Vehicles	1.022		13.0	13.0	13.0	13.0
J. Nondurables		1161.9	1187.4	1213.6	1240.3	1267.6
K. Services	1.031	1941.4	2001.6	2063.6	2127.6	2193.6
N. Residential	1.005	199.6	200.6	201.6	202.6	203.6
O. (Houses)			1.4	1.4	1.4	1.4
Q. Structures	1.008	213.9	215.6	217.4	219.1	220.9
R. Equipment	1.035	336.0	347.7	359.9	372.5	385.6
S. Inventories	1.010		15.4	15.6	15.7	15.9
			10.4	14.6	19.3	24.4	30.1
U. Exports	1.050	370.9	393.2	416.8	441.8	468.3
V. Imports	1.060	360.5	378.5	397.5	417.3	438.2
W. Government	1.015	756.7	768.0	779.5	791.2	803.1

P. Cyclical Patterns

Growth Rates	Growth Periods		1985	1986	1987	1988	1989
1.027	1967–84	*E. IPI	--	--	--	--	--
1.045	1966–84	*H. Dur	--	--	--	--	--
		*I. Total MV	--	--	--	--	--
1.022	1968–88	*J. Non	--	--	--	--	--
1.031	1978–87	*K. Ser	--	--	--	--	--
1.005	1971–83	*N. Res	--	--	--	--	--
		*O. HS	--	--	--	--	--
1.008	1970–78	*Q. Str	--	--	--	--	--
1.035	1965–91	*R. Eqt	--	--	--	--	--
1.010		*S. Inv	--	--	--	--	--
1.060	1968–88	*U. Exp	--	--	--	--	--
1.050	1969–76	*V. Imp	--	--	--	--	--
1.015	1967–87	*W. Gov	--	--	--	--	--

EXHIBIT 11.8 (continued)

Real Dollars

1990	1991	1992	1993	1994	1995	1996	1997	1998	1999	2000	2001	2002	2003	2004	2005	2006	2007	2008	2009	2010	
36.7	8078.9	8244.4	8383.8	8604.2	6742.9	6907.4	7082.9	7216.7	7513.6	7939.4	8107.9	8099.9	8387.6	8640.1	9462.0	9710.1	9813.6	10194.6	10803.5	11631.3	C. GDP
106.1	104.3	107.7	112.1	118.1	118.1	125.8	130.0	130.8	137.0	146.4	150.3	143.6	144.5	151.4	166.3	170.8	163.2	164.2	172.0	189.0	*E. IPI
130.7	4105.8	4219.8	4339.8	3929.8	4577.8	4692.4	4793.0	4816.9	4997.1	5207.7	5286.6	5309.4	5462.1	5668.7	5971.7	6064.0	6066.2	6262.0	6536.0	6693.5	G. PER
493.3	462.0	488.5	524.1	562.0	579.8	611.8	634.9	640.1	689.0	720.0	722.3	709.5	734.0	790.1	891.7	894.5	878.7	909.0	978.4	1104.3	*H. Dur
10.6	10.0	9.5	8.4	8.4	14.9	15.4	15.2	15.2	14.0	14.2	12.5	10.8	13.0	13.7	14.7	12.5	10.8	13.0	14.0	14.7	*I. Car
316.1	1302.9	1321.8	1348.9	1390.5	1421.9	1441.9	1459.6	1464.2	1511.4	1575.5	1594.1	1596.6	1631.7	1684.3	1755.7	1776.4	1779.2	1818.3	1876.9	1956.6	*J. Non
321.3	2341.0	2409.4	2466.8	1977.3	2577.0	2639.6	2699.1	2712.6	2796.7	2912.2	2972.5	3003.3	3096.4	3192.4	3324.3	3393.1	3426.3	3534.6	3680.6	3832.7	*K. Ser
816.7	738.6	791.3	856.3	961.6	1010.2	1057.6	1119.6	1127.4	1222.2	1316.8	1273.5	1103.2	1084.7	1166.2	1303.1	1263.8	1133.9	1110.6	1198.3	1401.0	L. DOM
605.8	741.2	783.4	836.5	921.9	975.9	1043.3	1093.3	1102.7	1197.2	1291.3	1243.9	1107.1	1086.0	1167.7	1304.5	1295.2	1133.7	1110.5	1198.1	1400.8	M. FIX
220.6	193.4	225.8	242.7	269.0	262.8	277.0	279.9	280.3	315.5	355.1	310.5	246.5	247.7	268.9	286.4	250.5	198.8	199.6	220.9	246.7	*N. Res
225.3	1014.4	1206.0	1293.3	1421.7	1357.3	1464.8	1440.7	1431.7	1588.0	1470.0	1218.0	1064.0	1372.0	1554.0	1750.0	1218.0	1064.0	1372.0	1596.0	1750.0	*O. HS
585.2	547.7	557.9	593.8	653.0	714.3	767.6	813.4	822.4	881.7	936.2	933.4	860.6	838.3	898.6	1018.1	1014.8	934.9	910.6	977.2	1152.2	P. BUS
203.3	181.6	169.2	186.3	168.9	181.1	189.9	203.4	205.4	211.2	221.4	223.1	213.7	208.9	214.8	225.2	227.0	217.4	212.5	218.5	233.5	*Q. Str
381.9	366.2	386.7	427.6	484.1	534.5	579.5	610.0	617.0	670.6	714.9	710.3	646.9	629.4	684.0	792.9	787.8	717.5	698.1	758.7	918.7	*R. Eqt
11.0	-2.6	7.9	19.8	59.7	33.1	14.0	26.3	24.8	25.0	25.5	29.6	-3.9	-1.4	-1.4	-1.5	-1.5	0.2	0.2	0.2	0.2	*S. Inv
-61.9	-22.3	-29.5	-74.5	-108.1	-107.6	-116.7	-103.0	-103.9	-90.4	-75.0	-57.4	-37.4	-14.7	10.8	39.4	71.4	107.1	147.0	191.2	240.2	
564.4	599.9	639.4	660.6	715.1	775.4	825.1	893.3	905.2	969.1	1037.5	1110.7	1189.2	1273.1	1363.0	1459.2	1562.2	1672.5	1790.6	1917.0	2052.4	*U. Exp
626.3	622.2	668.9	735.1	823.3	883.0	941.8	996.3	1009.1	1059.5	1112.5	1168.1	1226.5	1287.8	1352.2	1419.8	1490.8	1565.4	1643.8	1725.8	1812.1	*V. Imp
932.6	946.2	945.2	929.8	1259.9	1260.2	1273.3	1286.5	1287.1	1384.8	1489.9	1603.0	1724.6	1855.5	1996.4	2147.9	2310.9	2486.3	2675.0	2876.1	3096.5	*W. Gov

1990	1991	1992	1993	1994	1995	1996	1997	1998	1999	2000	2001	2002	2003	2004	2005	2006	2007	2008	2009	2010

1990	1991	1992	1993	1994	1995	1996	1997	1998	1999	2000	2001	2002	2003	2004	2005	2006	2007	2008	2009	2010	Trends
108.9	111.8	114.6	117.9	121.1	124.4	127.6	131.2	134.8	138.4	142.1	146.0	149.9	154.0	158.1	162.4	166.6	171.3	175.9	180.6	185.5	*E. IPI
445.5	465.6	486.5	508.4	531.3	555.2	580.2	606.3	633.6	662.1	691.9	723.1	755.6	789.6	825.1	862.3	901.1	941.6	984.0	1028.3	1074.5	*H. Dur
13.0	13.0	13.0	13.0	13.0	13.0	13.0	13.0	13.0	13.0	13.0	13.0	13.0	13.0	13.0	13.0	13.0	13.0	13.0	13.0	13.0	*I. Car
295.4	1323.9	1353.1	1382.8	1413.3	1444.3	1476.1	1506.6	1541.8	1575.7	1610.4	1645.6	1682.0	1719.0	1756.8	1795.5	1835.0	1875.4	1916.6	1958.8	2001.9	*J. Non
281.6	2331.7	2403.9	2478.5	2555.3	2634.5	2716.2	2800.4	2887.2	2976.7	3069.0	3164.1	3262.2	3363.3	3467.6	3575.1	3685.9	3800.2	3918.0	4039.5	4164.7	*K. Ser
204.6	206.7	206.7	207.7	208.8	209.8	210.9	211.9	213.0	214.0	215.1	216.2	217.3	218.4	219.4	220.5	221.6	222.8	223.9	225.0	226.1	*N. Res
1.4	1.4	1.4	1.4	1.4	1.4	1.4	1.4	1.4	1.4	1.4	1.4	1.4	1.4	1.4	1.4	1.4	1.4	1.4	1.4	1.4	*O. HS
222.6	224.4	226.2	228.0	229.8	231.7	233.5	235.4	237.3	239.2	241.1	243.0	245.0	246.9	248.9	250.9	252.9	254.9	257.0	259.0	261.1	*Q. Str
399.0	413.0	427.5	442.4	457.9	473.9	490.5	507.7	525.5	543.9	562.9	582.6	603.0	624.1	645.9	666.5	691.9	716.2	741.2	767.2	794.0	*R. Eqt
16.0	16.2	16.3	16.5	16.7	16.8	17.0	17.2	17.4	17.5	17.7	18.1	18.2	18.4	18.6	18.8	18.8	19.0	19.2	19.4	19.6	*S. Inv
36.2	43.0	50.4	58.5	67.4	77.0	87.5	98.9	111.3	124.8	139.4	155.3	172.5	191.1	211.2	233.0	256.6	282.0	309.5	339.1	371.1	
496.4	526.1	557.7	591.2	626.6	664.2	704.1	746.3	791.1	838.6	888.9	942.2	996.8	1058.7	1122.2	1189.6	1260.9	1336.6	1415.8	1501.8	1591.9	*U. Exp
460.1	483.1	507.3	532.6	559.3	587.2	616.6	647.4	679.8	713.8	749.5	787.0	826.3	867.6	911.0	956.5	1004.4	1054.6	1107.3	1162.7	1220.8	*V. Imp
815.1	827.4	839.6	852.4	865.1	878.1	891.3	904.7	918.2	932.0	946.0	960.2	974.6	989.2	1004.0	1019.1	1034.4	1049.9	1065.7	1081.6	1097.9	*W. Gov

1990	1991	1992	1993	1994	1995	1996	1997	1998	1999	2000	2001	2002	2003	2004	2005	2006	2007	2008	2009	2010	Cycles
--	--	--	--	--	--	--	--	1.02	1.04	1.00	0.93	0.98	1.02	1.07	1.00	0.93	0.98	1.02	1.07	1.00	*E. IPI
--	--	--	--	--	--	--	--	1.03	1.00	0.96	0.94	0.99	1.03	1.08	0.96	0.94	0.99	1.03	1.08	0.96	*H. Dur
--	--	--	--	--	--	--	--	1.08	1.09	0.96	0.83	1.00	1.05	1.13	0.96	0.83	1.00	1.08	1.13	0.96	*I. Car
--	--	--	--	--	--	--	--	1.01	1.02	0.99	0.98	1.00	1.01	1.02	0.99	0.98	1.00	1.01	1.02	0.99	*J. Non
--	--	--	--	--	--	--	--	1.00	1.01	0.99	0.98	1.00	1.00	1.01	0.99	0.98	1.00	1.01	1.01	0.99	*K. Ser
--	--	--	--	--	--	--	--	1.12	1.12	0.87	0.79	1.00	1.08	1.08	0.87	0.79	1.00	1.10	1.12	0.87	*N. Res
--	--	--	--	--	--	--	--	1.12	1.05	0.87	0.78	0.98	1.11	1.25	0.87	0.76	0.98	1.14	1.25	0.87	*O. HS
--	--	--	--	--	--	--	--	1.02	1.04	1.00	0.95	0.97	1.02	1.04	1.00	0.95	0.97	1.02	1.06	1.00	*Q. Str
--	--	--	--	--	--	--	--	1.05	1.03	0.96	0.88	0.94	1.05	1.12	0.96	0.88	0.94	1.05	1.17	0.96	*R. Eqt
--	--	--	--	--	--	--	--	1.00	1.01	1.15	-0.13	0.35	1.04	1.00	1.00	-0.13	0.95	1.00	1.02	0.95	*S. Inv
--	--	--	--	--	--	--	--	1.01	1.01	1.01	1.01	1.01	1.01	1.01	1.01	1.01	1.01	1.01	1.01	1.01	*U. Exp
--	--	--	--	--	--	--	--	1.00	1.00	1.00	1.00	1.00	1.00	1.00	1.00	1.00	1.00	1.00	1.00	1.00	*V. Imp
--	--	--	--	--	--	--	--	1.06	1.06	1.06	1.06	1.06	1.06	1.06	1.06	1.06	1.06	1.06	1.06	1.06	*W. Gov

    Final Model. The top table is the final model. The forecasts in the top table for 1996, 1997, and 1998 are the same forecasts that appear on page 4 of Turning Points. The forecasts for the years 1999 through 2010, are derived by multiplying the figures together from the bottom two tables! That's it! At the upper left, is a summary table with 1985=100.

3

EXHIBIT 11.8 (continued)

THE ALL OTHER CATEGORY

How To Read An ARRM

An ARRM is an Average Recession Recovery Model, usually averaging data from the nine post World War II recessions or recoveries. The ARRM shown in this graph is the Consumer Price Index (CPI)   In the graph, the solid line (ARRM9) is the average CPI across all nine post WWII recoveries and indexed to 100 in the second quarter of 1991...the trough of this our most recent recession.

Against this line, we superimpose the boxed line of actual data in this tenth business cycle. The closer the two lines are to one another, the more representative the new cycle is to the average of the prior cycles.

The two lines of small triangles above and below the solid ARRM line describe plus and minus one standard deviation of the historical data. These two lines can be interpreted as a band within which 2-out-of-3 of the historical observations fall. The line with the small x's represents our forecast for the current cycle. The ARRM Model is a powerful tool that can be useful in scenario planning, as well as, for forecasting various product lines or product groups.

Z1-1. Consumer Price Index (CPI)
ARRMt Model

New Book In Press

Cycles, Trends, and Turning Points:
Forecasting Techniques for Marketing and Sales

This book is intended for marketing and sales people who are interested in practical forecasting techniques. It makes use of the proprietary models used for years in Turning Points and Micrometrics.

For additional information, please call:

John V. Crosby
602-957-1445

Lagniappe (lan yap), is a popular term in Southern Louisiana and Southeast Texas meaning, "a little something extra".

Over the years, we have mentioned, with great respect, the National Bureau of Economic Research (NBER). The NBER is a private nonprofit research organization that was founded in 1920. It is devoted to the quantitative analysis of the American economy. The NBER is the organization that defines the business cycle peak and trough dates. They can be reached via the Internet at www.nber.org.

John V. Crosby, Publisher

EXHIBIT 11.8 (continued)

12

Long-Term Company Forecasts

WHAT IS MEANT by a long-term company forecast? What level of detail does it entail? How far out does it go? How accurate does it have to be? These questions and others like them are addressed repeatedly by marketing and sales professionals.

Long-term company forecasts fall within the strategic marketer's primary role and responsibilities. The long-term forecast is the company's look ahead and is critical to successful technology and product-line migration, as well as serving as a reference point for future capital planning, profitability, and cash-flow analyses. Implicit in the long-term forecast is the definition of certain served markets, share-of-market assumptions, current and new technologies required, and proposed product lines. Also implicit in this model are assumptions about unit volume, unit selling prices, and unit costs. An effective long-term company forecast will contain all of these elements.

LEVEL OF DETAIL

What level of detail to include in a forecast is frequently a topic of discussion—and usually a controversial one. Opinion varies from those who want to construct a bottom-up forecast moving from specific part numbers to models to product lines, to others who are comfortable with forecasting major product lines or product groups using a top-down approach.

Our recommendation is to anchor the forecast in the size and growth rates of your company's major served markets. This should also include current and projected information about your company's current and projected share of market. Another recommendation is to forecast at the technology, product group or family, and product line levels. We do not recommend that the long-term forecast go to the part-number level of detail. This level of detail is simply wasted, as the specific part numbers are likely to change as the market develops. We do recommend that units and dollars be forecast for each of the major product lines or product families.

FORECAST HORIZON

The forecast horizon, or how far out to forecast, is really a function of many factors: the economy, the type of industry in which your company is a participant, the length of time needed to develop new technologies, the planning and construction time for new facilities, cost of new facilities, product lifetimes, skilled labor availability, and so on. For most industries, a long-term forecast of five to ten years is adequate. The exception is companies dealing with replenishable natural resources, such as timber, which may require a twenty-five- to fifty-year forecast! For long-term forecasts, we propose a format as shown in Exhibit 12.1. This format is especially appropriate, as it permits a review of the actual versus the short-term and mid-term forecasts in the context of the long-term forecast.

FORECAST ACCURACY

Issues of forecast accuracy usually fall into two broad categories: what level of accuracy is required to run the business effectively, and what level of accuracy can be achieved in a cost-effective manner. In a dynamic environment, there is constant interplay between these two positions.

Strategic Marketing Revenue Forecast (5 Year × Year)					
	1998	1999	2000	2001	2002
Product Line A					
Product Line B					
Product Line C					
Totals					

EXHIBIT 12.1 Sample format for the long-term forecast

The first issue, what level of accuracy is required to run the business effectively, is answerable only by the key executives in the company. The more flexible and responsive the organization, the wider the margin of error acceptable (within limits) in the forecast. For example, as the time to market is reduced more and more, the tactical marketing and operations people in the organization can capitalize on emerging market trends in a much more timely manner. This means that the actual product can be developed in time to hit the market window even if the forecast called for the product to be developed at a later time. All members of the organization should remember is that no one can predict the future with certainty. Every forecast is constructed through a set of probabilities. The key is to explore multiple possibilities and to be prepared for a number of future situations rather than just one.

As to the second issue, overall there is an accuracy advantage of forecasting at the product-line or product-family level that involves the principle of aggregation. This principle holds that as you move from specific part numbers to groups of part numbers to product lines and groups of product lines, the aggregation of the detail into larger and larger groups takes advantage of offsetting variance and reduces the volatility of the numbers. The forecast accuracy that can be expected for long-term forecasts is in the range of 3 to 5 percent the first few years and about twice that in the later years.

PART IV

Forecasting and
Tactical Marketing

13

Short-Term and Near-Term Forecasts

SHORT-TERM FORECASTS are much more detailed in scope and content than long-term forecasts. They are key to the current operation of the business and may be used for near-term staffing decisions, factory loading, revenue and profitability planning, cash-flow analyses, and material procurement. Short-term forecasts may be weekly, monthly, or quarterly, depending on the needs of the company. While short-term forecasts are often created using a bottom-up approach, in this chapter we explore both the bottom-up and top-down approaches.

REVIEWING STRATEGIC ASSUMPTIONS

To stay connected with the primary goals and objectives of the company and to focus the short-term forecasting efforts, it is helpful to review the strategic assumptions found in the business plan or in the strategic marketing plan. These strategic assumptions set forth the primary markets to be served, the major product lines or families to be offered, and the projected unit volumes. Reaffirming, or redirecting if necessary, the strategic assumptions tends to focus the short-term forecasting efforts on the critical few market segments and product lines expected to contribute most to the company's revenue and profitability goals. In other words, short-term forecasting should be viewed as a tool to support the goals and objectives of the business and not as a routine exercise.

Within this context, short-term forecasts can serve to validate similarities and reconcile differences in the long-term forecast. For example, if there is a difference between the two types of forecasts, how do we explain it? Were the initial assumptions in the long-term forecasts off target in quantities, timing, or both? What is the revised view, and how can this information be fed back to strategic marketing so they can update their next long-term forecast?

TYPES OF FORECASTS

There are many different types of forecasts beyond the conventional sales forecast. There are short-term forecasts created by tactical marketing that link to the previously discussed longer-term forecasts of strategic marketing. Industry forecasts and share-of-market forecasts are valuable for reviewing product-line penetration goals and competitive activity. Capacity forecasts help operations plan for requisite manufacturing, distribution, or storefront resources. There are also short-term revenue and profitability forecasts that serve as the lifeblood of successful companies.

LEVEL OF DETAIL

There is no single answer to the level-of-detail question. The level selected for the forecast is dictated by the expected use of the forecast and, in some cases, by the available information. Economic data, for example, are available in constant and nominal dollars for many sectors of the economy. Industry data, on the other hand, are usually available in both units and dollars but are often reported in nominal dollars only and, as a result, contain an embedded inflation error.

Most industry associations collect historical data and report the information to their members. We recommend linking the economic data to industry data, to company and product-line data. This helps maintain the short-term forecasts in the context of broader change and minimizes surprise errors.

Data specific to the company are most helpful when placed initially in the context of the government and industry association data and then moved to more specific and unique product-family, group, and line data. At this point you may want to create a series of product groupings that facilitate manufacturing and ordering of materials. For example, if common part types or raw material needs are of interest, then forecasts that are aggregates of critical part-number detail are appropriate.

FORECAST HORIZON

The horizon or time period that the forecast covers differs based on the purpose of the forecast and the situation or context in which it is generated. If it is believed that we are coming up on a turning point and it is critical to anticipate the turning point as closely as possible, then we may want to forecast over a few days or few weeks. On the other hand, if we are interested in a revenue forecast, then we probably will focus on the next three months. We may also be interested in a two- or four-quarter rolling forecast. Regardless of the specific horizon, most short-term forecasts cover a maximum of a two-year period. With the two-year forecast within the scope of the longer-term strategic forecast, the two-year period is often used to link tactical marketing's forecast to strategic marketing and use that comparison to update the strategic planning assumptions. The two-year forecast, however, generally has less detail than the shorter-horizon forecasts.

FORECAST ACCURACY

Level of detail and horizon are two obvious factors influencing forecast accuracy. The key question to ask is what level of accuracy is required for the forecast. Forecasts at the part-number level—that is, those with a greater level of detail—carry a greater probability of error than forecasts that are aggregates of several part numbers.

A good reference point for forecast accuracy is the irregular component of the seasonal adjustment process. Over many forecasts, the greatest accuracy attainable consistently is equal to the irregular component. If the forecast period is a month, and the horizon is three months, and the variable's monthly irregular component is plus or minus 10 percent, then the best accuracy is plus or minus 10 percent! This does not mean that, on occasion, you cannot achieve greater accuracy, but on average, your lowest forecast error will be 10 percent—or said another way, your best forecast accuracy will be 90 percent.

A major factor in accurate forecasts is structure. How the data are structured and organized helps reduce errors of omission and errors of commission, as discussed in the following section.

FORECAST ANALYSIS [FORAN]

A structure and format useful in short-term forecasting is one in which the forecaster can see the results of prior forecasts to modify future forecasts accordingly. It is also advisable to standardize the content and format of

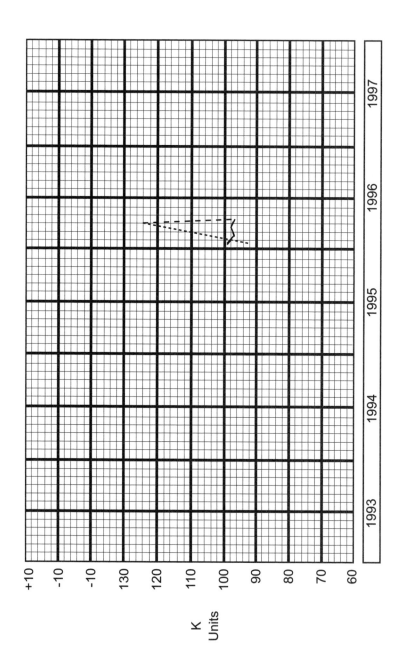

	A	B	C	D	E	F	G	H	I	J	K	L	M	N	O	P
			HISTORICAL DATA					MONTHLY FORECAST				1st MONTH REALIZATION				
														% Realization		
Month	Cycle %Chg	Trend - Cycle	Seasonally Adjusted	Seasonal Factor	Standard Month	Trading Day Factor	Original Data	1st Month Out	2nd Month Out	3rd Month Out	Three Month Total	NF1 Original	NF1 Adjusted	Actual Forecast	Optimal Forecast	R%
OCT.	1.4	94.7	97.1	93.4			90.7	86.9	87.6	105.3		-14.7	5.2	4.4	2.5	
NOV.	4.5	99.0	94.9	94.5			89.5	90.3	109.5	93.2		-1.3	-2.5	-.9	-4.3	
DEC.	-.7	98.3	105.2	113.8			119.7	107.3	98.9	102.9		33.7	11.1	11.6	7.0	
JAN.	.9	99.2	95.0	96.5			91.7	92.6	94.4	95.2		-23.4	-9.7	-1.0	-4.2	
FEB.	-2.2	97.0	97.4	104.1			101.4	97.2	98.9	98.0		10.6	2.5	4.3	.4	
MAR.	.9	97.9	98.7	126.6			125.0	120.9	93.4	91.5		23.3	1.3	3.4	.8	
APR.			97.5	98.8			96.3	97.3	96.4	109.6		-23.0	-1.2	-1.0		
MAY				97.5				94.8	107.2	54.2						
JUNE				110.5												
JULY				56.4												
AUG.				92.6												
SEPT.				115.2												
OCT.				93.4												
NOV.				94.5												
DEC.				113.8												
D%:	B - 2 / B - 3	Moving Average MCD: 3		E/D		G/F					H+I+J	18.6	4.8	3.8	3.2	63%
%			E/D									G/(G-1)	C/(C-1)	G/H	(C-1)/(B-1)	(M-N)/(M-O)

EXHIBIT 13.1 Sample FORAN work sheet for short-term forecasts

the short-term forecasts, whether the horizon is one month, three months, six months, or longer. As a working model, we present a format in Exhibit 13.1. The form can be created in one of the standard spreadsheet programs such as Microsoft Excel or Lotus 1-2-3. The example is adopted from a forecasting model called FORAN (forecast analysis) that was developed initially by Robert L. McLaughlin. The FORAN work sheet in Exhibit 13.1 covers a three-month forecast horizon. For a longer or shorter horizon, simply subtract or add the desired number of months. The work sheet consists of four parts: historical data, monthly forecasts, forecast realization, and a graph showing percent change and level of the variable being forecast. At the bottom of the form are simple formulas showing how the values in each column are computed.

The terms in the work sheet require some description and definition:

Historical Data

The historical data section consists of seven columns, labeled Cycle % Change, Trend-Cycle, Seasonally Adjusted, Seasonal Factor, Standard Month, Trading Day Factor, and Original Data. Let's assume we are entering data for an actual forecast.

We begin with the *seasonal factors*. The seasonal factors are generated by X-11 (as discussed in Chapter 5) or some other appropriate seasonal adjusting program. These factors are computed once a year and entered in column D for the entire year. The seasonal factors for January through December 1996 are as follows:

January	96.5
February	104.1
March	126.6
April	98.8
May	97.5
June	110.5
July	56.4
August	92.6
September	115.2
October	93.4
November	94.5
December	113.8

Next is *original data.* Original data are entered in column G opposite the appropriate month. In our example, the original data for 1996 are as follows:

January	91.7
February	101.4
March	125.0
April	96.3

We are not using trading-day factors in this example, but if we were, the next step would be to enter the trading day factor in column F. The following step would be to compute the standard month by dividing the original data by the trading-day factor and placing that answer in column E. The seasonal factors were entered first, so we jump to column C, *seasonally adjusted data,* and enter the following data:

January	95.0
February	97.4
March	98.7
April	97.5

Because we are not using columns E and F, the numbers in column C were computed by dividing the original data by the seasonal factor. For January, divide 91.7 by its seasonal factor of 96.5, and the seasonally adjusted value becomes 95.0. The actual procedure is $(91.7 \div 96.5) \times 100 = 95.03$.

Next, we smooth the data in column C using a three-month moving average to compute the *trend-cycle* component which is placed in column B. Remember that we want to center a three-month moving average, so we compute the seasonally adjusted data (column C) for February, March, and April and enter it in column B opposite March.

February	97.4
March	98.7
April	97.5

$$293.6 \div 3 = 97.87 \text{ or } 97.9$$

Column A, *cycle percent change,* is computed for March by dividing 97.9 by 97.0, the previous month's figure, to yield 0.9 percent. The actual computation is as follows:

$$((97.9 \div 97.0) \times 100) - 100 = 0.93\%$$

Forecast Generation

Now that the historical data are organized and entered, we are ready to generate a forecast. Each month the data are analyzed and graphed to prepare for the next forecast period. Using our example, we are now in the month of May and are forecasting 94.8 for May, 107.2 for June, and 54.2 for July (the next three months shown in the second section of the work sheet, monthly forecast). The actual data for the month will be reported by accounting, and we could then compute the percent realization in the last section. But for illustrative purposes, let's look at how we computed the percent realization for April.

Forecast Realization

The percent realization assumes, in this example, that we are tracking on the actual versus the first month of the forecast. Column L, NF1 original, is the percent change from the preceding month for the original data in column G. NF1 is the naive forecast 1 which basically says that there will be *no change!* Next month will be the same as last month. If we compute the percent change from this month to last month, we have the percent change of an NF1 forecast versus actual. This is the error reference our forecast must beat if our forecast is better than NF1. The value for April is –23.0 percent.

The same process is used for column M, NF1 adjusted, only we use the numbers in column C. The NF1 adjusted percent change for April is –1.2 percent. Now the real question is: How well did our forecast do against the NF1 benchmarks? That calculation is shown in column N, actual forecast. The actual forecast realization for April is determined by computing the percent change from the first month's forecast to the actual data for April. In this case 97.3 is the first month's forecast, and 96.3 is the actual. The percent change is –1.03, or rounded off, –1.0. This is interpreted as forecasting 97 percent of the change. Optimal forecast is the percent change of the irregulars and is computed using columns B and C.

The last computation is the realization percentage. Realization percentage is the percent change successfully predicted and is computed by keeping a running average of the five columns (L, M, N, O, and P) without regard to sign. In the example, we show a running total opposite December. If you follow the computations, M – N divided by M – O, we arrive at 63 percent of the change successfully predicted. That is a good number. Over a long period, two-thirds of the change successfully predicted is very respectable performance!

Graph

The graph is a key component of the FORAN work sheet. The top portion is a column chart of the data in column A, cycle percent change. The solid line is a graph of column B, trend-cycle. The dotted line signifies the original data shown in column G. Taken all together, the FORAN work sheet provides a structured approach to short-term forecasting. Each of your company's major product lines can be shown on a single sheet.

14

Forecasting New Products

WITH ANY NEW-PRODUCT FORECAST, the challenge lies in the assumptions made by the forecaster. In some cases the new product is an extension of a prior product, so historical data of some sort can be utilized. In other cases, the product is new to a market that exists, in kind, but not specifically in terms of the features and benefits of the product. Another case may involve a new product and a new market (this is the toughest).

New-product forecasts may be generated for different reasons. One type of forecast may be used to determine feasibility; another may be used for capacity planning; another for competitive analysis; and another for both capacity planning and revenue projections. These different types of forecasts have different levels of acceptable forecast error, and so the forecaster must document the assumptions made during the construction of the forecast model.

CONVENTIONAL APPROACHES

There are three conventional approaches typically employed in forecasting new products: expert opinion, the logistic or S-curve, and historical data from analogous or look-alike products. Expert opinion, either from a single expert or from a panel of experts, basically relies on the experience and belief system of the experts. One or more people may have considerable experience in a specific industry which usually qualifies them as "expert." The forecast of the new product is generated from their anticipation of what might occur, given what similar events have occurred in the past. Their belief system is tempered by current environmental and market factors and what they view as likely to occur. Occasionally, historical data are used or referred to but are generally not employed in the forecasting process.

The logistic curve is a standard mathematical approach used for forecasting growth functions. The underlying premise of the S-curve holds that the rate of growth is proportional to the amount of growth realized *and* to the amount of growth remaining to be realized. The assumptions are that if either of these growth quantities is small, then the rate of growth will be low. The S-curve is used regularly in forecasting growth functions in biology and medicine and forecasting the maturation and spread of technology. A contemporary book on the S-curve and how it is used in a variety of applications is Theodore Modis's *Predictions, Society's Telltale Signature Reveals the Past and Forecasts the Future* (New York: Simon and Schuster, 1992).

An analogous approach uses information and historical data about similar products to forecast future demand for new products. The accuracy of this approach is dependent on the degree of similarity between the analogous products and the new products and the similarity between prior economic conditions and introductory dates and the economic conditions and introductory period of the planned new products. With this approach, monthly or quarterly historical data can be seasonally adjusted, but it is difficult to control for economic conditions and different introductory periods. An alternate approach to these three approaches, and one that warrants consideration, is the *Average Experience Model (AEM)*.

AVERAGE EXPERIENCE MODEL (AEM)

As explained in Chapter 6, the AEM (pronounced "aim") is a special case of the Average Recession Recovery Model (ARRM) and can be used, among other things, to forecast new products. In ARRMs, it is the peak and trough dates that are indexed and set equal to 100. The AEM can be used in all of the foregoing applications, plus it can take into consideration differences in economic conditions and introductory periods. Exhibit 14.1 illustrates several applications of the AEM approach.

In the top curve in Exhibit 14.1, we see an AEM for a series of S-curves showing the historical growth pattern of several previous products, all indexed to a common introductory date. The idea behind the AEM is that we can take the average of these six S-curves, for example, and use it as the

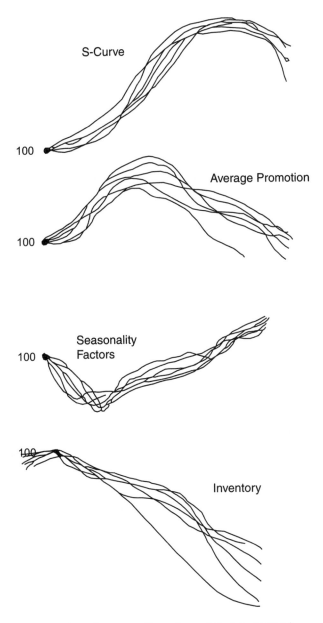

S-Curve

Average Promotion

100

100

Seasonality
Factors

100

100

Inventory

EXHIBIT 14.1 Examples of Average Experience Models (AEMs)

baseline for a new-product forecast. When we average a series of similar S-curves, the extreme values are attenuated, and the forecast becomes the central value. When the underlying data have been seasonally adjusted, then variability is due to different introductory time periods—for example, June or July versus early September. Like the ARRMs, AEMs also require the use of seasonally adjusted data.

The second example illustrates the use of the AEM in forecasting the average boost in demand following a special promotion. Often it is difficult to forecast the increased demand, but with the AEM, a model of an *average promotion* (APROM) can be constructed and used to establish a baseline or reference point for the increased demand resulting from a special promotion. Also of interest is the shape and time duration of the return to a steady state demand. This application is useful in evaluating the effects of advertising dollars. It is also helpful to operations, as they can use the baseline forecast to quantify the level of increased production output needed to satisfy customers' peaked interests as a result of the promotion.

Seasonal factors can also be evaluated using the Average Experience Model. In the example shown, we are interested in developing a longer-term forecast and therefore want to use an average of the past six years of seasonal factors. We create the model by indexing the seasonal factors to the start of the year and then average the six years. That's all there is to it!

The last example illustrates how the AEM can be used to model and forecast a decrease in inventory levels. Conversely, the same concept could be employed to forecast an increase in inventory levels.

SELECTING THE DATA

We have shown using the examples in Exhibit 14.1 that there are many possible applications for the Average Experience Model. Keep in mind that the data, if monthly or quarterly, must be seasonally adjusted prior to the construction of the model if the model is to be accurate and representative of the deseasonalized average.

When you're constructing an AEM using actual data from prior product introductions that belong to the same product line or same class of products, the seasonally adjusted data can be used intact, as they are from the same product family. For new products that do not have any directly applicable historical data, you can create a composite by selecting key features of the new product that you believe will be critical factors in the customers' decision to buy. If you are an electronics firm, for example, and your new product is some sort of a telecommunication device, you may want to look at prior introductory data for telecom devices that share speed or size, and use those data as a proxy. If you are a home builder, you may want to analyze prior sales by square foot and select a subset of home model data for use in the AEM. Many different examples could be discussed. There is no one correct answer; the choice depends on your company's products, markets served, and critical feature set.

COMPOSITE DATA MODEL

When you mix data gathered from different products, you are constructing a *composite data model*—composite in the sense that the data set is composed of data from different products. When a composite data set is used, it is also important to compute a weighted average of the seasonal factors for the different products, if they are different.

TRACKING ACTUAL VERSUS THE MODEL

We use the AEM as a baseline or reference forecast for new products. The AEM line is the equivalent of the ARRM line in Chapter 6. Once we begin plotting actual data against the AEM line, we can determine if our assumptions were correct and the data set representative of the market demand for the new product by how much the actual data deviate from the AEM line. Exhibit 14.2 provides an example of an AEM line (the solid line) and the

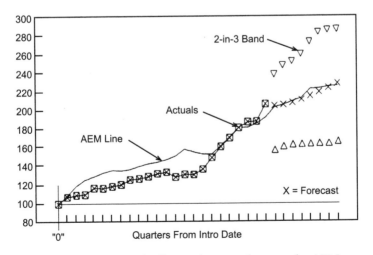

EXHIBIT 14.2 Tracking example illustrating actual versus the AEM

actual plus the forecast. Note that the introductory date is shown as "zero" to indicate the onset of the AEM. The hatch marks on the x-axis are the quarters following the introduction of the new product. The "X"s are the forecast. Note how the AEM line serves as a reference point and a beginning when there were no data! When the values are indexed, as shown on the y-axis, there is an additional advantage in that the numbers can be read directly as a percentage increase from the introduction.

15

Forecasting
Turning Points

TURNING POINTS ARE DEFINED as major peaks or troughs, followed by a change in direction, of an otherwise continuous data series. The change in direction may be steep and abrupt or shallow and gradual. With few exceptions, turning points are followed by significant changes in the performance of key economic variables, so advance knowledge about an impending turning point can provide substantial advantage to those persons who can anticipate, interpret, and capitalize on such events. The primary responsibility for monitoring and reporting on changes in various economic variables falls to tactical marketing.

Since forecasting turning points is a difficult task, we explore several approaches, with each level increasing in complexity and sophistication. The tools include using simple leading indicators as a recession and recovery barometer, a three-color system created from the interplay between leading and coinciding indicators, an array or pyramid of indicators together with a straw man of impending change, and finally a sophisticated approach to monitoring rates of change between related variables called a paired index. We recommend using the approach that is the least complex yet gives you the advance information desired.

LEADING INDICATORS

In Chapter 8 we explored various economic indicators and how they can be used with company data. By far the simplest indicator of change is the

199

performance of the composite index of leading indicators and its component series. As noted, the indicators, formerly published by the Department of Commerce Bureau of Economic Analysis, are now published by the Conference Board, a nonprofit organization. The Conference Board changed the composition of the indicator package in December 1996 and published its revised indicators in January 1997. In a single chart, it shows the amount of lead time for each of the prior six recessions. The chart is reproduced in Exhibit 15.1. The Conference Board adds, "A downward movement in the composite index of leading indicators of 2 percent (annual rate) or more over six months, coupled with declines in the majority of the component series, is needed before a recession warning can be considered reliable." This is the simplest and most direct approach, but there are limitations. For example, and as you can see from the chart, there are two "false positives" (a recession signal not followed by a recession), plus in the last two recessions the leading indicators did not signal a recession until two and three months after the fact. If you add to this lack of lead time the observation that the leading indicators themselves are not current, then the leading indicators as a sole predictor of a turning point would be inadequate. The delay in reporting runs an average of one month to three months.

Another leading indicator, the Purchasing Manager's Index (PMI), is available on the first of every month and therefore has zero delay. A graph of the PMI is shown in Exhibit 15.2 and is reproduced from the August 1990 issue of *NAPM Insights*. The original article explains:

The Purchasing Manager's Index (PMI) covering all business cycles since 1950, with shaded areas indicating recessions, as determined by the National

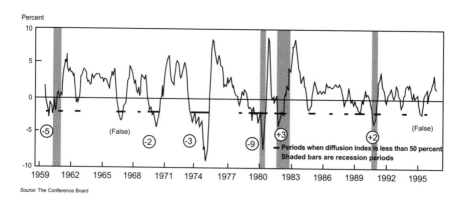

EXHIBIT 15.1 Leading indicators and their lead times

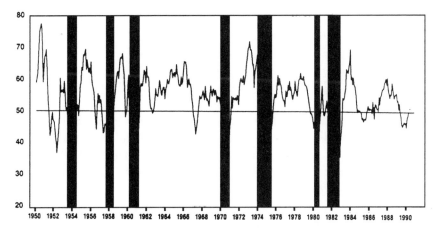

EXHIBIT 15.2 The Purchasing Manager's Index (PMI) as a leading indicator
(reprinted from *NAPM Insights*)

> *Bureau of Economic Research. On average, the PMI signaled a cyclical peak
> about 13.3 months (a range of 6 to 21 months) before the previous seven reces-
> sions. It indicated a cyclical trough about 4 months (a range of 1 to 9 months)
> before the official terminal month of the recession. Although a PMI below 50%
> generally indicates a decline in the manufacturing economy, it would need to
> fall below 44% before registering a decline in real GNP. (page 23).*

The PMI, like the leading indicators, also suffers from false positives.
Exhibit 15.3 shows a graph from the July 1996 issue of *Purchasing Today* indicating that the index dropped below 44.5% in early 1996 but the economy did
not tip into recession.

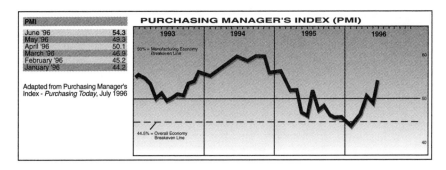

EXHIBIT 15.3 The PMI below 50 percent and no recession (reprinted from
Purchasing Today)

Another approach, one that is just a bit more complex, is the three-color system for signaling change.

THREE-COLOR SYSTEM

The three-color system for signaling change is a graphic enhancement to the use of leading and coinciding indicators. It is a straightforward and colorful approach that is easily understood. Developed originally by Robert L. McLaughlin as a graphic means of communicating with management, it has been widely copied.

The concept is simple. Stoplights are universal, and we capitalize on the wide acceptance of the meaning attached to the colors green, yellow, and red. As you would expect, green means "all systems go," with the economy seen as continuing to expand, and no perceived threat of a turning point. Yellow indicates that caution is in order in that patterns of change are beginning to emerge, but it is too soon to conclude that a turning point is imminent. Red, on the other hand, indicates danger and is used to signal that a turning point is at hand.

One of the three colors is selected, based on the interaction of the leading and coinciding indicators. We select green when the leading indicators and the coinciding indicators are both increasing. Yellow is selected when the leading indicator turns down but the coinciding indicator continues to

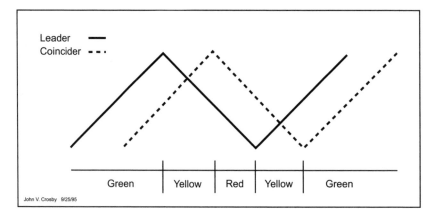

EXHIBIT 15.4 Graph of the three-color system for signaling change

rise. Red is selected when both the leading and coinciding indicators turn down. This is shown graphically in Exhibit 15.4. Our experience has been that management is quick to relate to a visual warning system of this type. The three-color system can also be incorporated into a broader management system. For example, when the marketing organization issues a yellow warning, various levels of contingency planning could kick in that would help prepare the organization for the possibility of a turning point.

PYRAMID OF INDICATORS AND THE STRAW MAN

Another approach to forecasting turning points, one that is more complex, is the pyramid of indicators. This concept, also developed by Robert L. McLaughlin, makes use of a rather large number of indicators that, in the past, have reached turning points themselves before a turning point was reached in the general economy. In this regard, a change in the pattern of indicators can be useful in forecasting turning points in the overall economy.

This concept makes use of several subconcepts: first, leading indicators reach turning points before the broader economy; two, different indicators lead general economic turning points by varying time periods—there are very long leaders (policy leaders), long leaders (factory leaders), and short leaders (roughly coinciders); and three, the greater the number of leading indicators reaching a turning point, the greater the probability that a turning point in the general economy will follow within a short time. These concepts are illustrated in Exhibit 15.5, a pyramid of indicators used to forecast a turning point in the June 1991 issue of *Turning Points*. Note that the pyramid was showing June 1991 as the end of the last recession.

There are 30 indicators in the pyramid, arranged in descending order of average lead time. Each indicator's *Business Conditions Digest* series number (now the *Business Cycle Indicators* published by the Conference Board) is referenced, together with the respective average lead times. The shaded area containing "O"s is the chain of indicators, or the imaginary line that identifies the average peaks joined in time. The left or right position of the chain of indicators is determined by the straw man—the hypothesized date of the end of the last recession. In the example shown, the hypothesized onset was June 1991. The chain of indicators was then positioned to the left of the onset date by a distance equal to the average lead times of the indicators.

Now, if the recession were to end as hypothesized, we would expect to see two-thirds or maybe three-fourths of the indicators trough (marked L for low) either on the chain of indicators or slightly to the left of the chain. If we

Note: The indicators in CAPS are policy indicators.

Leading indicators	Series No.	Avg Ld Time (Mos)
MONEY SUPPLY chg (M2)	102	9.9
Sensitive Producer Prices	98	9.1
MONEY SUPPLY chg (M1)	85	8.1
Long Leading Indicator	990	8.0
MONEY SUPPLY (M2)	106*	5.6
Housing Permits	29*	4.9
Housing Starts	28	4.9
Stock Market	19*	4.7
Factory Delivery Lags	32*	4.0
MONEY SUPPLY (M1)	105	3.9
Plant/Equipment Orders	20*	3.9
Consumer Expectations (UofM)	83*	3.9
Prices/Unit Labor Costs	26Q	3.8
Credit Market Funds	110Q	3.3
New Businesses	13	3.2
Residential Investment	89Q	3.1
Sensitive Material Prices	99*	2.8
The Leading Indicator	910*	2.6
Profits to Income (%)	22Q	2.3
Real Cash Flow	16Q	2.3
Mfg Orders (Nondefense)	35Q	2.3
Consumer Sentiment	27	2.3
Production, Consumer Goods	58	2.3
Total Inventories (chg in $)	75	2.3
InstallmentCredit (chg in $)	31	2.1
Mfrs' New Orders, Consumer	113	2.1
Production, Nondurables	8*	2.0
Ratio, Coincident/Lagging	74	2.0
Average Weekly Hours, Mfg	940	1.9
	1*	1.6
Mean		3.8
Std Dev		2.2

In the Strawman above, 24 of the 30 indicators had bottomed out either on or before the chain of circles thereby offering strong support for June as the strawman month for the end of the recession.
The NBER Business Cycle Dating Committee announced in December 1992, that the official end of the recession was March 1991.

EXHIBIT 15.5 The pyramid of indicators

count the ones in Exhibit 15.5 that have troughed, we come up with twenty-four out of thirty, or 80 percent. This suggests that the end of the recession as hypothesized is probably June or even a little earlier. In retrospect, we know that the last recession ended in March of 1991—roughly three months earlier than this straw man was indicating.

Next, we explore the last and perhaps most sophisticated approach to forecasting turning points, the paired index.

PAIRED INDEX

The paired index consists of two variables, for example orders and sales, that are related in time. In this case, orders precede sales by some period of time. The paired index further holds that a change in the order rate will precede a change in the sales rate. The idea, then, is to use the lead of one variable to predict subsequent changes in the other variable. In our example, we would like to use changes in the order rate to predict changes in the sales rate. The general concept is presented graphically in Exhibit 15.6. The paired index consists of a panel of three graphs. The solid line in the bottom graph, sales billed (S/B), is the variable in which we are interested. The dotted line, orders received (O/R), is the leading variable. The middle graph displays rate of change, or the momentum of the two variables. The top graph shows the interactions between the two variables. The pattern of change in the three panels is used to forecast the dependent variable.

As shown in Exhibit 15.6, the objective is to forecast the sales-billed turning point, marked by the vertical dashed line in the tenth month. Here, the orders received is a perfect predictor of the sales-billed indicator; in a real-world situation they are almost never perfect. Consequently, a paired index also includes rates of change to highlight the momentum and interactions of the variables.

Bottom graph (volumes): For each of the two variables, sales billed (S/B) and orders received (O/R), 100 equals the arithmetic mean of the first twelve months of data. The solid line is always the coincider and the dashed line the leader.

Middle graph (momentum): The two curves in the middle show the monthly percent change in the two lower curves. In a paired index, the rate of change gravitates toward 100 when its volume in the lower graph approaches a turning point.

Top graph (interaction): The solid line in the upper curve is generated by dividing the O/R by S/B each month and multiplying the result by 100. Where

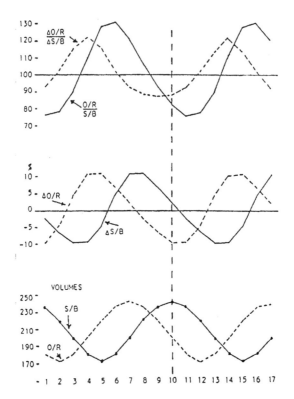

EXHIBIT 15.6 The paired index

the gap between the two volume curves is the greatest, the solid line in the upper curve will be the greatest distance above 100 (as shown in the sixth month).

If there is a lead-lag relationship between the two variables shown by the lower curves, a paired index will look like this example. In a paired index, if all the curves peak (or trough) except the sales-billed curve, that is the strongest indication of an impending peak (or trough) in the variable or indicator you are trying to predict.

Let's look at a couple of real examples from the last recession. Exhibit 15.7 illustrates two paired indexes: housing permits versus housing starts and the leading indicator versus industrial production. In each case we were interested in forecasting the time course of the curve labeled "C" in the bottom panels. We note that the curves in the middle and top panels turned upward, which confirmed that the coinciding variable had also turned up.

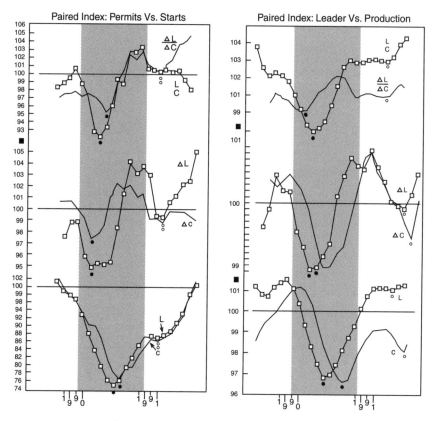

EXHIBIT 15.7 Examples of the paired index

16

The Revenue Forecast

ONE OF THE MOST IMPORTANT FORECASTS generated by tactical marketing is the revenue forecast. Revenue forecasts may cover a period of time as short as a few months or as long as a few years. These forecasts should be in units and dollars and are used by all members of management to plan their respective functions. The revenue forecast is tactical marketing's best estimate of what the company can expect, in revenue or billings, over the period of time covered by the forecast.

THE THREE B'S: BOOKINGS, BACKLOG, AND BILLINGS

Bookings, backlog, and billings are three key measures of the health of any company. *Bookings* refers to the quantity of orders booked for either present, near-term, or longer-term delivery. Bookings forecasts are the strict purview of the salespeople and discussed in Chapter 19. *Backlog* refers to the aggregate quantity of orders that have been booked and are to be scheduled, manufactured, and shipped over some period of time. Backlog forecasts are usually the responsibility of the sales department in conjunction with operations or production control and planning. Changes in the backlog can be a valuable early indicator of changes in the marketplace or in the factory. *Billings* refers to the quantity of goods shipped *and* billed to the customer. If your company is on an accrual basis, then the dollar value of the goods billed equals revenue. If your company is on a cash basis, then revenue equals the amount of billings collected. It is important to keep straight the definitions of bookings, backlog, and billings.

FORECASTING REVENUE

For discussion purposes, we will assume an accrual basis in which billings is the same as revenue. Within the context of our relational model of marketing and sales, tactical marketing is responsible for generating the revenue forecast. A sample revenue forecast is shown in Exhibit 16.1.

In the sample, the columns represent the various product families. Perhaps internal to the tactical marketing organization, these data may be further broken down to the product-line level, but for our purposes this level is adequate. Two years of monthly and quarterly unit data are shown. The data are not seasonally adjusted and are in the same format as management would receive them.

At the top of the forecast, the actual numbers are shown and are identified by an asterisk to the left of the month. Actuals run through May and provide an opportunity to compute forecast versus actual as the year unfolds, rather than waiting until year-end. The two-year tactical marketing forecast is shown by month and by quarter. At the very bottom there are four years of forecast data. These data are from the long-term strategic marketing forecast and are useful for placing the tactical marketing forecast in context.

LEVEL OF DETAIL

In the sample forecast, the level of detail is the product family, and the unit of measure is units. It is preferable to have two forecasts: one in units and the other in dollars. The unit forecast should be generated using market assumptions and market considerations and not from unit demand estimated by the sales force. The dollar forecast can be generated using certain assumptions for average selling prices which can be linked to the unit forecast to create the dollar forecast.

The two-year tactical marketing revenue forecast is described in months, quarters, and years. This level of detail facilitates the close coordination of marketing events such as product introductions and also matches with the

EXHIBIT 16.1 Sample revenue forecast

Column groups: CONSUMER GOODS = Mixer, Blend, Knife; PERSONAL CARE = Hair, Comb, Other, Total; then Total Cons; COMMERCIAL = Soda Fount, Other, Total Comm; then Grand Total.

	Period	Days	Mixer	Blend	Knife	Hair	Comb	Other	Total	Total Cons	Soda Fount	Other	Total Comm	Grand Total
Actual	'Jan	19	4931	5017	1036	3666	210	2792	6668	17652	414	25	439	18091
	'Feb	20	4957	5805	1159	3924	326	3377	7627	19548	407	25	432	19980
	'Mar	25	4994	5844	1223	3898	342	3390	7630	19691	430	25	455	20145
			14882	16666	3418	11488	878	9559	21925	56891	1251	75	1326	58217
	'Apr	19	4724	5593	1112	4033	430	3371	7834	19283	439	25	464	19727
	'May	20	5071	5695	1119	4301	419	3223	7943	19828	455	25	480	20308
	'Jun	24	5200	5900	1250	4625	210	3325	8160	20510	450	25	475	20925
			14995	17188	3481	12959	1059	9919	23937	59601	1344	75	1419	61020
Short-term	Jul	10	4400	5075	1065	3035	290	2945	6270	16810	475	25	500	17310
	Aug	20	4700	5200	1150	2880	303	3065	6248	17300	480	25	505	17805
	Sep	24	5000	5620	1235	3750	215	3255	7220	19075	500	25	525	19600
			14100	15895	3450	9665	810	9265	19740	53185	1455	75	1530	54715
	Oct	20	4300	5300	1150	3185	330	3205	6700	17650	465	25	490	18140
	Nov	20	4300	4920	1020	3600	280	2820	6900	17140	480	25	505	17645
	Dec	27	4270	4465	955	3920	255	2805	7060	16750	495	25	520	17270
			13070	14635	3125	10885	865	8910	20660	51540	1440	75	1515	53055
	1996		57047	64434	13474	44997	3612	37653	86262	221127	5690	300	5790	227007
Medium-term	Jan	19	4600	4400	870	4475	165	2270	6910	16780	435	25	460	17240
	Feb	20	5000	4900	930	5180	275	2570	8025	18855	430	25	455	19330
	Mar	25	5380	5200	960	5455	390	2630	8475	20015	465	25	490	20505
			14980	14500	2760	15110	830	7470	23410	55650	1350	75	1425	57075
	Apr	19	5700	5000	960	4895	250	2405	7550	19210	450	25	475	19685
	May	19	5810	4920	975	4940	420	2400	7760	19505	685	25	710	20015
	Jun	25	5800	5380	1003	5340	305	3045	8690	20865	530	25	555	21420
			17310	15300	2970	15175	975	7850	24000	59580	1465	75	1540	61120
	Jul	10	4900	4485	925	3520	155	2175	5850	16160	505	25	530	16690
	Aug	20	3850	4680	985	3920	120	2400	6440	15955	515	25	540	18695
	Sep	24	4240	5330	1090	5200	195	2205	7600	18260	520	25	545	18885
			12990	14495	3000	12640	470	6780	19890	50375	1540	75	1615	51990
Long-term	Oct	20	4430	5100	1050	5380	210	2310	7900	18430	500	25	525	19005
	Nov	18	4620	4860	1015	5350	250	2450	8050	18545	505	25	530	19075
	Dec	24	4500	5110	1000	4425	260	2485	7170	17780	490	25	515	18295
			13550	15070	3065	15155	720	7245	23120	54805	1495	75	1570	56375
	1997		58830	59365	11795	58080	2995	29344	90420	220410	5850	300	6150	226560
	1998		60200	63400	12400	58950	3000	30300	92250	228250	6000	300	6300	234550
	1999		62000	63000	13500	60000	3500	32000	93500	238000	6200	300	6500	242500
	2000		64000	67000	14300	42000	4000	33000	99000	244000	6400	300	6700	251200
	2001		65000	68000	15000	63000	5000	35000	103000	251000	6600	300	6900	257900

company's fiscal periods. We recommend that the revenue forecast and actual performance be compared and reconciled on a monthly and quarterly basis. This way, there are no surprises!

FORECAST HORIZON

Why two years? We recommend a two-year horizon because it spans two fiscal years, so there is less chance of interrupted sales momentum from one year to the next. Another reason is that a two-year horizon usually provides adequate lead time for new-product development within the context of current technology, so tactical marketing feels a greater sense of control and contribution. A third, related reason is that tactical marketing can anticipate and plan for conversion from one product model to the succeeding model. As new products are introduced, product-conversion planning is essential in minimizing lost revenue, unwanted inventory gains, and excess quantities of obsolete product.

The format for the two-year forecast can be as shown in Exhibit 16.1, or an alternate format can be used as shown in Exhibit 16.2. The format in Exhibit 16.2 is used for forecasting specific models or part types as an aid in product-conversion planning and forecasting. The added benefit of this type of format is that it can be used to track changes in the forecast. This format is called a stagger chart or waterfall chart and is widely used in the semiconductor and microelectronics industry.

A third sample format involves the first four quarters in months and quarters and the second four quarters in quarters only. This minimizes the level of detail for tactical marketing, yet still satisfies the need for a two-year forecast. The formats in Exhibits 16.1 and 16.2 can both be modified to accommodate this approach.

PREFERRED FORECAST ACCURACY

Tactical marketing's two-year forecast at the product-line or product-family level of detail should be accurate to within plus or minus 3 to 5 percent, one to two quarters out; plus or minus 5 to 10 percent, four to six quarters out; and plus or minus 10 to 15 percent at the two-year horizon. Remember that this is a tactical marketing revenue forecast and not a bookings forecast generated by the sales organization. In Part V we explore forecasting by the sales force.

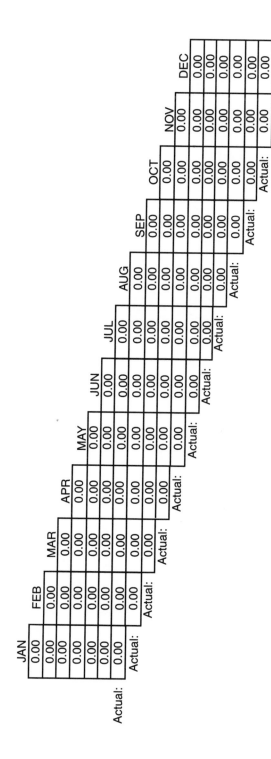

EXHIBIT 16.2 An alternate sample of the revenue forecast

PART V

Forecasting and Sales

17

Marketing and Sales as a Relational Process

THE IDEA FOR DESCRIBING marketing and sales as a relational process emerged over a number of years of working with and managing the two functions. It is not uncommon for there to be a lack of clarity or perhaps even disputes over what marketing and sales are responsibile for and to whom they report. For example, which function is primarily responsible for tracking and understanding the competition and communicating that information to the wider organization? Which function is responsible for revenue projections (forecasts)? Sales forecasts? Which function is responsible for defining the size or capacity of the facilities needed to satisfy the revenue projections? Which function is responsible for profits? And on and on.

Our approach was to develop a relational model for marketing and sales that has at its core the customer and the customer's company—the account. These concepts were developed fully in my book, *Managing the Big Sale: A Relational Approach to Marketing Strategies, Tactics, and Selling* (Lincolnwood, Ill.: NTC Business Books, 1996) and are only summarized here to illustrate how marketing and sales have different responsibilities for forecasting over varying horizons. The key is for marketing and sales to overlap somewhat in principal roles yet be mutually responsible and accountable to each other, especially when the role overlap is confusing, uncertain, or redundant. See Exhibit 17.1.

EXHIBIT 17.1 The relational
nature of marketing and sales

THE ACCOUNT DEVELOPMENT CYCLE

To keep the multiple roles of strategic marketing, tactical marketing, and sales focused, we introduced the notion of the account development cycle, a broadly structured approach describing how marketing and sales can work together to serve the needs and wants of their customers. This model, shown in Exhibit 17.2, provides the context for relational responsibility, as all three functions (strategic marketing, tactical marketing, and sales) are collectively responsible to the customer. Following is a summary of the major elements of the account development cycle drawn from *Managing the Big Sale.* For

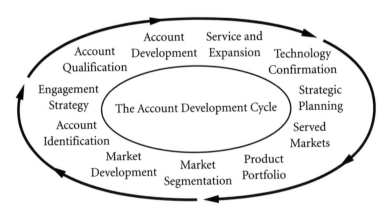

EXHIBIT 17.2 The account development cycle

each of the three sections, outlining primary responsibilities for the function, refer to Exhibit 17.2.

"The terms marketing and sales are often used interchangeably but, especially in the context of a complex sale, they are not the same. Marketing involves a long planning horizon and, broadly speaking, is primarily responsible for such functions as: the definition of technologies, identification of products and services, delineation of served markets, product positioning, product pricing, and the definition and achievement of specific revenue and profit goals. Sales, on the other hand, has a much narrower focus and utilizes marketing's plans and analyses to call on identified prospective accounts, build personal relationships with qualified buyers, identify specific opportunities, close sales, and provide ongoing service to each of the many customers within the target accounts. In addition, salespeople provide a valuable view of the current marketplace through their day-to-day interaction with the customer. Clearly, the two functions are different, yet they are interdependent.

"To be successful, marketing and sales must function relationally, which means that the roles and responsibilities of each are defined in terms of the other's needs and from the perspective of the customers. For example, because the primary role of sales is to sell products and services at a level of price, quality, and performance acceptable to the customer, the sales force can be successful only if the roles and responsibilities of marketing are defined and practiced in a manner complementary to both sales and the customer. By the same token, if marketing's primary role is to deliver profit and market share for the company, then the role of sales must be defined in a manner complementary to both marketing and the customer, in other words, to find and service customers who want the company's products and services. When viewed relationally, the question of what constitutes a satisfied customer or a successful marketing or sales organization shifts away from looking at one or the other function and, instead, focuses on the patterns of interaction that take place between marketing and sales in response to customers' needs.

"As the level of interaction increases and the relationship between marketing and sales strengthens, the level of complexity increases significantly. While specific time frames and functions vary with the specific industry, the levels of responsibility, detail, and different views of the future do not. Sales tends to focus on the immediate or very near term. A good rule of thumb for strategic marketing's planning horizon is five to ten years; for tactical marketing, one to three years; and for sales, the current fiscal year."

STRATEGIC MARKETING

"The primary responsibilities of strategic marketing include *strategic planning*, definition of *served markets*, creation of the *product portfolio*, and *market segmentation*. Satisfying these primary areas involves working within a planning horizon of five to ten years and includes defining specific product lines or product groups, conducting market and marketing research, segmentation studies, developing descriptions of likely product applications, conducting major competitive analyses, and generating a broad range of pro forma financials. Implicit in this approach are discussions and decisions about current and projected technologies that will be needed to realize the projected goals and objectives of the business plan.

"In terms of products, the planning level of strategic marketing is restricted to the product group or the product family. Expected quantities and their dollar value are derived from market growth rates and share-of-market assumptions. This takes advantage of the principle of aggregation, using product mix and market research data, and provides ample leeway for tactical marketing planners to expand the planning process as new information becomes available.

"The planning horizon for strategic marketing is typically five to ten years. This means a minimum of a five-year revenue and profit plan is required for each of the major product families involved. If new technologies are to be developed, the five-year plan must take that into consideration and show the source and application of funds to pay for the new development. Planned cost reductions would also have to occur for the margin goals to be met. The plan would also describe the slope of the cost improvement curve.

"Forecasting, at the strategic marketing level, must include knowledge of what's happening in the national economy. The following questions must be considered: How is the economy structured? Which microsectors of the economy contain data about our products? What will be the relationship of the projected product groups or product families to the national economy? Will the product family move in a procyclical fashion or will it move in a more contracyclical manner? What will be the impact of any recessionary periods that may occur while we bring the new products to market?"

TACTICAL MARKETING

"While strategic marketing has primary responsibility for the definition of served markets, tactical marketing has the primary responsibility for *market development*. Market development typically takes the form of expansion, contraction, or redefinition of one or more of the served market segments. For example, strategic marketing may have originally defined the served market for color laser printers consisting mainly of networked desktop applications. Tactical marketing, working with sales, may discover new information showing that there are growth and profit opportunities if the served market application is redefined by the individual home-based professional.

"Tactical marketing is also primarily responsible for *account identification* and *engagement strategy*. A broad selection of electronic data sources is available to help identify prospective target accounts. Marketing tacticians screen the 'long list' of possible customers to produce a short list of prospective target accounts for sales, saving an incredible amount of time and money.

"Once the short list of prospective target accounts has been generated, marketing tacticians prepare detailed target account profiles including the identification of the most likely competitors. These profiles identify each target account in terms of size, product lines, markets served, share-of-market by product line, position in the marketplace, profitability, major customers by product line, major competitors by product line, management structure, key personnel by function, and potential sales opportunities by product line. These profiles are combined with product data sheets, marketing communications, and positioning materials to form the sales kits. The sales kits are used by marketing tacticians to train the salespeople. These materials help the salespeople understand the engagement strategy and how the critical features and benefits of the various products and product lines can help them plan how to engage their respective accounts."

SALES

"Sales is responsible for *account qualification, account development, account service and expansion,* and *technology confirmation.* Account qualification defines the process of contacting and meeting with various key people within the target account to understand and quantify their respective needs and wants. The qualification process also determines the importance and urgency of the needs and wants and assesses whether or not the opportunities being discussed have been funded. Once the account is qualified, the process of account development can proceed.

"The early stages of the account development process may take several weeks or several months, depending on the complexity of the products and whether the target account is a new or existing account and whether the products are new or existing. For example, if it is a new account, then the salesperson must build basic confidence of the decision makers by acquainting them with the company. After building the necessary relationships, the salesperson identifies and quantifies one or more specific sales opportunities, makes the appropriate presentations, and tracks each opportunity through its respective selling cycle. Generally, different product lines require somewhat different selling cycles. Knowing where each opportunity is in the selling cycle can be very useful when the salesperson is asked to submit a bookings forecast.

"Account service and expansion follow the sale. With complex sales, the key to effective service is to first understand the many different and often competing expectations of the various customers within the account. It is essential to understand what is important to the key people and to structure the service review around those expectations. The concept of service is different for different accounts and might include monthly or quarterly meetings where summary statistics on quality, delivery, price changes, stocking requests, and inventory positions are presented. Wherever possible, the use of graphs is recommended.

"Asking salespeople to be responsible for technology confirmation or redirection may seem strange, but this is a neglected area. The salespeople are usually very knowledgeable about how their company's products and services satisfy or do not satisfy the needs and wants of the marketplace. Unfortunately, few companies have an effective means of gathering this valuable information. We propose that the account review process be used as the vehicle to gather such information.

"Regularly held account reviews include a detailed business won/business lost analysis for each of the sales opportunities identified. Sharing information by sales, tactical marketing, and strategic marketing provides a unique opportunity to discuss what is working well and what requires improvement. This discussion provides the opportunity to reaffirm or redirect the strategies and tactics being used."

18

Sales Opportunity Tracking

WITHIN THE CONTEXT of the relational approach, marketing is responsible for revenue (billings) forecasting, and sales is responsible for bookings forecasting. If marketing is responsible for technology and product development, then they are the best equipped to forecast the level and mix of sales revenue expected from the targeted markets. This includes identifying prospective target accounts and crafting the engagement strategy believed to be effective. This shared or relational responsibility between marketing and sales greatly reduces the uncertainty for the sales force, as they can focus essentially on prequalified prospective accounts.

This process is not infallible. Sales, to be effective, must plan and execute the transfer of primary responsibility from marketing and construct assertively the detailed sales approach needed to identify and close the targeted sales opportunities. It is these opportunities, or bookings, that the sales force forecasts.

Sales forecasts only bookings expected for products that have been defined as sales opportunities and are somewhere "in the selling cycle." By "in the selling cycle," we mean that an initial meeting has been held with specific people within the account and a specific opportunity has been defined. For an opportunity to be defined, there must be a product identified, quantities estimated, targeted delivery dates defined, and so on. By forecasting only defined opportunities that are somewhere in the selling cycle, the accuracy of the bookings forecast increases considerably!

Step	Cumulative Probability of Close
1. Initial contact	0.1
2. First call/follow-up	0.2
3. ID decision makers	0.3
4. ID confirm	0.3
5. ID installed base	0.4
6. ID opportunity/needs	0.5
7. Formal presentation	0.6
8. Confirm product line	0.7
9. Determine pricing	0.7
10. Demo/product evaluation	0.8
11. Issues/concerns	0.8
12. Negotiation	0.9
13. Close/receive P.O.	1.0

EXHIBIT 18.1 Steps in the selling cycle

THE SELLING CYCLE

What is the selling cycle? The selling cycle is an abstraction of the key steps leading to a successful sale. Although the steps, and the elapsed time between them, are different for each industry and type of product, certain steps are similar across all industries. An example of key steps in the selling cycle is shown in Exhibit 18.1. In actual practice, members of the marketing and sales organization would meet to discuss what they consider to be the key steps in the selling cycle and the preferred elapsed time between each step. This is a key component of the relational responsibility of marketing and sales, as it permits the transfer process to be realized via discussions and negotiations about the selling cycle. Once defined, the selling cycle provides a backbone for both organizations to track progress against the sales goals.

ASSUMPTIONS

The assumptions behind the selling cycle hold that there is a preferred number of steps leading to a successful sale and that the elapsed time between those steps is as important to the success of the sale as are the actual steps. For example, if a customer in an account has been contacted but not followed up on for several weeks, do you think that the salesperson can simply contact the customer whenever he or she wants and pick up where they left off? Highly unlikely! When the salesperson does contact the customer, the customer's response may range from saying nothing to being rude and abusive. The net result is usually a lost sale and a very unhappy and often vocal customer.

If your company has been in business for a period of time, and you have an effective sales force, then you have the basic raw material on hand to construct a draft of the selling cycle. To start, simply identify the top 20 percent of your sales force that generates 80 percent of the bookings and invite them to a roundtable discussion about their approach to selling. Begin by asking each of them to think about an especially successful sale about which they felt proud and satisfied, and then ask each to tell his or her story from start to finish in the presence of the other expert salespeople.

Take detailed notes of each presentation, and try to outline a broad set of steps that can be used later in follow-up discussions. Continue until all have told their stories, and then ask for an open discussion about what seemed to work well for people. Edit your notes, and if there appears to be significant differences between salespeople when selling the same types of products, explore these differences in greater detail, and arrive at a consensus on the key steps in the selling cycle and what the experts believe to be the preferred elapsed time between steps.

The assumption is that as each step in the selling cycle is accomplished in a satisfactory manner, the probability of the next step's also being completed satisfactorily increases accordingly, the goal being to close the sale. Now, if the cumulative probability of a successful close increases as each successive step in the selling cycle is satisfied, and we know the preferred elapsed time between steps, we have the elements for an effective bookings forecast.

STEPS IN THE SELLING CYCLE

The selling cycle is the key to successful target-account development. Each product line in each served market has its own preferred cycle or sequence of activities that, when followed, tends to yield favorable sales results. The selling cycle is further complicated by the type of target account being developed. New accounts, for example, require extra steps and additional time, regardless of the product lines involved. These extra steps permit the salespeople to introduce themselves and offer the prospective customers information about your company.

Broadly speaking, the sequence of the selling cycle begins with a general introduction of people, companies, and products. In these early steps, questions are asked about philosophy, performance, quality, reliability, and price. Only when the participants perceive there to be a potential fit among the people, products, and companies will the opportunity for more specific discussions be presented. For some companies, these early meetings take a considerable amount of time and effort. These early steps usually consist of one to two-hour meetings with people throughout the organization. Having slides or overheads that are geared to the differing needs and wants of the various groups is valuable and saves a considerable amount of the salesperson's time.

During these early meetings, the more effective salespeople ask a lot of questions and seek to learn who the customers are, what their needs and wants are, the names and titles of the person or persons who can make the decision, and how the company's decision-making process works. Exhibit 18.2 shows an example of a general selling cycle used by a major account rep for

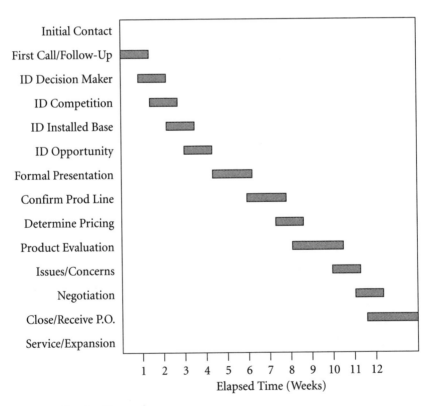

EXHIBIT 18.2 A selling cycle

a microcomputer manufacturer. The steps listed are checkpoints. Additional steps too detailed to track and too specific to list occur within these steps. For example, ID Decision Maker may include several meetings with people at different levels of the organization. This sequence helps the account rep effectively track his or her progress.

The length of the individual horizontal bars relates to the average length of time a given step takes to accomplish. Knowing the time required to accomplish specific tasks enables a salesperson to schedule his or her personal selling time more effectively. Knowing the overall time it takes for the salesperson to progress through the selling cycle also gives sales management insight into whether the salespeople will achieve their sales quota. The selling cycle can be used as well to review sales effectiveness and improve the accuracy of bookings forecasts. The steps in the selling cycle can also be arrayed horizontally, as shown in Exhibit 18.3. With this approach, a simple spreadsheet can be used to organize and track the progress of each opportunity through the selling cycle. It is obvious, as well, that the more complex the sale of your product, the longer will be your selling cycle.

CUMULATIVE PROBABILITIES

Cumulative probability is a method of applying weights to dependent events that are sequential in nature. For example, the cumulative probability of closing a sale successfully is much *lower* early in the selling cycle and much *higher* later in the selling cycle. As we advance successfully from one step to the next, the cumulative probability that our efforts will result in a sale is increasing. (Please note that this does not suggest that you multiply the dollar value of your defined opportunity by the cumulative probability to arrive at an adjusted forecast quantity! Defined opportunities are usually won or lost in their entirety: you do not win a portion or lose a portion of the total opportunity on which you are working. You forecast the full dollar value of each defined opportunity, as we shall see later.)

The cumulative probability is simply a way of adding confidence to the accuracy of your near-term forecast numbers. For example, embedded in the selling cycle is the preferred elapsed time between steps. For defined opportunities that are early in their respective selling cycles, it will take longer to close the sale, as there are a greater number of remaining steps left to be successfully navigated before we can close the sale. This way of looking at sales places the more accurate forecasts in the near term and the less accurate forecasts further out.

SALES OPPORTUNITY BOOKING FORECAST

Number	Opportunity	Amount	Step 1	Step 2	Step 3	Step 4	Step 5	Step 6	Step 7	Step 8	Step 9	Step 10	Step 11	Step 12	Step 13	Comments
1 Plan	Alpha Co.	$750K	Dec-97	Dec-97	Jan-98	Jan-98	Feb-98	Feb-98	Mar-98	Mar-98	Apr-98	Apr-98	May-98	May-98	Jun-98	
1 Actual																
2 Plan	Beta Co.	$500K														
2 Actual																
3 Plan	Gamma Co.	$600K														
3 Actual																
4 Plan																
4 Actual																
5 Plan																
5 Actual																

EXHIBIT 18.3 Sales opportunity booking forecast

STAYING ON TRACK

Staying on track, or certainly, getting back on track once you have deviated from your plan, is always a challenge. We propose that as a starting point you use the elapsed times in the selling cycle to project the dates on which you will complete each step in the cycle. You can use any number of scheduling or calendaring software, or a spreadsheet program such as Microsoft Excel or Lotus 1-2-3. An example that builds on an earlier spreadsheet model is shown in Exhibit 18.4.

In this example there are two lines for each defined opportunity. The top line shows the planned completion dates for each step in the selling cycle, and the bottom line shows the actual dates on which each step was completed. Using an approach like this not only helps you stay on track but also accomplishes two additional things. One, it provides an accurate comparison of planned versus actual elapsed time between steps in the selling cycle and can therefore provide valuable data confirming your prior assumptions. Second, if you are drifting off the planned dates, you can determine the impact of this on your future numbers and take corrective action early.

SALES MANAGEMENT

Sales management really has a nice tool here. For example, sales management can review with each salesperson the status of his or her defined opportunities and whether the person is likely to stay on track or drift off. They can sum the total dollar value of each salesperson's defined opportunities and determine the percentage contribution of each salesperson and each region to the overall goals of the company. Tracking likewise can help sales management determine the number of salespeople needed to generate the revenue numbers projected by marketing. It also provides a good platform for working with individual salespeople on sales call planning.

Perhaps the most value is found in sales management's ability to correctly anticipate and forecast the bookings necessary to support the revenue plan. A simple way of looking at this is presented in Exhibit 18.5. This table shows sales management the dollar value of all defined opportunities and whether they are likely to close in the quarter of interest.

SALES OPPORTUNITY BOOKING FORECAST																	
Number	Opportunity	Amount	Step 1	Step 2	Step 3	Step 4	Step 5	Step 6	Step 7	Step 8	Step 9	Step 10	Step 11	Step 12	Step 13	Comments
1 Plan	Alpha Co.	$750K	Dec-97	Dec-97	Jan-98	Jan-98	Feb-98	Feb-98	Mar-98	Mar-98	Apr-98	Apr-98	May-98	May-98	Jun-98	
1 Actual		$750K	Dec-97	Dec-97	Jan-98	Feb-98										
2 Plan	Beta Co.	$500K														
2 Actual																
3 Plan	Gamma Co.	$600K														
3 Actual																
4 Plan																
4 Actual																
5 Plan																
5 Actual																

EXHIBIT 18.4 Tracking sales opportunities through the selling cycle

Sales Opportunity Review . . .

■ Summary by Confidence Level

	Tot.	.1	.3	.5	.6	.7	.8
Opptys	24	1	5	10	5	3	0
% Total	100	4	21	42	21	13	0
Value (K$)	1750	50	250	1000	200	250	0
% Total	3	3	14	57	11	14	0

EXHIBIT 18.5 A sales management tool

19

The Bookings Forecast

THE PURPOSE OF ASKING the sales force to generate a bookings forecast versus a billings or revenue forecast is simply to place accountability for booking the order with the sales force. By focusing on bookings, the salespeople are 100 percent in control of their own destiny. A key part of the relational approach to marketing and sales is the clearer understanding of roles and responsibilities. A key benefit for the sales organization is that they are no longer asked to prospect or to ask the customers what their future needs might be. Rather, the salesperson is responsible for identifying the specific sales opportunity, selecting the appropriate product line, and sizing the opportunity in terms of units and dollars over what time period. This permits more face-to-face selling time for the salespeople. Remember from our discussion in the previous chapter that only the expected bookings are forecast for each defined opportunity.

The bookings forecast is a forecast of expected orders to be written or booked at some time in the future. A booking may be a single order for a type and quantity of goods to be shipped on a certain date, in its entirety, or it could be for a larger quantity of goods that are to be shipped over an extended period. Both types of bookings are handled in the same manner. Remember, if the opportunity is not defined and quantified, it does not become a part of the bookings forecast. To do so would mean that the salesperson is guessing, and that is the biggest problem with sales forecasting today.

For the bookings forecast to be accurate, the salesperson must apply the appropriate selling cycle, because it is the overall length of the selling cycle and the elapsed time between steps that is key to generating an accurate forecast. The new-order selling cycle, for example, has 13 steps, with preferred elapsed times between steps as shown in Exhibit 19.1. If we choose an initial contact date and then use the preferred elapsed times, in weeks, to plan or pace the sale through the various steps, we see the dates below the steps as shown in Exhibit 19.2. Look at these dates as a plan or a map of how you, as the salesperson, are going to move the sale through the selling cycle successfully. This example shows that the order for 1,200 units and $3,600,000 will close (be booked) the week of October 3, 1997. Note in Exhibit 19.2 that we have added a row immediately below the ABC Co. as a means of tracking actual versus plan. Some expert salespeople also add a calculated field that shows how many days they are ahead or behind the plan.

When it is time to generate a bookings forecast, simply locate the month that your plan indicates that you will close that opportunity, and place the unit and or dollar value in that month. In our example (see Exhibit 19.3), the bookings forecast indicates that 1,200 units or $3,600,000, will be booked in October. Continue this process for each of the defined opportunities. As the time progresses and a new 12-month forecast is requested, simply drop the current month and add a month. If you are on track with each of your defined opportunities, then updating the bookings forecast is relatively quick and

Step	Weeks of Elapsed and Cumulative Time	
1. Initial contact	start	start
2. First call/follow-up	1	1
3. Introduce company	2	3
4. ID decision makers	2	5
5. ID installed based	2	7
6. ID opportunity/needs	2	9
7. Formal presentation	2	11
8. Confirm product line	2	13
9. Determine pricing	2	15
10. Demo/product evaluation	2	17
11. Issues/concerns	2	19
12. Negotiation	3	23
13. Close/receive P.O.	2	25

EXHIBIT 19.1 Steps and elapsed times in the selling cycle

| Account | Opportunity | Product | Bookings Forecast | | Step 1 | Step 2 | Step 3 | Step 4 | Step 5 | Step 6 | Step 7 | Step 8 | Step 9 | Step 10 | Step 11 | Step 12 | Step 13 | Comments |
			Units	Dollars	4/18/97	4/25/97	5/9/97	5/23/97	6/6/97	6/20/97	7/3/97	7/18/97	8/1/97	8/15/97	9/5/97	9/19/97	10/3/97	
ABC Co.	Laptop	FLB-200	1 2	3600														
Tracking					4/18/97	4/24/97	5/6/97											

EXHIBIT 19.2 Bookings plan by sales opportunity

| Account | Opportunity | Product | Bookings Forecast (units) | | Apr | May | Jun | Jul | Aug | Sep | Oct | Nov | Dec | Jan | Feb | Mar | Comments |
			Units	Dollars													
ABC Co.	Laptop	FLB-200	1200	3600000	0	0	0	0	0	0	1200	0	0	0	0	0	

EXHIBIT 19.3 Sample bookings forecast

straightforward. If, for example, there are opportunities that were planned to book in the current month and are still valid but for one reason or another failed to make the month cutoff, roll them over into the new current month.

LEVEL OF DETAIL

The level of detail appropriate for the bookings forecast is the specific part number of the product in which the customer is interested. The fact that you as the salesperson are forecasting only product for which there is a defined opportunity that is active in the selling cycle is a considerable advantage over guessing what product type and the quantities in which the customer might be interested.

Quantities are forecast in units. In the example shown, the opportunity was for 1,200 FLB-200 laptop units worth some $3,600,000. By your forecasting in units, other functional areas within the company can use the bookings forecast directly without having to know prices and whether or not some sort of a special price promotion was in effect.

FORECAST HORIZON

In the case of a bookings forecast of the type being discussed here, the forecast horizon really becomes a factor of the length of the selling cycle. A good rule of thumb is for the horizon to be roughly twice the length of the selling cycle. In the previous example the selling cycle was approximately twenty-five weeks long, so a twelve-month rolling bookings forecast would be appropriate. For companies whose products have a very short selling cycle, we would recommend a minimum forecast horizon of three months.

FORECAST ACCURACY

The accuracy of the bookings forecast is directly dependent on the close ratio for each salesperson. Varying with the industry and the type of product or service sold, close ratios may run anywhere from 2:10 to 1:2. Remember that these numbers usually emerge from salespeople doing their own prospecting and qualifying. Within the context of the relational model, marketing has prequalified the accounts but has not defined specific opportunities. If there is to be fallout, it will occur at the opportunity-definition step in the selling cycle. Once you have passed that step, and assuming that you have a number of opportunities across a number of companies, your close ratio and hence the forecast accuracy should be in the range of 85 to 95 percent at the six-month horizon. Within a three-month horizon, your bookings forecast accuracy should be in excess of 95 percent.

PART VI

Monitoring Forecast Accuracy

20

Measures of Forecast Accuracy

MEASURES OF FORECAST ACCURACY are important to understanding the source and nature of forecast error so that the accuracy of the forecasting process can be continually improved. To continually improve something, you must first understand what you are attempting to measure, and second, have meaningful metrics by which to measure. It is also important to sort out answers to the question of "what is good enough."

People who *use* forecasts are most interested in a straightforward measure of forecast accuracy—that is, *forecast versus actual.* In other words, how close did the forecast come to the actual numbers? *Forecasters,* on the other hand, must understand many different measures of forecast accuracy if they are to continually improve their forecast accuracy. Note that measures of forecast accuracy become issues for management only when the actual results deviate substantially from the forecast.

WHAT IS GOOD ENOUGH?

Earlier in the book, we explored various methodological approaches to forecasting. One such method involved the two naive approaches: naive 1 and naive 2. Recall that naive forecast 1 holds that tomorrow will be the same as today. In other words, naive 1 is a "no change" model. Naive 2 is also a "no change in the rate of change" model and holds that the rate of increase or decrease will be the same from today to tomorrow as it was from yesterday to today. This is a constant-rate-change model. The naive models are often used as standards against which the accuracy of other forecasts are measured.

The question remains: What is good enough? A forecast that is good enough balances the time and money to prepare it against the value it provides. For example, do we need a point forecast that is accurate to less than 1 percent, or can we live with a range of forecast values? Unfortunately the answer varies by type and nature of product and service, as well as by company. The key seems to rest in understanding the response envelope of your company. For example, is the nature of your business such that you can accelerate or decelerate the flow of product to accommodate variance in forecast accuracy? If so, what do you estimate that stretch and compress function to look like? Can you accommodate plus or minus 10 percent? Plus or minus 15 percent? More? Less? These are the primary questions to ask when specifying forecast accuracy.

Once again, if we look at marketing and sales as a relational process, then forecasting responsibilities can be shared across functions. This results in increased dialogue between organizational functions, which serves to enhance the use of forecast information.

CONVENTIONAL MEASURES

There are many conventional measures of forecast accuracy. Many of these are modifications to a common theme of measuring forecast error from one forecast period to another. This method generates both positive and negative errors. When these errors are summed and divided by the number of errors, the result is the average error or *mean error* (ME). This approach usually produces the lowest error score, as the positive and negative errors cancel out. Another approach eliminates the positive and negative errors canceling by computing the average error without regard to sign. This is done by averaging the absolute values of the errors. This approach is called the *mean absolute deviation* (MAD).

A third approach, called the *mean squared error* (MSE), also gets rid of the positive and negative errors and amplifies the error measure by squaring each error term, summing them, and computing the average.

These three approaches all follow from the measurement of forecast error as a percentage. Since we are measuring forecast accuracy, subtract the actual from the forecast, divide by the actual, and multiply the answer by 100. In notation it looks like:

$$PE = \frac{\text{Forecast} - \text{Actual}}{\text{Actual}} \times 100$$

The sign of the answer in this calculation is also of value. If the PE is negative, then the forecast is less than the actual. If it is positive, then the actual is greater than the forecast. The other percent error measures are *mean percent error* (MPE) and *mean absolute percent error* (MAPE). In MPE the individual PEs are summed and the mean computed. The MAPE does the same thing but without regard to sign—that is, it uses absolute values.

THE BOTTOM LINE: FORECAST VERSUS ACTUAL

The bottom line for most companies is knowing how much the forecast deviated from the actual. In other words, what is the forecast versus actual for the key areas of interest. This focus also helps gather meaningful information to in turn help answer the question of what is good enough. For example, if you are tracking and reporting on forecast error or forecast accuracy, and you find that the organization is still achieving its goals even though forecast error is higher than planned, you have some information that suggests that your initial forecast-accuracy goals were too high.

In my experience, the preferred way to present forecast accuracy is in terms of percent error or percent accurate. Percent error was demonstrated in the preceding section and is a satisfactory way of presenting forecast error. If you are interested in presenting forecast accuracy, then simply subtract the PE from 100, and report that number. If you are working from a historical data series, your forecast accuracy, over time, can be only as good as the irregular component of the seasonally adjusted series. For example, if the irregular component varies plus or minus 10 percent, period to period, then over time your forecast error will not be less than plus or minus 10 percent. In fact, it would probably be no better than plus or minus 15 percent except on those chance events.

CONTROL CHARTS

Most factories today have extensive quality-control systems that are essential in achieving and maintaining the level of quality demanded by today's consumers. Control charts, or Shewhart control charts, are an essential element of any comprehensive quality-management system. Devised by W. A. Shewhart in 1924 as a graphic method of detecting assignable causes of variation in a manufacturing process—that is, deviation of actual manufactured part measures compared with specification values—control charts can also be used to monitor forecast accuracy in a couple of different ways.

For example, if we use percent error as a measure of forecast accuracy, then "zero" becomes the desired specification value for forecast error. Positive deviations describe forecast errors in which the forecast value was greater than the actual value, and negative deviations describe forecast errors in which the forecast value was less than the actual value. See Exhibit 20.1. Control charts can also be used to track trends or bias in forecast accuracy. For example, if forecast errors continue to be positive, then there is bias in the direction of forecast values greater than actual values. Conversely, if forecast errors continue on the negative side, then there is bias in the direction of forecast values less than actual values. Increasing or decreasing trends in errors and bias can also be detected using control charts.

Adding upper and lower control limits to control charts enhances the usefulness of the control chart as a tool. Control limits are used in many ways.

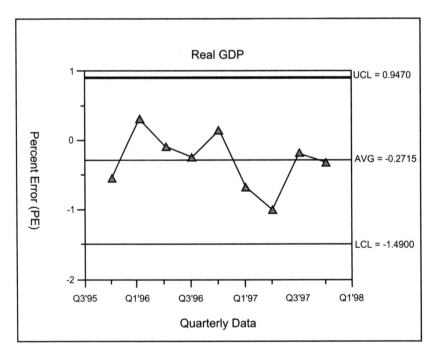

EXHIBIT 20.1 Actual versus forecast expressed graphically as a positive or negative value

For example, in a manufacturing process, the limits may signify the upper and lower tolerance limits of a process parameter, or they could be used to determine the variability of a process for which there is no specification. In the latter, the upper and lower limits are defined as the plus or minus 3-sigma or 6-sigma variance of the actual data. Limits computed in this manner serve as a reference point for consistency of the process without intervention. If the limits are too broad, new limits can be established, and specific intervention will be required to operate within these new limits.

The establishment of upper and lower control limits is influenced by the level of forecast accuracy required. When forecast errors are tracked, decisions about needed accuracy can be grounded in data rather than opinion. For example, if the users of your forecasts can still achieve their goals with a forecast error of 10 percent when they have been insisting on a forecast error of 5 percent, relaxing the expectation of forecast accuracy could reduce the cost of the forecast and make it available that much sooner if 10 percent accuracy versus 5 percent accuracy is acceptable! Exhibit 20.2 illustrates upper and lower control limits.

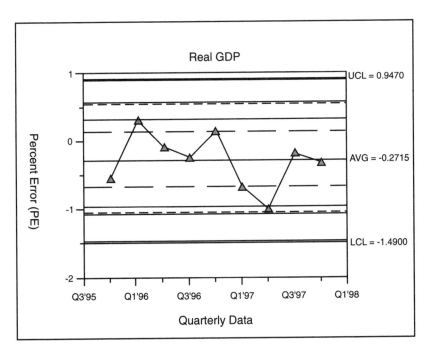

EXHIBIT 20.2 Sample control chart with upper and lower limits

PERCENT CHANGE SUCCESSFULLY PREDICTED

Percent change successfully predicted (PCSP) is a highly refined approach to measuring forecast accuracy and was developed originally by my friend and colleague Bob McLaughlin. The concept of PCSP holds that the real challenge to the forecaster is to predict as much of the change in data series as possible. For example, if we compare the forecast accuracy of two forecasters where forecaster A reports a forecast error of 4 percent and forecaster B reports a forecast error of 8 percent, can we conclude that forecaster A is twice as good as forecaster B? No, not without knowing the percent change in the underlying data series. For the example noted, if the percent change in the data series for forecaster A and B was 1 percent and 16 percent, respectively, then the conclusion would be that forecaster B was the better forecaster. Forecaster A would have been better off using NF1!

The bottom line being forecast versus actual, the concepts of PCSP are really useful as a tool for forecasters as they seek to improve their forecasting accuracy. To that end, the PCSP can also be combined with the control chart to yield a powerful tool for measuring forecast accuracy. From experience, we know that really good forecasters average about 60 percent of the change successfully predicted. Therefore, we could set 60 percent as the control chart mean and monitor our performance against the target.

21

Closing the Loop

THIS FINAL CHAPTER ILLUSTRATES how the forecasting loop can be closed. We began this journey with the view that forecasting is both art and science—art, in terms of where to look, what to present, and how to use graphics to communicate forecast information in a way that our intended audience can understand and follow; and science, in that effective forecasts make use of many different methods of computation drawn from various schools of thought. The best course is to be open-minded to those things that work and not be overinvested in a methodology just for the sake of the methodology.

We reviewed the broad class of time series and explained the major elements of seasonal adjustment and why it is essential to accurate forecasting. With a review of the basic tools, we introduced our Average Recession Recovery Model (ARRM) and companion Average Experience Model (AEM) as special cases of time series and explained their benefits.

Next we highlighted the unique needs of strategic marketing and illustrated how their forecasts really had to be more macro and longer-term than the forecasts of tactical marketing and day-to-day operations. This includes being aware of what is happening in the broader economies of the world and linking macroeconomic factors to the industries, technologies, markets, product families, and product lines. We explained how strategic marketing's longer-term forecasts are used for capacity and capital appropriations planning. The forecast horizon for strategic marketing was defined as five years.

Tactical marketing, on the other hand, is focused on the near term, with a forecast horizon of two years. Tactical marketing develops products within the broad technologies defined by strategic marketing and serving, at a minimum, the same markets defined by strategic marketing. It is essential that any differences between the views of the two marketing functions be identified, understood, and reconciled as soon as possible. Forecast level is the product line, forecast periods are quarters, and level of detail is in units and dollars. Tactical marketing's responsibility was defined as extending to the identification of prospective target accounts and the development of sales kits for use in sales training.

While strategic and tactical marketing are responsible for revenue and profitability, sales is responsible for booking the order. They are focused in the here and now and are responsible for calling on, developing, closing, and servicing their respective accounts. Within our model, sales forecasts only those opportunities that have been identified within each of the target accounts. The salespeople track each opportunity through its respective selling cycle and use the elapsed times as a pacing or planning process for forecasting when each opportunity is planned to close. This planned close becomes a booked order. This approach to field sales forecasting eliminates all of the guesswork in forecasting and places the salesperson more in charge of day-to-day selling efforts. The monthly or quarterly target account review is the venue for communicating progress on each account and coordinating the collective efforts of strategic marketing, tactical marketing, and sales.

MARKETING AND SALES AS A RELATIONAL PROCESS

The basic idea behind our approach is to parse the overall planning and forecasting tasks into strategic marketing, tactical marketing, and sales subtasks and tie the subtasks together through communication, cooperation, and collaboration. In this way, the field salespeople do not have to spend a lot of time trying to estimate what each of their clients might buy over the next several months and can, instead, focus on closing the defined opportunities within each of their target accounts. The anticipated close date and the units and dollars involved for each of these opportunities constitute the bookings forecast.

Members of tactical marketing create the revenue forecast that drives short-term and near-term product development and factory planning activities based on their perception of the needs and wants of each of the application domains within each of the served market segments. With tactical marketing responsible for revenue and profitability, there is a vested interest in helping the sales force focus on the prospective target accounts believed by tactical marketing to yield the planned results.

Strategic marketing maintains the longer look ahead, monitors current product-development activities within the context of current technology, and develops the next-generation technologies. Strategic marketing also takes the lead in business-planning efforts and prepares pro forma financials of new-product families and new technologies.

A summary of the forecasting contributions of the three functions is shown in Exhibit 21.1.

Strategic Marketing Revenue Forecast
(5 Year × Year)

	1998	1999	2000	2001	2002
Product Line A					
Product Line B					
Product Line C					
Total					

Tactical Marketing Revenue Forecast (2 Year × Quarter)

	Q11998	Q21998	Q31998	Q41998	1998	Q11999	Q21999	Q31999	Q41999	1999
Product Line A										
Product Line B										
Product Line C										
Total										

Tactical Marketing Revenue Forecast
(1 Year × Quarter)

	Q11998	Q21998	Q31998	Q41998	1998
Product Line A					
Product Line B					
Product Line C					

Sales Marketing Revenue Forecast
(1 Year × Quarter)

	Q11998	Q21998	Q31998	Q41998	1998
A 123 Part No.					
A 234 Part No.					
A 345 Part No.					

EXHIBIT 21.1 Summary of forecast contributions (blank work sheet)

THE FORECAST CYCLE

A number of companies require their salespeople to generate an unconstrained demand forecast for their territory each month by product type, in units and dollars, for the next six to twelve months. These individual forecasts are then summed, or rolled up, at various levels to create an aggregate forecast. For example, the forecasts of each salesperson in the Southwest territory are rolled up into a forecast for the Southwest region. The Southwest region is, in turn, added to the Northwest, Central, Southeast, and Northeast regions to create the U.S. forecast. This aggregate forecast is often "judged" at each level of sales and marketing management, adding time to the process and distorting the data. It is not uncommon for a field-generated bottom-up demand forecast of this sort to take several weeks to generate. It is also notoriously inaccurate because forecasts generated in this manner are frequently confused with goals or quotas.

Working within marketing and sales in the context of the relational approach, lengthy forecast cycles are a thing of the past. Strategic marketing, for example, generates its long-term five-year forecast annually and updates it once a year during the strategic business-planning cycle. Tactical marketing, working within the guidelines set by strategic marketing, generates a two- to three-year forecast at the product-line level of detail by quarter and in units and dollars. This is the short-term operating forecast used for revenue, capacity, and profitability planning and is updated quarterly. Members of sales, working with the prospective target accounts defined by tactical marketing, call on the target account, identify opportunities, and move the account through the steps in the selling cycle to book the order. The bookings forecast is simply a reporting of the projected close date of each of their opportunities, summed across all salespeople.

With this approach to forecasting, field salespeople are forecasting only opportunities that have been identified and that are somewhere in the selling cycle. If there are no defined opportunities being worked, there is no bookings forecast. Also, with each opportunity defined in terms of product, unit volume, and sales price, the accuracy of the bookings forecast is no longer left to chance. The specifics are known, which in turn greatly facilitates the factory's ability to build the correct product at the appropriate time.

STRATEGIC MARKETING FORECASTS [REVENUE]

Strategic marketing forecasts are generated in dollars and for broad sectors of the company. It is not uncommon for a technology company to forecast revenue by technology. Using technology as an example, the forecast might

Strategic Marketing Revenue Forecast (5 Year × Year)					
	1998	1999	2000	2001	2002
Alpha Technology	1,500	750	200	100	100
Product Line A					
Product Line B					
Product Line C					
Beta Technology	1,000	1,500	1,500	1,200	800
Product Line D					
Product Line E					
Product Line F					
Gamma Technology	200	850	1,500	2,000	2,500
Product Line G					
Product Line H					
Product Line I					
Total	2,700	3,100	3,200	3,300	3,400

EXHIBIT 21.2 Strategic marketing revenue forecast by technology

look as shown in Exhibit 21.2. Note how the dollar value of Beta Technology tails off as Gamma Technology replaces it.

TACTICAL MARKETING FORECASTS (BILLINGS)

Forecasts generated by tactical marketing are more detailed, yet cover a shorter horizon. In our example the level of detail is at the product-line level, involves units and dollars, and spans a horizon of two years. It is at this level of detail that the tactical marketing forecast would pick up the planned shift from technology category B to C—or extend category B if the strategic forecast of demand is premature or less than anticipated. This interaction and adjustment of the different marketing forecasts adds significant value to the company. The tactical marketing forecast is updated each quarter.

As those responsible for the tactical marketing function generate their short-term forecasts, they construct an audit trail of their assumptions and later use them to develop criteria for the selection of prospective target accounts for the salespeople. At the same time, tactical marketing is creating possible application scenarios, using the company's products and technologies. These application areas are called application domains and are critical in the development of the sales kits and in the training of salespeople. See Exhibit 21.3.

Tactical Marketing Revenue Forecast (2 Year × Quarter)

	Q11998	Q21998	Q31998	Q41998	1998	Q11999	Q21999	Q31999	Q41999	1999
Alpha Technology	400	400	400	300	1,500	250	200	150	150	750
Product Line A										
Product Line B										
Product Line C										
Beta Technology	100	200	300	400	1,000	500	400	300	300	1,500
Product Line D										
Product Line E										
Product Line F										
Gamma Technology	0	0	25	175	200	175	200	225	250	850
Product Line G										
Product Line H										
Product Line I										
Total					2,700					3,100

EXHIBIT 21.3 Tactical marketing revenue forecast

SALES FORECASTS (BOOKINGS)

The bookings forecast is generated by sales. It is a forecast of the sales opportunities they will close and includes specific accounts, specific products, specific quantities, specific dollars, and a specific time frame (usually a month) in which the order will be booked. Because no salesperson is able to close all of the sales on which he or she is working, the bookings forecast contains a total value greater than that needed to support marketing's revenue plan. For example, if the revenue plan calls for $100K, and the sales force has an average close ratio of one-third, then for management to be confident that the revenue numbers will be supported, the amount of bookings in position to close should equal $300K. See Exhibit 21.4.

From Exhibit 21.4, for illustration purposes, assume that product line A and Customer A account for all of Alpha Technology's sales in 1999. Then the sales opportunity booking forecast should show a greater dollar volume to allow for lost bookings. For example, using a close ratio of 1:3, we need sales opportunities totaling $2,250 to support a planned revenue of $8,750.

If the company is a new start-up, and the sales force wants to be somewhat conservative, they can guardband the revenue numbers even more by offsetting the time in which the bookings must be made to support the revenue. In the example shown in Exhibit 21.5, the backlog is offset one month from the revenue plan, and the bookings forecast is offset an additional month from the backlog plan. This provides some breathing room for a new sales force or for a company that cannot afford to miss its revenue forecast.

ALTERNATIVE SUPPORTING SOLUTIONS

Remember that forecasts are only tools to help you run the business more effectively. Forecasts, in and of themselves, have no value; their entire value is in their contribution to increased operating effectiveness. Look for alternative supporting solutions when the old ways no longer work. Our movement to a bookings forecast using defined opportunities rather than a broad guesstimate of what the customer intends to buy is an example of an alternative solution. Another alternative solution to rapidly changing forecast content would be to reduce manufacturing cycle time to the shortest possible time and manufacture to order rather than to forecast. Many other examples of alternative solutions could be provided. Suffice it to say that forecasting, however complex or sophisticated, is still a tool for effective business management. And like any good tool, it must be kept sharp and well maintained to be ready when needed.

Sales Opportunity Booking Forecast (1 Year × Month × Quarter)

	Jan	Feb	Mar	Q11999	Apr	May	Jun	Q21999	Jul	Aug	Sep	Q31999	Oct	Nov	Dec	Q41999	1999
Customer A																	
A 123 Part No.	300	300	150	750	250	250	100	600	200	200	50	450	200	200	50	450	2250
Customer B																	
A 234 Part No.																	
Customer C																	
A 345 Part No.																	
A 456 Part No.																	
Customer D																	
A 123 Part No.																	
A 234 Part No.																	

Note: For illustration purposes, only product line A part numbers are shown for Alpha Technology.

EXHIBIT 21.4 Sales opportunity booking forecast

SALES OPPORTUNITY BOOKING FORECAST

	Jan	Feb	Mar	Q1 1998	Apr	May	Jun	Q2 1998	Jul	Aug	Sep	Q3 1998	Oct	Nov	Dec	Q4 1998	1998
Customer A																	
A 123 Part No.	1000*																
Customer B																		
A 234 Part No.																		
Customer C																		
A 345 Part No.																		
A 456 Part No.																		
Customer D																		
A 123 Part No.																		
A 234 Part No.																		

BACKLOG FORECAST

	Jan	Feb	Mar	Q1 1998	Apr	May	Jun	Q2 1998	Jul	Aug	Sep	Q3 1998	Oct	Nov	Dec	Q4 1998	1998
Customer A																	
A 123 Part No.		1000*															
Customer B																		
A 234 Part No.																		
Customer C																		
A 345 Part No.																		
A 456 Part No.																		
Customer D																		
A 123 Part No.																		
A 234 Part No.																		

REVENUE (BILLINGS) FORECAST

	Jan	Feb	Mar	Q1 1998	Apr	May	Jun	Q2 1998	Jul	Aug	Sep	Q3 1998	Oct	Nov	Dec	Q4 1998	1998
Customer A																	
A 123 Part No.			1000*														
Customer B																		
A 234 Part No.																		
Customer C																		
A 345 Part No.																		
A 456 Part No.																		
Customer D																		
A 123 Part No.																		
A 234 Part No.																		

Note: For illustration purposes, only product line A part numbers are shown.

*Single values are shown for illustration purposes only.

EXHIBIT 21.5 Sample offset forecasts

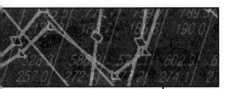

Further Reading

Armstrong, J. C. "Forecasting with Econometric Methods: Folklore Versus Fact." *Journal of Business* 1978, S1: 549–600.

Box, G. E. P., and G. M. Jenkins. *Time Series Analysis, Forecasting, and Control*, 2nd ed. San Francisco: Holden Day, 1976.

Brown, R. G. *Smoothing, Forecasting, and Prediction of Discrete Time Series*. Englewood Cliffs, N. J.: Prentice Hall, 1963.

Chow, W. M. "Adaptive Control of the Exponential Smoothing Constant." *Journal of Industrial Engineering*, 16 (5), 1965.

Delurgio, S. A., and C. D. Bhame. *Forecasting Systems for Operations Management*. Homewood, Ill.: Business One Irwin, 1991.

Fabricant, Solomon. Toward a Firmer Basis of Economic Policy: The Founding of the Natural Bureau of Economic Research. Cambridge, Mass.: NBER, Inc., 1984.

Gardner, E. S. "Exponential Smoothing: The State of the Art." *Journal of Forecasting* 4 (1985): 1–28.

Hanke, J. E., and A. G. Reitsch. *Business Forecasting*, 5th ed. Englewood Cliffs, N. J.: Prentice Hall, 1995.

Holt, C. C., et al. *Planning Production, Inventories, and Work Force*. Englewood Cliffs, N. J.: Prentice Hall, 1960.

Lewandowski, Rudolf. "An Integrated Approach to Medium and Long-Term Forecasting, the Marketing-Mix System." In *The Handbook of Forecasting: A Manager's Guide*, S. Makridakis and S. C. Wheelwright (eds.). New York: John Wiley & Sons, 1982.

Makridakis, S., et al. *The Forecasting Accuracy of Major Time Series Methods*. New York: John Wiley & Sons, 1984.

Makridakis, S., and M. Hibon. "Accuracy of Forecasting: An Empirical Investigation (with discussion)." *Journal of the Royal Statistical Society* 142 (1979) (A), part 2: 97–145.

McLaughlin, R. L. "Forecasting Models: Sophisticated or Naive?" *Journal of Forecasting* 2 (3) (1983): 274–76.

———. *Forecasting Techniques for Decision Making*, 5th ed. Rockville, MD.: Control Data Management Institute, 1989.

McLeary, R. and R. A. Hay. *Applied Time Series Analysis for the Social Sciences*. Beverly Hills, CA: Sage Publications, 1980.

Parzen, E. "Forecasting and Whitening Filter Estimation," in *Forecasting*, 12, S. Makridakis and S. C. Wheelwright (eds.). TMS/North-Holland, Amsterdam, 1979.

Roberts, S. D., and R. Reed. "The Development of a Self-Adaptive Forecasting Technique." *AIIE Transactions*, 6, 1969.

Slovic, P. "Psychological Study of Human Judgment: Implications for Investment Decision Making." *Journal of Finance* 27 (1972): 779–99.

Winters, P. R. "Forecasting Sales by Exponentially Weighted Moving Averages." *Management Science* 6(1960): 324–42.

Appendix A:
Numerical List of
SIC Short Titles

A PARTIAL LIST OF the official SIC titles of the divisions and the two-digit major groups, three-digit industry groups, and four-digit industries are shown in Part I. For various reasons, including presentation of statistical tables, it is desirable to have a standard list of short SIC titles so that all agencies may use the same short titles for the same codes as long as the titles fit the space requirements of the publication.

The standard short titles that follow have been limited to thirty-six spaces for four-digit industry codes and thirty-eight spaces for two-digit major group and three-digit industry group codes. Where a two-digit major group or three-digit industry group contains only a single four-digit industry, the two-digit or three-digit titles are allowed thirty-six rather than thirty-eight spaces. If the official SIC title falls within the foregoing short title space limitation, it is generally used without change.

It is understood, of course, that just as a title itself is not sufficient to define an industry, so too a short title may not appear to represent the same content as the official title. Content can be defined only by reference to the official titles and descriptions for the relevant division, major group, industry group, and industry.

A. AGRICULTURE, FORESTRY, AND FISHING

Code	Short Title	Code	Short Title
01	**AGRICULTURAL PRODUCTION—CROPS**	0214	Sheep and goats
		0219	General livestock, nec
011	Cash Grains	**024**	**Dairy Farms**
0111	Wheat	0241	Dairy farms
0112	Rice	**025**	**Poultry and Eggs**
0115	Corn	0251	Broiler, fryer, and roaster
0116	Soybeans		chickens
0119	Cash grains, nec	0252	Chicken eggs
013	**Field Crops, Except Cash Grains**	0253	Turkeys and turkey eggs
		0254	Poultry hatcheries
0131	Cotton	0259	Poultry and eggs, nec
0132	Tobacco	**027**	**Animal Specialties**
0133	Sugarcane and sugar beets	0271	Fur-bearing animals and rabbits
0134	Irish Potatoes	0272	Horses and other equines
0139	Field crops, except cash grains, nec	0273	Animal aquaculture
016	**Vegetables and Melons**	0279	Animal specialties, nec
0161	Vegetables and melons	**029**	**General Farms, Primarily Animal**
017	**Fruits and Tree Nuts**	0291	General farms, primarily animal
0171	Berry crops		
0172	Grapes		
0173	Tree nuts	**07**	**AGRICULTURAL SERVICES**
0174	Citrus fruits	**071**	**Soil Preparation Services**
0175	Deciduous tree fruits	0711	Soil preparation services
0179	Fruits and tree nuts, nec	**072**	**Crop Services**
018	**Horticultural Specialties**	0721	Crop planting and protecting
0181	Ornamental nursery products	0722	Crop harvesting
0182	Food crops grown under cover	0723	Crop preparation services for market
019	**General Farms, Primarily Crop**	0724	Cotton ginning
0191	General farms, primarily crop	**074**	**Veterinary Services**
		0741	Veterinary services for livestock
02	**AGRICULTURAL PRODUCTION— LIVESTOCK**	0742	Veterinary services, specialties
		075	**Animal Services, Except Veterinary**
021	**Livestock, Except Dairy and Poultry**	0751	Livestock services, exc. veterinary
0211	Beef cattle feedlots		
0212	Beef cattle, except feedlots		
0213	Hogs		

Code	Short Title	Code	Short Title
0752	Animal specialty services	0831	Forest products
076	**Farm Labor and Management Services**	**085**	**Forestry Services**
		0851	Forestry services
0761	Farm labor contractors		
0762	Farm management services	**09**	**FISHING, HUNTING, AND TRAPPING**
078	**Landscape and Horticultural Services**	**091**	**Commercial Fishing**
0781	Landscape counseling and planning	0912	Finfish
		0913	Shellfish
0782	Lawn and garden services	0919	Miscellaneous marine products
0783	Ornamental shrub and tree services	**092**	**Fish Hatcheries and Preserves**
		0921	Fish hatcheries and preserves
08	**FORESTRY**	**097**	**Hunting, Trapping, Game Propagation**
081	**Timber Tracts**	0971	Hunting, trapping, game propagation
0811	Timber tracts		
083	**Forest Products**		

B. MINING

Code	Short Title	Code	Short Title
10	**METAL MINING**	1094	Uranium-radium-vanadium ores
101	**Iron Ores**	1099	Metal ores, nec
1011	Iron ores		
102	**Copper Ores**	**12**	**COAL MINING**
1021	Copper ores	**122**	**Bituminous Coal and Lignite Mining**
103	**Lead and Zinc Ores**	1221	Bituminous coal and lignite—surface
1031	Lead and zinc ores		
104	**Gold and Silver Ores**	1222	Bituminous coal—underground
1041	Gold ores		
1044	Silver ores	**123**	**Anthracite Mining**
106	**Ferroalloy Ores, Except Vanadium**	1231	Anthracite Mining
		124	**Coal Mining Services**
1061	Ferroalloy ores, except vanadium	1241	Coal mining services
		13	**OIL AND GAS EXTRACTION**
108	**Metal Mining Services**	**131**	**Crude Petroleum and Natural Gas**
1081	Metal mining services		
109	**Miscellaneous Metal Ore**		

Code	Short Title	Code	Short Title
1311	Crude petroleum and natural gas	1446	Industrial sand
132	**Natural Gas Liquids**	**145**	**Clay, Ceramic, & Refractory Minerals**
1321	Natural gas liquids	1455	Kaolin and ball clay
138	**Oil and Gas Field Services**	1459	Clay and related minerals, nec
1381	Drilling oil and gas wells	**147**	**Chemical and Fertilizer Minerals**
1382	Oil and gas exploration services	1474	Potash, soda, and borate minerals
1389	Oil and gas field services, nec	1475	Phosphate rock
14	**NONMETALLIC MINERALS, EXCEPT FUELS**	1479	Chemical and fertilizer mining, nec
141	**Dimension Stone**	**148**	**Nonmetallic Minerals Services**
1411	Dimension stone	1481	Nonmetallic minerals services
142	**Crushed and Broken Stone**	**149**	**Miscellaneous Nonmetallic Minerals**
1422	Crushed and broken limestone	1499	Miscellaneous nonmetallic minerals
1423	Crushed and broken granite		
1429	Crushed and broken stone, nec		
144	**Sand and Gravel**		
1442	Construction sand and gravel		

C. CONSTRUCTION

Code	Short Title	Code	Short Title
15	**GENERAL BUILDING CONTRACTORS**	**16**	**HEAVY CONSTRUCTION, EX. BUILDING**
152	**Residential Building Construction**	**161**	**Highway and Street Construction**
1521	Single-family housing construction	1611	Highway and street construction
1522	Residential construction, nec	**162**	**Heavy Construction, Except Highway**
153	**Operative Builders**	1622	Bridge, tunnel, & elevated highway
1531	Operative builders	1623	Water, sewer, and utility lines
154	**Nonresidential Building Construction**	1629	Heavy construction, nec
1541	Industrial buildings and warehouses	**17**	**SPECIAL TRADE CONTRACTORS**
1542	Nonresidential construction, nec	**171**	**Plumbing, Heating, Air-Conditioning**

Code	Short Title	Code	Short Title
1711	Plumbing, heating, air-conditioning	**176**	**Roofing, Siding, and Sheet Metal Work**
172	**Painting and Paper Hanging**	1761	Roofing, siding, and sheet metal work
1721	Painting and paper hanging	**177**	**Concrete Work**
173	**Electrical Work**	1771	Concrete work
1731	Electrical work	**178**	**Water Well Drilling**
174	**Masonry, Stonework, and Plastering**	1781	Water well drilling
1741	Masonry and other stonework	**179**	**Misc. Special Trade Contractors**
1742	Plastering, drywall, and insulation	1791	Structural steel erection
1743	Terrazzo, tile, marble, mosaic work	1793	Glass and glazing work
175	**Carpentry and Floor Work**	1794	Excavation work
1751	Carpentry work	1795	Wrecking and demolition work
1752	Floor laying and floor work, nec	1796	Installing building equipment, nec
		1799	Special trade contractors, nec

D. MANUFACTURING

Code	Short Title	Code	Short Title
20	**FOOD AND KINDRED PRODUCTS**	2033	Canned fruits and vegetables
201	**Meat Products**	2034	Dehydrated fruits, vegetables, soups
2011	Meat packing plants	2035	Pickles, sauces, and salad dressings
2013	Sausages and other prepared meats	2037	Frozen fruits and vegetables
2015	Poultry slaughtering and processing	2038	Frozen specialties, nec
202	**Dairy Products**	**204**	**Grain Mill Products**
2021	Creamery butter	2041	Flour and other grain mill products
2022	Cheese, natural and processed	2043	Cereal breakfast foods
2023	Dry, condensed, evaporated products	2044	Rice milling
2024	Ice cream and frozen desserts	2045	Prepared flour mixes and doughs
2026	Fluid milk	2046	Wet corn milling
203	**Preserved Fruits and Vegetables**	2047	Dog and cat food
2032	Canned specialties	2048	Prepared feeds, nec
		205	**Bakery Products**

Code	Short Title	Code	Short Title
2051	Bread, cake, and related products	2098	Macaroni and spaghetti
2052	Cookies and crackers	2099	Food preparations, nec
2053	Frozen bakery products, except bread	**21**	**TOBACCO PRODUCTS**
206	**Sugar and Confectionery Products**	**211**	**Cigarettes**
		2111	Cigarettes
2061	Raw cane sugar	**212**	**Cigars**
2062	Cane sugar refining	2121	Cigars
2063	Beet sugar	**213**	**Chewing and Smoking Tobacco**
2064	Candy & other confectionery products	2131	Chewing and smoking tobacco
2066	Chocolate and cocoa products	**214**	**Tobacco Stemming and Redrying**
2067	Chewing gum	2141	Tobacco stemming and redrying
2068	Salted and roasted nuts and seeds		
207	**Fats and Oils**	**22**	**TEXTILE MILL PRODUCTS**
2074	Cottonseed oil mills	**221**	**Broadwoven Fabric Mills, Cotton**
2075	Soybean oil mills		
2076	Vegetable oil mills, nec	2211	Broadwoven fabric mills, cotton
2077	Animal and marine fats and oils	**222**	**Broadwoven Fabric Mills, Manmade**
2079	Edible fats and oils, nec	2221	Broadwoven fabric mills, manmade
208	**Beverages**		
2082	Malt beverages	**223**	**Broadwoven Fabric Mills, Wool**
2083	Malt		
2084	Wines, brandy, and brandy spirits	2231	Broadwoven fabric mills, wool
2085	Distilled and blended liquors	**224**	**Narrow Fabric Mills**
2086	Bottled and canned soft drinks	2241	Narrow fabric mills
2087	Flavoring extracts and syrups, nec	**225**	**Knitting Mills**
		2251	Women's hosier, except socks
209	**Misc. Food and Kindred Products**	2252	Hosiery, nec
		2253	Knit outerwear mills
2091	Canned and cured fish and seafoods	2254	Knit underwear mills
		2257	Weft knit fabric mills
2092	Fresh or frozen prepared fish	2258	Lace & warp knit fabric mills
2095	Roasted coffee	2259	Knitting mills, nec
2096	Potato chips and similar snacks	**226**	**Textile Finishing, Except Wool**
2097	Manufactured ice	2261	Finishing plants, cotton

Code	Short Title	Code	Short Title
2262	Finishing plants, manmade	2341	Women's and children's underwear
2269	Finishing plants, nec		
227	**Carpets and Rugs**	2342	Bras, girdles, and allied garments
2273	Carpets and rugs		
228	**Yarn and Thread Mills**	**235**	**Hats, Caps, and Millinery**
2281	Yarn spinning mills	2353	Hats, caps, and millinery
2282	Throwing and winding mills	**236**	**Girls' and Children's Outerwear**
2284	Thread mills		
229	**Miscellaneous Textile Goods**	2361	Girls' & children's dresses, blouses
2295	Coated fabrics, not rubberized		
2296	Tire cord and fabrics	2369	Girls' and children's outerwear, nec
2297	Nonwoven fabrics		
2298	Cordage and twine	**237**	**Fur Goods**
2299	Textile goods, nec	2371	Fur goods
		238	**Miscellaneous Apparel and Accessories**
23	**APPAREL AND OTHER TEXTILE PRODUCTS**		
		2381	Fabric dress and work gloves
231	**Men's and Boys' Suits and Coats**	2384	Robes and dressing gowns
		2385	Waterproof outerwear
2311	Men's and boys' suits and coats	2386	Leather and sheep-lined clothing
232	**Men's and Boys' Furnishings**		
2321	Men's and boys' shirts	2387	Apparel belts
2322	Men's & boys' underwear & nightwear	2389	Apparel and accessories, nec
		239	**Misc. Fabricated Textile Products**
2323	Men's and boys' neckwear		
2325	Men's and boys' trousers and slacks	2391	Curtains and draperies
		2392	Housefurnishings, nec
2326	Men's and boys' work clothing	2393	Textile bags
2329	Men's and boys' clothing, nec	2394	Canvas and related products
233	**Women's and Misses' Outerwear**	2395	Pleating and stitching
		2396	Automative and apparel trimmings
2331	Women's and misses' blouses & shirts		
		2397	Schiffli machine embroideries
2335	Women's, juniors', & misses' dresses	2399	Fabricated textile products, nec
		24	**LUMBER AND WOOD PRODUCTS**
2337	Women's and misses' suits and coats		
		241	**Logging**
2339	Women's and misses' outerwear, nec	2411	Logging
		242	**Sawmills and Planing Mills**
234	**Women's and Children's Undergarments**		

Code	Short Title	Code	Short Title
2421	Sawmills and planing mills, general	**253**	**Public Building & Related Furniture**
2426	Hardwood dimension & flooring mills	2531	Public building & related furniture
2429	Special product sawmills, nec	**254**	**Partitions and Fixtures**
243	**Millwork, Plywood & Structural Members**	2541	Wood partitions and fixtures
2431	Millwork	2542	Partitions and fixtures, except wood
2434	Wood kitchen cabinets	**259**	**Miscellaneous Furniture and Fixtures**
2435	Hardwood veneer and plywood	2591	Drapery hardware & blinds & shades
2436	Softwood veneer and plywood	2599	Furniture and fixtures, nec
2439	Structural wood members, nec		
244	**Wood Containers**	**26**	**PAPER AND ALLIED PRODUCTS**
2441	Nailed wood boxes and shook	**261**	**Pulp Mills**
2448	Wood pallets and skids	2611	Pulp mills
2449	Wood containers, nec	**262**	**Paper Mills**
245	**Wood Buildings and Mobile Homes**	2621	Paper mills
2451	Mobile homes	**263**	**Paperboard mills**
2452	Prefabricated wood buildings	2631	Paperboard mills
249	**Miscellaneous Wood Products**	**265**	**Paperboard Containers and Boxes**
2491	Wood preserving	2652	Setup paperboard boxes
2493	Reconstituted wood products	2653	Corrugated and solid fiber boxes
2499	Wood products, nec	2655	Fiber cans, drums & similar products
25	**FURNITURE AND FIXTURES**	2656	Sanitary food containers
251	**Household Furniture**	2657	Folding paperboard boxes
2511	Wood household furniture	**267**	**Misc. Converted Paper Products**
2512	Upholstered household furniture	2671	Paper coated & laminated, packaging
2514	Metal household furniture	2672	Paper coated and laminated, nec
2515	Mattresses and bedsprings	2673	Bags: plastics, laminated, & coated
2517	Wood TV and radio cabinets	2674	Bags: uncoated paper & multiwall
2519	Household furniture, nec		
252	**Office Furniture**		
2521	Wood office furniture		
2522	Office furniture, except wood		

Code	Short Title	Code	Short Title
2675	Die-cut paper and board	2819	Industrial inorganic chemicals, nec
2676	Sanitary paper products		
2677	Envelopes	**282**	**Plastics Materials and Synthetics**
2678	Stantionery products		
2679	Converted paper products, nec	2821	Plastics materials and resins
		2822	Synthetic rubber
27	**PRINTING AND PUBLISHING**	2823	Cellulosic manmade fibers
		2824	Organic fibers, noncellulosic
271	**Newspapers**	**283**	**Drugs**
2711	Newspapers	2833	Medicinals and botanicals
272	**Periodicals**	2834	Pharmaceutical preparations
2721	Periodicals	2835	Diagnostic substances
273	**Books**	2836	Biological products exc. diagnostic
2731	Book Publishing		
2732	Book printing	**284**	**Soap, Cleaners, and Toilet Goods**
274	**Miscellaneous Publishing**		
2741	Miscellaneous publishing	2841	Soap and other detergents
275	**Commercial Printing**	2842	Polishes and sanitation goods
2752	Commercial printing, lithographic		
		2843	Surface active agents
2754	Commercial printing, gravure	2844	Toilet preparations
2759	Commercial printing, nec	**285**	**Paints and Allied Products**
276	**Manifold Business Forms**	2851	Paints and allied products
2761	Manifold business forms	**286**	**Industrial Organic Chemicals**
277	**Greeting Cards**	2861	Gum and wood chemicals
2771	Greeting cards	2865	Cyclic crudes and intermediates
278	**Blankbooks and Bookbinding**		
2782	Blankbooks and looseleaf binders	2869	Industrial organic chemicals, nec
		287	**Agricultural Chemicals**
2789	Bookbinding and related work	2873	Nitrogenous fertilizers
279	**Printing Trade Services**	2874	Phosphatic fertilizers
2791	Typesetting	2875	Fertilizers, mixing only
2796	Platemaking services	2879	Agricultural chemicals, nec
		289	**Miscellaneous Chemical Products**
28	**CHEMICALS AND ALLIED PRODUCTS**		
		2891	Adhesives and sealants
281	**Industrial Inorganic Chemicals**	2892	Explosives
		2893	Printing ink
2812	Alkalies and chlorine	2895	Carbon black
2813	Industrial gases	2899	Chemical preparations, nec
2816	Inorganic pigments		

Code	Short Title	Code	Short Title
29	**PETROLEUM AND COAL PRODUCTS**	3086	Plastics foam products
		3087	Custom compound purchased resins
291	**Petroleum Refining**		
2911	Petroleum refining	3088	Plastic plumbing fixtures
295	**Asphalt Paving and Roofing Materials**	3089	Plastics products, nec
2951	Asphalt paving mixtures and blocks	**31**	**LEATHER AND LEATHER PRODUCTS**
2952	Asphalt felts and coatings	**311**	**Leather Tanning and Finishing**
299	**Misc. Petroleum and Coal Products**	3111	Leather tanning and finishing
		313	**Footwear Cut Stock**
2992	Lubricating oils and greases	3131	Footwear cut stock
2999	Petroleum and coal products, nec	**314**	**Footwear, Except Rubber**
		3142	House slippers
		3143	Men's footwear, except athletic
30	**RUBBER AND MISC. PLASTICS PRODUCTS**	3144	Women's footwear, except athletic
301	**Tires and Inner Tubes**	3149	Footwear, except rubber, nec
3011	Tires and inner tubes	**315**	**Leather Gloves and Mittens**
302	**Rubber and Plastics Footwear**	3151	Leather gloves and mittens
3021	Rubber and plastics footwear	**316**	**Luggage**
305	**Hose & Belting & Gaskets & Packing**	3161	Luggage
		317	**Handbags and Personal Leather Goods**
3052	Rubber & plastics hose & belting	3171	Women's handbags and purses
3053	Gaskets, packing and sealing devices	3172	Personal leather goods, nec
		319	**Leather Goods, NEC**
306	**Fabricated Rubber Products, Nec**	3199	Leather goods, nec
3061	Mechanical rubber goods	**32**	**STONE, CLAY, AND GLASS PRODUCTS**
3069	Fabricated Rubber Products		
308	**Miscellaneous Plastics Products, NEC**	**321**	**Flat Glass**
		3211	Flat glass
3081	Unsupported plastics film & sheet	**322**	**Glass and Glassware, Pressed or Blown**
3082	Unsupported plastics profile shapes	3221	Glass containers
		3229	Pressed and blown glass, nec
3083	Laminated plastics plate & sheet	**323**	**Products of Purchased Glass**
		3231	Products of purchased glass
3084	Plastics pipe	**324**	**Cement, Hydraulic**
3085	Plastics bottles	3241	Cement, hydraulic

Code	Short Title	Code	Short Title
325	**Structural Clay Products**	**332**	**Iron and Steel Foundries**
3251	Brick and structural clay tile	3321	Gray and ductile iron foundries
3253	Ceramic wall and floor tile	3322	Malleable iron foundries
3255	Clay refractories	3324	Steel investments foundries
3259	Structural clay products, nec	3325	Steel foundries, nec
326	**Pottery and Related Products**	**333**	**Primary Nonferrous Metals**
3261	Vitreous plumbing fixtures	3331	Primary copper
3262	Vitreous china table & kitchenware	3334	Primary aluminum
3263	Semivitreous table & kitchenware	3339	Primary nonferrous metals, nec
		334	**Secondary Nonferrous Metals**
3264	Porcelain electrical supplies	3341	Secondary nonferrous metals
3269	Pottery products, nec	**335**	**Nonferrous Rolling and Drawing**
327	**Concrete, Gypsum, and Plaster Products**	3351	Copper rolling and drawing
3271	Concrete block and brick	3353	Aluminum sheet, plate, and foil
3272	Concrete products, nec	3354	Aluminum extruded products
3273	Ready-mixed concrete	3355	Aluminum rolling and drawing, nec
3274	Lime	3356	Nonferrous rolling and drawing, nec
3275	Gypsum products		
328	**Cut Stone and Stone Products**	3357	Nonferrous wiredrawing & insulating
3281	Cut stone and stone products	**336**	**Nonferrous Foundries (Castings)**
329	**Misc. Nonmetallic Mineral Products**	3363	Aluminum die-castings
3291	Abrasive products	3364	Nonferrous die-casting exc. aluminum
3292	Asbestos products	3365	Aluminum foundries
3295	Minerals, ground or treated	3366	Copper foundries
3296	Mineral wool	3369	Nonferrous foundries, nec
3297	Nonclay refractories	**339**	**Miscellaneous Primary Metal Products**
3299	Nonmetallic mineral products, nec	3398	Metal heat treating
		3399	Primary metal products, nec
33	**PRIMARY METAL INDUSTRIES**	**34**	**FABRICATED METAL PRODUCTS**
331	**Blast Furnace and Basic Steel Products**	**341**	**Metal Cans and Shipping Containers**
3312	Blast furnaces and steel mills	3411	Metal cans
3313	Electrometallurgical products		
3315	Steel wire and related products		
3316	Cold finishing of steel shapes		
3317	Steel pipe and tubes		

Code	Short Title	Code	Short Title
3412	Metal barrels, drums, and pails	3483	Ammunition, exc, for small arms, nec
342	**Cutlery, Handtools, and Hardware**	3484	Small arms
3421	Cutlery	3489	Ordnance and accessories, nec
3423	Hand and edge tools, nec	**349**	**Misc. Fabricated Metal Products**
3425	Saw blades and handsaws	3491	Industrial valves
3429	Hardware, nec	3492	Fluid power valves & hose fittings
343	**Plumbing and Heating, Except Electric**	3493	Steel springs, except wire
3431	Metal sanitary ware	3494	Valves and pipe fittings, nec
3432	Plumbing fixture fittings and trim	3495	Wire springs
3433	Heating equipment, except electric	3496	Misc. fabricated wire products
		3497	Metal foil and leaf
344	**Fabricated Structural Metal Products**	3498	Fabricated pipe and fittings
		3499	Fabricated metal products, nec
3441	Fabricated structural metal		
3442	Metal doors, sash, and trim	**35**	**INDUSTRIAL MACHINERY AND EQUIPMENT**
3443	Fabricated plate work (boiler shops)	**351**	**Engines and Turbines**
3444	Sheet metal work	3511	Turbines and turbine generator sets
3446	Architectural metal work	3519	Internal combustion engines, nec
3448	Prefabricated metal buildings		
3449	Miscellaneous metal work	**352**	**Farm and Garden Machinery**
345	**Screw Machine Products, Bolts, Etc.**	3523	Farm machinery and equipment
3451	Screw machine products	3524	Lawn and garden equipment
3452	Bolts, nuts, rivets, and washers	**353**	**Construction and Related Machinery**
346	**Metal Forgings and Stampings**	3531	Construction machinery
3462	Iron and steel forgings	3532	Mining Machinery
3463	Nonferrous forgings	3533	Oil and gas field machinery
3465	Automative stampings	3534	Elevators and moving stairways
3466	Crowns and closures	3535	Conveyors and conveying equipment
3469	Metal stampings, nec	3536	Hoists, cranes, and monorails
347	**Metal Services, NEC**	3537	Industrial trucks and tractors
3471	Plating and polishing	**354**	**Metalworking Machinery**
3479	Metal coating and allied services	3541	Machine tools, metal cutting types
348	**Ordnance and Accessories, NEC**		
3482	Small arms ammunition		

Code	Short Title	Code	Short Title
3542	Machine tools, metal forming types	3579	Office machines, nec
3543	Industrial patterns	**358**	**Refrigeration and Service Machinery**
3544	Special dies, tools, jigs & fixtures	3581	Automatic vending machines
3545	Machine tool accessories	3582	Commercial laundry equipment
3546	Power-driven handtools	3585	Refrigeration and heating equipment
3547	Rolling mill machinery		
3548	Welding apparatus	3586	Measuring and dispensing pumps
3549	Metalworking machinery, nec		
		3589	Service industry machinery, nec
355	**Special Industry Machinery**		
3552	Textile machinery	**359**	**Industrial Machinery, NEC**
3553	Woodworking machinery	3592	Carburetors, pistons, rings, valves
3554	Paper industries machinery		
3555	Printing trades machinery	3593	Fluid power cylinders & actuators
3556	Food products machinery		
3559	Special industry machinery, nec	3594	Fluid power pumps and motors
		3596	Scales and balances, exc. laboratory
356	**General Industrial Machinery**		
3561	Pumps and pumping equipment	3599	Industrial machinery, nec
3562	Ball and roller bearings	**36**	**ELECTRONIC & OTHER ELECTRIC EQUIPMENT**
3563	Air and gas compressors		
3564	Blowers and fans	**361**	**Electric Distrubtion Equipment**
3565	Packaging machinery		
3566	Speed changers, drives, and gears	3612	Transformers, except electronic
		3613	Switchgear and switchboard apparatus
3567	Industrial furnaces and ovens		
3568	Power transmission equipment, nec	**362**	**Electrical Industrial Apparatus**
		3621	Motors and generators
3569	General industrial machinery, nec	3624	Carbon and graphite products
		3625	Relays and industrial controls
357	**Computer and Office Equipment**	3629	Electrical industrial apparatus, nec
3571	Electronic computers		
3572	Computer storage devices	**363**	**Household Appliances**
3575	Computer terminals	3631	Household cooking equipment
3577	Computer peripheral equipment, nec	3632	Household refrigerators and freezers
3578	Calculating and accounting equipment	3633	Household laundry equipment

Code	Short Title	Code	Short Title
3634	Electric housewares and fans	3692	Primary batteries, dry and wet
3635	Household vacuum cleaners	3694	Engine electrical equipment
3639	Household appliances, nec	3695	Magnetic and optical recording media
364	**Electric Lighting and Wiring Equipment**	3699	Electrical equipment & supplies, nec
3641	Electric lamps		
3643	Current-carrying wiring devices	**37**	**TRANSPORTATION EQUIPMENT**
3644	Noncurrent-carrying wiring devices	**371**	**Motor Vehicles and Equipment**
3645	Residential lighting fixtures	3711	Motor vehicles and car bodies
3646	Commercial lighting fixtures	3713	Truck and bus bodies
3647	Vehicular lighting equipment	3714	Motor vehicles parts and accessories
3648	Lighting equipment, nec	3715	Truck trailers
365	**Household Audio and Video Equipment**	3716	Motor homes
3651	Household audio and video equipment	**372**	**Aircraft and Parts**
		3721	Aircraft
3652	Prerecorded records and tapes	3724	Aircraft engines and engine parts
366	**Communications Equipment**	3728	Aircraft parts and equipment, nec
3661	Telephone and telegraph apparatus	**373**	**Ship and Boat Building and Repairing**
3663	Radio & TV communications equipment	3731	Ship building and repairing
3669	Communications equipment, nec	3732	Boat building and repairing
367	**Electronic Components and Accessories**	**374**	**Railroad Equipment**
		3743	Railroad equipment
3671	Electron tubes	**375**	**Motorcycles, Bicycles, and Parts**
3672	Printed circuit boards		
3674	Semiconductors and related devices	3751	Motorcycles, bicycles, and parts
3675	Electronic capacitors	**376**	**Guided Missiles, Space Vehicles, Parts**
3676	Electronic resistors		
3677	Electronic coils and transformers	3761	Guided missiles and space vehicles
3678	Electronic connectors	3764	Space propulsion units and parts
3679	Electronic components, nec		
369	**Misc. Electrical Equipment & Supplies**	3769	Space vehicle equipment, nec
		379	**Miscellaneous Transportation Equipment**
3691	Storage batteries		

Code	Short Title	Code	Short Title
3792	Travel trailers and campers	**387**	**Watches, Clocks, Watchcases & Parts**
3795	Tanks and tank components		
3799	Transportation equipment, nec	3873	Watches, clocks, watchcases & parts
38	**INSTRUMENTS AND RELATED PRODUCTS**		
		39	**MISCELLANEOUS MANUFACTURING INDUSTRIES**
381	**Search and Navigation Equipment**		
3812	Search and navigation equipment	**391**	**Jewelry, Silverware, and Plated Ware**
382	**Measuring and Controlling Devices**	3911	Jewelry, precious metal
		3914	Silverware and plated ware
3821	Laboratory apparatus and furniture	3915	Jewelers' materials & lapidary work
3822	Environmental controls	**393**	**Musical Instruments**
3823	Process control instruments	3931	Musical instruments
3824	Fluid meters and counting devices	**394**	**Toys and Sporting Goods**
		3942	Dolls and stuffed toys
3825	Instruments to measure electricity	3944	Games, toys, and children's vehicles
3826	Analytical instruments	3949	Sporting and athletic goods, nec
3827	Optical instruments and lenses	**395**	**Pens, Pencils, Office, & Art Supplies**
3829	Measuring & controlling devices, nec		
		3951	Pens and mechanical pencils
384	**Medical Instruments and Supplies**	3952	Lead pencils and art goods
		3953	Marking Devices
3841	Surgical and medical instruments	3955	Carbon paper and inked ribbons
3842	Surgical appliances and supplies	**396**	**Costume Jewelry and Notions**
		3961	Costume jewelry
3843	Dental equipment and supplies	3965	Fasteners, buttons, needle, & pins
3844	X-ray apparatus and tubes	**399**	**Miscellaneous Manufactures**
3845	Electromedical equipment	3991	Brooms and brushes
385	**Ophthalmic Goods**	3993	Signs and advertising specialities
3851	Ophthalmic goods		
386	**Photographic Equipment and Supplies**	3995	Burial caskets
		3996	Hard surface floor coverings, nec
3861	Photographic equipment and supplies	3999	Manufacturing industries, nec

E. TRANSPORTATION AND PUBLIC UTILITIES

Code	Short Title
40	**RAILROAD TRANSPORTATION**
401	**Railroads**
4011	Railroads, line-haul operating
4013	Switching and terminal services
41	**LOCAL AND INTERURBAN PASSENGER TRANSIT**
411	**Local and Suburban Transportation**
4111	Local and suburban transit
4119	Local passenger transportation, nec
412	**Taxicabs**
4121	Taxicabs
413	**Intercity and Rural Bus Transportation**
4131	Intercity & rural bus transportation
414	**Bus Charter Service**
4141	Local bus charter service
4142	Bus charter service, except local
415	**School Buses**
4151	School buses
417	**Bus Terminal and Service Facilities**
4173	Bus terminal and service facilities
42	**TRUCKING AND WAREHOUSING**
421	**Trucking & Courier Services, Ex. Air**
4212	Local trucking, without storage
4213	Trucking, except local
4214	Local trucking with storage
4215	Courier services, except by air

Code	Short Title
422	**Public Warehousing and Storage**
4221	Farm product warehousing and storage
4222	Refrigerated warehousing and storage
4225	General warehousing and storage
4226	Special warehousing and storage, nec
423	**Trucking Terminal Facilities**
4231	Trucking terminal facilities
43	**U.S. POSTAL SERVICE**
431	**U.S. Postal Service**
4311	U.S. Postal Service
44	**WATER TRANSPORTATION**
441	**Deep Sea Foreign Trans. of Freight**
4412	Deep sea foreign trans. of freight
442	**Deep Sea Domestic Trans. of Freight**
4424	Deep sea domestic trans. of freight
443	**Freight Trans. on the Great Lakes**
4432	Freight trans. on the Great Lakes
444	**Water Transportation of Freight, NEC**
4449	Water transportation of freight, nec
448	**Water Transportation of Passengers**
4481	Deep sea passenger trans., ex. ferry
4482	Ferries

Code	Short Title	Code	Short Title
4489	Water passenger transportation, nec	474	**Rental of Railroad Cars**
		4741	Rental of railroad cars
449	**Water Transportation Services**	**478**	**Miscellaneous Transportation Services**
4491	Marine cargo handling		
4492	Towing and tugboat services	4783	Packing and crating
4493	Marinas	4785	Inspection & fixed facilities
4499	Water transportation services, nec	4789	Transportation servies, nec
		48	**COMMUNICATIONS**
45	**TRANSPORTATION BY AIR**	**481**	**Telephone Communications**
451	**Air Transportation, Scheduled**	4812	Radiotelephone communications
4512	Air Transportation, scheduled		
4513	Air courier services	4813	Telephone communications, exc. radio
452	**Air Transportation, Nonscheduled**	**482**	**Telegraph & Other Communications**
4522	Air transportation, nonscheduled	4822	Telegraph & other communications
458	**Airports, Flying Fields, & Services**	**483**	**Radio and Television Broadcasting**
4581	Airports, flying fields, & services	4832	Radio broadcasting stations
		4833	Television broadcasting stations
46	**PIPELINES, EXCEPT NATURAL GAS**	**484**	**Cable and Other Pay TV Services**
461	**Pipelines, Except Natural Gas**	4841	Cable and other pay TV services
4612	Crude petroleum pipelines		
4613	Refined petroleum pipelines	**489**	**Communications Services, NEC**
4619	Pipelines, nec	4899	Communications services, nec
47	**TRANSPORTATION SERVICES**	**49**	**ELECTRIC, GAS, AND SANITARY SERVICES**
472	**Passenger Transportation Arrangement**	**491**	**Electric Services**
		4911	Electric services
4724	Travel agencies	**492**	**Gas Production and Distribution**
4725	Tour operators		
4729	Passenger transport arrangement, nec	4922	Natural gas transmission
473	**Freight Transportation Arrangement**	4923	Gas transmission and distribution
4731	Freight Transportation arrangement	4924	Natural gas distribution

Code	Short Title	Code	Short Title
4925	Gas production and/or distribution	495	**Sanitary Services**
493	**Combination Utility Services**	4952	Sewerage systems
4931	Electric and other services combined	4953	Refuse systems
		4959	Sanitary services, nec
4932	Gas and other services combined	496	**Steam and Air-Conditioning Supply**
4939	Combination utilities, nec	4961	Steam and air-conditioning supply
494	**Water Supply**	**497**	**Irrigation Systems**
4941	Water supply	4971	Irrigation systems

F. WHOLESALE TRADE

Code	Short Title	Code	Short Title
50	**WHOLESALE TRADE— DURABLE GOODS**	5043	Photographic equipment and supplies
501	**Motor Vehicles, Parts, and Supplies**	5044	Office equipment
		5045	Computers, peripherals & software
5012	Automobile and other motor vehicles	5046	Commercial equipment, nec
5013	Motor vehicle supplies and new parts	5047	Medical and hospital equipment
5014	Tires and tubes	5048	Ophthalmic goods
5015	Motor vehicle parts, used	5049	Professional equipment, nec
502	**Furniture and Homefurnishings**	**505**	**Metals and Minerals, Except Petroleum**
5021	Furniture	5051	Metals service centers and offices
5023	Homefurnishings	5052	Coal and other minerals and ores
503	**Lumber and Construction Materials**	**506**	**Electrical Goods**
5031	Lumber, plywood, and millwork	5063	Electrical apparatus and equipment
5032	Brick, stone, & related materials	5064	Electrical appliances, TV & radios
5033	Roofing, siding, & insulation	5065	Electronic parts and equipment
5039	Construction materials, nec	**507**	**Hardware, Plumbing & Heating Equipment**
504	**Professional & Commercial Equipment**		

Code	Short Title	Code	Short Title
5072	Hardware	5131	Piece goods & notions
5074	Plumbing & hydronic heating supplies	5136	Men's and boys' clothing
5075	Warm air heating & air-conditioning	5137	Women's and children's clothing
5078	Refrigeration equipment and supplies	5139	Footwear
508	**Machinery, Equipment and Supplies**	**514**	**Groceries and Related Products**
5082	Construction and mining machinery	5141	Groceries, general line
5083	Farm and garden machinery	5142	Packaged frozen foods
5084	Industrial machinery and equipment	5143	Dairy products, exc. dried or canned
5085	Industrial supplies	5144	Poultry and poultry products
5087	Service establishment equipment	5145	Confectionery
5088	Transportation equipment & supplies	5146	Fish and seafoods
509	**Miscellaneous Durable Goods**	5147	Meats and meat products
5091	Sporting & recreational goods	5148	Fresh fruits and vegetables
5092	Toys and hobby goods and supplies	5149	Groceries and related products, nec
5093	Scrap and waste materials	**515**	**Farm-Product Raw Materials**
5094	Jewelry & precious stones	5153	Grain and field beans
5099	Durable goods, nec	5154	Livestock
		5159	Farm-product raw materials, nec
51	**WHOLESALE TRADE—NONDURABLE GOODS**	**516**	**Chemicals and Allied Products**
511	**Paper and Paper Products**	5162	Plastics materials & basic shapes
5111	Printing and writing paper	5169	Chemicals & allied products, nec
5112	Stationery and office supplies	**517**	**Petroleum and Petroleum Products**
5113	Industrial & Personal service paper	5171	Petroleum bulk stations & terminals
512	**Drugs, Proprietaries, and Sundries**	5172	Petroleum products, nec
5122	Drugs, proprietaries, and sundries	**518**	**Beer, Wine, and Distilled Beverages**
513	**Apparel, Piece Goods, and Notions**	5181	Beer and ale
		5182	Wine and distilled beverages
		519	**Misc. Nondurable Goods**
		5191	Farm supplies

Code	Short Title	Code	Short Title
5192	Books, periodicals & newspapers	5194	Tobacco and tobacco products
		5198	Paints, varnishes, and supplies
5193	Flowers & florists' supplies	5199	Nondurable goods, nec

G. RETAIL TRADE

Code	Short Title	Code	Short Title
52	**BUILDING MATERIALS & GARDEN SUPPLIES**	542	**Meat and Fish Markets**
		5421	Meat and fish markets
521	**Lumber and Other Building Materials**	543	**Fruit and Vegetable Markets**
		5431	Fruit and vegetable markets
5211	Lumber and other building materials	544	**Candy, Nut, and Confectionery Stores**
523	**Paint, Glass, and Wallpaper Stores**	5441	Candy, nut, and confectionery stores
5231	Paint, glass, and wallpaper stores	545	**Dairy Products Stores**
		5451	Dairy products stores
525	**Hardware Stores**	546	**Retail Bakeries**
5251	Hardware stores	5461	Retail bakeries
526	**Retail Nurseries and Garden Stores**	549	**Miscellaneous Food Stores**
		5499	Miscellaneous food stores
5261	Retail nurseries and garden stores	55	**AUTOMOTIVE DEALERS & SERVICE STATIONS**
527	**Mobile Home Dealers**		
5271	Mobile home dealers	551	**New and Used Car Dealers**
		5511	New and used car dealers
53	**GENERAL MERCHANDISE STORES**	552	**Used Car Dealers**
		5521	Used car dealers
531	**Department Stores**	553	**Auto and Home Supply Stores**
5311	Department stores	5531	Auto and home supply stores
533	**Variety Stores**	554	**Gasoline Service Stations**
5331	Variety stores	5541	Gasoline service stations
539	**Misc. General Merchandise Stores**	555	**Boat Dealers**
		5551	Boat dealers
5399	Misc. general merchandise stores	556	**Recreational Vehicle Dealers**
		5561	Recreational vehicle dealers
		557	**Motorcycle Dealers**
54	**FOOD STORES**	5571	Motorcycle dealers
541	**Grocery Stores**	559	**Automotive Dealers, NEC**
5411	Grocery stores	5599	Automotive dealers, nec

Code	Short Title	Code	Short Title
56	**APPAREL AND ACCESSORY STORES**	**58**	**EATING AND DRINKING PLACES**
561	**Men's & Boys' Clothing Stores**	**581**	**Eating and Drinking Places**
5611	Men's & boys' clothing stores	5812	Eating places
562	**Women's Clothing Stores**	5813	Drinking places
5621	Women's Clothing stores		
563	**Women's Accessory & Specialty Stores**	**59**	**MISCELLANEOUS RETAIL**
		591	**Drug Stores and Proprietary Stores**
5632	Women's accessory & specialty stores	5912	Drug stores and proprietary stores
564	**Children's and Infants' Wear Stores**	**592**	**Liquor Stores**
		5921	Liquor stores
5641	Children's and infants' wear stores	**593**	**Used Merchandise Stores**
		5932	Used merchandise stores
565	**Family Clothing Stores**	**594**	**Miscellaneous Shopping Goods Stores**
5651	Family clothing stores		
566	**Shoe Stores**	5941	Sporting goods and bicycle shops
5661	Shoe stores		
569	**Misc. Apparel & Accessory Stores**	5942	Book stores
		5943	Stationery stores
5699	Misc. apparel & accessory stores	5944	Jewelry stores
		5945	Hobby, toy, and game shops
		5946	Camera & photographic supply stores
57	**FURNITURE AND HOME-FURNISHINGS STORES**	5947	Gift, novelty, and souvenir shops
571	**Furniture and Homefurnishings Stores**	5948	Luggage and leather goods stores
5712	Furniture stores	5949	Sewing, needlework, and piece goods
5713	Floor covering stores		
5714	Drapery and upholstery stores	**596**	**Nonstore Retailers**
5719	Misc. homefurnishings stores	5961	Catalog and mail-order houses
572	**Household Appliance Stores**	5962	Merchandising machine operators
5722	Household appliance stores		
573	**Radio, Television, & Computer Stores**	5963	Direct selling establishments
		598	**Fuel Dealers**
5731	Radio, TV, & electronic stores	5983	Fuel oil dealers
5734	Computer and software stores	5984	Liquefied petroleum gas dealers
5735	Record & prerecorded tape stores		
5736	Musical instrument stores	5989	Fuel dealers, nec

Code	Short Title	Code	Short Title
599	**Retail Stores, NEC**	5994	News dealers and newsstands
5992	Florists	5995	Optical goods stores
5993	Tobacco stores and stands	5999	Miscellaneous retail stores, nec

H. FINANCE, INSURANCE, AND REAL ESTATE

Code	Short Title	Code	Short Title
60	**DEPOSITORY INSTITUTIONS**	6111	Federal & fed.-sponsored credit
601	**Central Reserve Depositories**	**614**	**Personal Credit Institutions**
6011	Federal reserve banks	6141	Personal credit institutions
6019	Central reserve depository, nec	**615**	**Business Credit Institutions**
602	**Commercial Banks**	6153	Short-term business credit
6021	National commercial banks	6159	Misc. business credit institutions
6022	State commercial banks		
6029	Commercial banks, nec	**616**	**Mortgage Bankers and Brokers**
603	**Savings Institutions**		
6035	Federal savings institutions	6162	Mortgage bankers and correspondents
6036	Savings institutions, except federal	6163	Loan brokers
606	**Credit Unions**		
6061	Federal credit unions	**62**	**SECURITY AND COMMODITY BROKERS**
6062	State credit unions		
608	**Foreign Bank & Branches & Agencies**	**621**	**Security Brokers and Dealers**
		6211	Security brokers and dealers
6081	Foreign bank & branches & agencies	**622**	**Commodity Contracts Brokers, Dealers**
6082	Foreign trade & international banks	6221	Commodity contracts brokers, dealers
609	**Functions Closely Related to Banking**	**623**	**Security and Commodity Exchanges**
6091	Nondeposit trust facilities	6231	Security and commodity exchanges
6099	Functions related to deposit banking	**628**	**Security and Commodity Services**
61	**NONDEPOSITORY INSTITUTIONS**	6282	Investment advice
		6289	Security & commodity services, nec
611	**Federal & Fed.-Sponsored Credit**		

Code	Short Title	Code	Short Title
63	**INSURANCE CARRIERS**	6514	Dwelling operators, exc. apartments
631	**Life Insurance**		
6311	Life insurance	6515	Mobile home site operators
632	**Medical Service and Health Insurance**	6517	Railroad property lessors
		6519	Real property lessors, nec
6321	Accident and health insurance	**653**	**Real Estate Agents and Managers**
6324	Hospital and medical service plans	6531	Real estate agents and managers
633	**Fire, Marine, and Casualty Insurance**	**654**	**Title Abstract Offices**
		6541	Title abstract offices
6331	Fire, marine, and casualty insurance	**655**	**Subdividers and Developers**
635	**Surety Insurance**	6552	Subdividers and developers, nec
6351	Surety insurance		
636	**Title Insurance**	6553	Cemetery subdividers and developers
6361	Title insurance		
637	**Pension, Health, and Welfare Funds**	**67**	**HOLDING AND OTHER INVESTMENT OFFICES**
6371	Pension, health and welfare funds	**671**	**Holding Offices**
639	**Insurance Carriers, NEC**	6712	Bank holding companies
6399	Insurance carriers, nec	6719	Holding companies, nec
		672	**Investment Offices**
64	**INSURANCE AGENTS, BROKERS & SERVICE**	6722	Management investment, open-end
641	**Insurance Agents, Brokers & Service**	6726	Investment offices, nec
		673	**Trusts**
6411	Insurance agents, brokers, & service	6732	Educational, religious, etc. trusts
		6733	Trusts, nec
65	**REAL ESTATE**	**679**	**Miscellaneous Investing**
651	**Real Estate Operators and Lessors**	6792	Oil royalty traders
		6794	Patent owners and lessors
6512	Nonresidential building operators	6798	Real estate investment trusts
6513	Apartment building operators	6799	Investors, nec

I. SERVICES

Code	Short Title	Code	Short Title
70	**HOTELS AND OTHER LODGING PLACES**	7241	Barber shops
701	**Hotels and Motels**	**725**	**Shoe Repair and Shoeshine Parlors**
7011	Hotels and motels	7251	Shoe repair and shoeshine parlors
702	**Rooming and Boarding Houses**	**726**	**Funeral Service and Crematories**
7021	Rooming and boarding houses	7261	Funeral service and crematories
703	**Camps and Recreational Vehicle Parks**	**729**	**Miscellaneous Personal Services**
7032	Sporting and recreational camps	7291	Tax return preparation services
7033	Trailer parks and campsites	7299	Miscellaneous personal services, nec
704	**Membership-Basis Organization Hotels**		
7041	Membership-basis organization hotels	**73**	**BUSINESS SERVICES**
		731	**Advertising**
72	**PERSONAL SERVICES**	7311	Advertising agencies
721	**Laundry, Cleaning, & Garment Services**	7312	Outdoor advertising services
7211	Power laundries, family & commercial	7313	Radio, TV, publisher representatives
7212	Garment pressing & cleaners' agents	7319	Advertising, nec
7213	Linen supply	**732**	**Credit Reporting and Collection**
7215	Coin-operated laundries and cleaning	7322	Adjustment & collection services
7216	Drycleaning plants, except rug	7323	Credit reporting services
7217	Carpet and upholstery cleaning	**733**	**Mailing, Reproduction, Stenographic**
7218	Industrial launderers	7331	Direct mail advertising services
7219	Laundry and garment services, nec	7334	Photocopying & duplicating services
722	**Photographic Studios, Portrait**	7335	Commercial photography
7221	Photographic studios, portrait	7336	Commercial art and graphic design
723	**Beauty Shops**	7338	Secretarial & court reporting
7231	Beauty shops	**734**	**Services to Buildings**
724	**Barber Shops**	7342	Disinfecting & pest control services

Code	Short Title	Code	Short Title
7349	Building maintenance services, nec	7513	Truck rental and leasing, no drivers
735	**Misc. Equipment Rental & Leasing**	7514	Passenger car rental
		7515	Passenger car leasing
7352	Medical equipment rental	7519	Utility trailer rental
7353	Heavy construction equipment rental	**752**	**Automobile Parking**
		7521	Automobile parking
7359	Equipment rental & leasing, nec	**753**	**Automotive Repair Shops**
736	**Personnel Supply Services**	7532	Top & body repair & paint shops
7361	Employment agencies		
7363	Help supply services	7533	Auto exhaust system repair shops
737	**Computer and Data Processing Services**	7534	Tire retreading and repair shops
7371	Computer programming services	7536	Automotive glass replacement shops
7372	Prepackaged software	7537	Automotive transmission repair shops
7373	Computer integrated systems design	7538	General automotive repair shops
7374	Data processing and preparation	7539	Automotive repair shops, nec
7375	Information retrieval services	**754**	**Automotive Services, Except Repair**
7376	Computer facilities management	7542	Carwashes
7377	Computer rental & leasing	7549	Automotive services, nec
7378	Computer maintenance & repair		
7379	Computer related services, nec	**76**	**MISCELLANEOUS REPAIR SERVICES**
738	**Miscellaneous Business Services**	**762**	**Electrical Repair Shops**
		7622	Radio and television repair
7381	Detective & armored car services	7623	Refrigeration service and repair
7382	Security systems services	7629	Electrical repair shops, nec
7383	News syndicates	**763**	**Watch, Clock, and Jewelry Repair**
7384	Photofinishing laboratories		
7389	Business services, nec	7631	Watch, clock, and jewelry repair
75	**AUTO REPAIR, SERVICES, AND PARKING**	**764**	**Reupholstery and Furniture Repair**
751	**Automotive Rentals, No Drivers**	7641	Reupholstery and furniture repair

Code	Short Title	Code	Short Title
769	**Miscellaneous Repair Shops**	7941	Sports clubs, managers, & promoters
7692	Welding repair	7948	Racing, including track operation
7694	Armature rewinding shops		
7699	Repair services, nec	**799**	**Misc. Amusement, Recreation Services**
78	**MOTION PICTURES**	7991	Physical fitness facilities
781	**Motion Picture Production & Services**	7992	Public gold courses
7812	Motion picture & video production	7993	Coin-operated amusement devices
7819	Services allied to motion pictures	7996	Amusement parks
782	**Motion Picture Distribution & Services**	7997	Membership sports & recreation clubs
7822	Motion picture and tape distribution	7999	Amusement and recreation, nec
7829	Motion picture distribution services	**80**	**HEALTH SERVICES**
783	**Motion Picture Theaters**	**801**	**Offices & Clinics of Medical Doctors**
7832	Motion picture theaters, ex drive-in	8011	Offices & clinics of medical doctors
7833	Drive-in motion picture theaters	**802**	**Offices and Clinics of Dentists**
784	**Video Tape Rental**	8021	Offices and clinics of dentists
7841	Video tape rental	**803**	**Offices of Osteopathic Physicians**
79	**AMUSEMENT & RECREATION SERVICES**	8031	Offices of osteopathic physicians
791	**Dance Studios, Schools, and Halls**	**804**	**Offices of Other Health Practitioners**
7911	Dance studios, schools, and halls	8041	Offices and clinics of chiropractors
792	**Producers, Orchestras, Entertainers**	8042	Offices and clinics of optometrists
7922	Theatrical producers and services	8043	Offices and clinics of podiatrists
7929	Entertainers & entertainment groups	8049	Offices of health practitioners, nec
793	**Bowling Centers**	**805**	**Nursing and Personal Care Facilities**
7933	Bowling centers	8051	Skilled nursing care facilities
794	**Commercial Sports**	8052	Intermediate care facilities
		8059	Nursing and personal care, nec

Code	Short Title	Code	Short Title
806	**Hospitals**	**83**	**SOCIAL SERVICES**
8062	General medical & surgical hospitals	**832**	**Individual and Family Services**
8063	Psychiatric hospitals	8322	Individual and family services
8069	Specialty hospitals exc. psychiatric	**833**	**Job Training and Related Services**
807	**Medical and Dental laboratories**	8331	Job training and related services
8071	Medical laboratories	**835**	**Child Day Care Services**
8072	Dental laboratories	8351	Child day care services
808	**Home Health Care Services**	**836**	**Residential Care**
8082	Home health care services	8361	Residential care
809	**Health and Allied Services, NEC**	**839**	**Social Services, NEC**
8092	Kidney dialysis centers	8399	Social services, nec
8093	Specialty outpatient clinics, nec	**84**	**MUSEUMS, BOTANICAL, ZOOLOGICAL GARDENS**
8099	Health and allied services, nec	**841**	**Museums and Art Galleries**
		8412	Museums and art galleries
81	**LEGAL SERVICES**	**842**	**Botanical and Zoological Gardens**
811	**Legal Services**	8422	Botanical and zoological gardens
8111	Legal services		
		86	**MEMBERSHIP ORGANIZATIONS**
82	**EDUCATIONAL SERVICES**	**861**	**Business Associations**
821	**Elementary and Secondary Schools**	8611	Business associations
8211	Elementary and secondary schools	**862**	**Professional Organizations**
822	**Colleges and Universities**	8621	Professional organizations
8221	Colleges and universities	**863**	**Labor Organizations**
8222	Junior colleges	8631	Labor organizations
823	**Libraries**	**864**	**Civic and Social Associations**
8231	Libraries	8641	Civic and social associations
824	**Vocational Schools**	**865**	**Political Organizations**
8243	Data processing schools	8651	Political organizations
8244	Business and secretarial schools	**866**	**Religious Organizations**
8249	Vocational schools, nec	8661	Religious organizations
829	**Schools & Educational Services, NEC**	**869**	**Membership Organizations, NEC**
8299	Schools & educational services, nec	8699	Membership organizations, nec

Code	Short Title	Code	Short Title
87	**ENGINEERING & MANAGEMENT SERVICES**	8734	Testing laboratories
871	**Engineering & Architectural Services**	874	**Management and Public Relations**
8711	Engineering services	8741	Management services
8712	Architectural services	8742	Management consulting services
8713	Surveying services	8743	Public relations services
872	**Accounting, Auditing, & Bookkeeping**	8744	Facilities support services
8721	Accounting, auditing, & bookkeeping	8748	Business consulting, nec
873	**Research and Testing Services**	88	**PRIVATE HOUSEHOLDS**
8731	Commercial physical research	881	Private Households
8732	Commercial nonphysical research	8811	Private households
8733	Noncommercial research organizations	89	**SERVICES, NEC**
		899	**Services, NEC**
		8999	Services, nec

J. PUBLIC ADMINISTRATION

Code	Short Title	Code	Short Title
91	**EXECUTIVE, LEGISLATIVE, AND GENERAL**	9221	Police protection
911	**Executive Offices**	9222	Legal counsel and prosecution
9111	Executive offices	9223	Correctional institutions
912	**Legislative Bodies**	9224	Fire protection
9121	Legislative bodies	9229	Public order and safety, nec
913	**Executive and Legislative Combined**	93	**FINANCE, TAXATION, & MONETARY POLICY**
9131	Executive and legislative combined	931	**Finance, Taxation, & Monetary Policy**
919	**General Government, NEC**	9311	Finance, taxation, & monetary policy
9199	General government, nec		
92	**JUSTICE, PUBLIC ORDER, AND SAFETY**	94	**ADMINISTRATION OF HUMAN RESOURCES**
921	**Courts**	941	**Admin. of Educational Programs**
9211	Courts		
922	**Public Order and Safety**		

Code	Short Title	Code	Short Title
9411	Admin. of educational programs	9611	Admin. of general economic programs
943	**Admin. of Public Health Programs**	**962**	**Regulation, Admin. of Transportation**
9431	Admin. of public health programs	9621	Regulation, admin. of transportation
944	**Admin. of Social & Manpower Programs**	**963**	**Regulation, Admin. of Utilities**
9441	Admin. of social & manpower programs	9631	Regulation, admin. of utilities
945	**Administration of Veterans' Affairs**	**964**	**Regulation of Agricultural Marketing**
9451	Administration of veterans' affairs	9641	Regulation of agricultural marketing
95	**ENVIRONMENTAL QUALITY AND HOUSING**	**965**	**Regulation Misc. Commercial Sectors**
951	**Environmental Quality**	9651	Regulations misc. commercial sectors
9511	Air, water, & solid waste management	**966**	**Space Research and Technology**
9512	Land, mineral, wildlife conservation	9661	Space research and technology
953	**Housing and Urban Development**	**97**	**NATIONAL SECURITY AND INTL. AFFAIRS**
9531	Housing programs	**971**	**National Security**
9532	Urban and community development	9711	National security
		972	**International Affairs**
96	**ADMINISTRATION OF ECONOMIC PROGRAMS**	9721	International affairs
961	**Admin. of General Economic Programs**		

K. NONCLASSIFIABLE ESTABLISHMENTS

Code	Short Title	Code	Short Title
99	**NONCLASSIFIABLE ESTABLISHMENTS**	9999	Nonclassifiable establishments
999	**Nonclassifiable Establishments**		

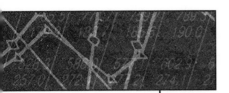

Appendix B:
X-11 Sample Printout

X-11.2 SEASONAL ADJUSTMENT PROGRAM
U.S. BUREAU OF THE CENSUS
STATISTICAL RESEARCH DIVISION
SEPTEMBER 1, 1988

THE X-11 PROGRAM IS DIVIDED INTO SEVEN MAJOR PARTS-
PART   DESCRIPTION
A. PRIOR ADJUSTMENTS, IF ANY
B. PRELIMINARY ESTIMATES OF IRREGULAR COMPONENT WEIGHTS
AND REGRESSION TRADING DAY FACTORS
C. FINAL ESTIMATES OF ABOVE
D. FINAL ESTIMATES OF SEASONAL, TREND-CYCLE AND IRREGULAR
COMPONENTS
E. ANALYTICAL TABLES
F. SUMMARY MEASURES
G. SLIDING SPANS DIAGNOSTICS, IF REQUESTED
TABLES ARE IDENTIFIED BY THEIR PART LETTER AND SEQUENCE WITHIN
THE PART. A GIVEN TABLE HAS THE SAME
IDENTIFICATION IN THE STANDARD, LONG AND FULL PRINTOUTS. THE SAME
NUMBER IS GIVEN TO CORRESPONDING
TABLES IN PARTS B,C, AND D. THUS, TABLES B10., C10. AND D10. ARE ALL TABLES
OF SEASONAL FACTORS
WHEN NO CORRESPONDING TABLE EXISTS THE SEQUENCE NO. IS NOT USED IN
THE PART. THUS, B8. AND D8. ARE
TABLES OF UNMODIFIED SI RATIOS BUT THERE IS NO C8

THIS SERIES RUN 09/22/96
SERIES TITLE-JPNIMP SHORT; UNADJUSTED IMPORTS
SERIES NO. JPNIMP
PERIOD COVERED - 1/74 TO 10/84
TYPE OF RUN - MULTIPLICATIVE SEASONAL ADJUSTMENT.
SHORT PRINTOUT. NO CHARTS
TRADING DAY REGRESSION ESTIMATES NOT APPLIED
SIGMA LIMITS FOR GRADUATING EXTREME VALUES ARE 1.5 AND 2.5
MOVING AVERAGES FOR SEASONAL FACTOR CURVES - J F M A M J J A S
O N D

3X5 3X5 3X5 3X5 3X5 3X5 3X5 3X5 3X5 3X5 3X5 3X5
JPNIMP 1/74 - 10 ≠ 84 MULTIPLICATIVE SEASONAL ADJUSTMENT SHORT
PRINTOUT

1 JPNIMP SHORT: UNADJUSTED IMPORTS P. 1, SERIES
JPNIMP

B 1. ORIGINAL SERIES

YEAR	JAN	FEB	MAR	APR	MAY	JUN	JUL	AUG	SEP	OCT	NOV	DEC	AVGE
1974	8355	7656	8093	9550	10304	9758	11758	11570	11276	11815	11242	11988	10280
1975	11909	9163	10064	9291	8083	8581	9526	9155	8406	9381	8671	10449	9390
1976	11567	9950	13083	12312	11846	13994	13545	14078	13304	12967	14269	14128	12920
1977	14116	11977	15416	14119	15454	16198	15207	17633	16242	16204	15591	18071	15519
1978	17844	18424	21037	21819	20101	20489	22172	20655	20648	21204	20246	19939	20382
1979	22473	18654	19851	23006	20920	23199	21833	22761	21887	22998	23491	21355	21869
1980	24965	22498	23852	25647	26566	26774	26134	25413	26420	25689	25918	27137	25584
1981	31961	23412	30531	32230	30305	31476	31407	35429	29101	36989	33265	30015	31343
1982	37200	27080	35866	37594	29404	29672	28879	38147	29042	32740	26951	24862	31453
1983	29532	28944	34402	35035	32933	33262	32596	36338	29757	40707	40257	38070	34319
1984	46138	36342	47582	46380	48891	45043	62596	50846	49401	50750	****	****	48397
AVG	23278	19464	23616	24271	23164	23495	25059	25639	23226	25586	21990	21601	

TABLE TOTAL- 3040694 MEAN- 23390 STD. DEVIATION- 11421
1 JPNIMP SHORT: UNADJUSTED IMPORTS P. 2, SERIES
JPNIMP

C17. FINAL WEIGHTS FOR IRREGULAR COMPONENT
GRADUATION RANGE FROM 1.5 TO 2.5 SIGMA

YEAR	JAN	FEB	MAR	APR	MAY	JUN	JUL	AUG	SEP	OCT	NOV	DEC	TOT
1974	100.00	100.00	0.00	100.00	42.30	14.00	100.00	100.00	100.00	100.00	100.00	100.00	956.30
1975	100.00	100.00	100.00	100.00	100.00	100.00	100.00	100.00	100.00	100.00	100.00	100.00	1200.00
1976	100.00	100.00	100.00	100.00	100.00	100.00	100.00	100.00	100.00	100.00	0.00	100.00	1100.00
1977	100.00	100.00	100.00	100.00	100.00	40.02	98.17	100.00	100.00	100.00	100.00	100.00	1138.20
1978	5.25	100.00	100.00	100.00	100.00	100.00	100.00	100.00	100.00	100.00	100.00	100.00	1105.25
1979	100.00	100.00	42.17	100.00	100.00	100.00	100.00	100.00	100.00	100.00	100.00	100.00	1142.17
1980	100.00	100.00	100.00	100.00	100.00	100.00	100.00	100.00	100.00	96.47	100.00	100.00	1196.47
1981	100.00	92.59	100.00	100.00	100.00	100.00	100.00	100.00	76.45	100.00	100.00	100.00	1169.04
1982	100.00	100.00	100.00	14.82	100.00	100.00	100.00	0.00	100.00	100.00	100.00	100.00	1014.82
1983	100.00	0.00	100.00	100.00	100.00	100.00	100.00	100.00	0.00	100.00	100.00	100.00	1000.00
1984	100.00	100.00	100.00	100.00	100.00	100.00	0.00	85.77	100.00	0.00	*****	*****	785.77

1 JPNIMP SHORT: UNADJUSTED IMPORTS P. 3, SERIES JPNIMP
D 8. FINAL UNMODIFIED SI RATIOS

YEAR	JAN	FEB	MAR	APR	MAY	JUN	JUL	AUG	SEP	OCT	NOV	DEC	AVGE
1974	101.81	88.67	88.80	99.32	101.74	92.11	106.75	101.73	96.72	100.09	95.58	104.27	98.13
1975	108.17	88.23	103.23	100.83	91.36	99.08	110.45	105.04	94.39	101.89	90.00	102.93	99.63
1976	107.62	87.58	109.76	99.24	92.58	107.08	102.07	104.88	98.45	95.60	105.18	104.04	101.17
1977	103.23	86.42	108.78	96.68	102.21	103.78	95.15	108.61	98.54	96.25	89.68	99.53	99.07
1978	94.05	93.41	103.75	106.23	97.59	99.41	107.21	99.22	98.31	100.41	95.82	94.79	99.19
1979	107.32	89.17	94.57	108.63	97.78	107.13	99.40	102.22	96.87	100.17	100.91	90.82	99.58
1980	105.17	93.54	97.56	102.88	104.61	104.24	101.36	98.03	100.91	96.66	95.45	97.62	99.84
1981	112.69	81.27	104.25	108.05	99.53	100.77	98.03	108.28	87.60	110.21	98.59	88.95	99.85
1982	110.96	81.98	111.05	119.48	95.42	97.63	95.66	127.13	97.96	112.41	94.30	87.70	102.64
1983	102.87	97.69	111.47	109.37	100.21	99.56	95.83	103.91	81.77	106.73	101.05	92.13	100.22
1984	108.67	83.81	107.71	102.87	105.74	94.64	127.55	100.75	95.39	95.90	*****	*****	102.30
AVG	105.69	88.34	103.72	104.87	98.98	100.49	103.59	105.44	95.17	101.49	96.66	96.28	

TABLE TOTAL- 13014.95
1 JPNIMP SHORT: UNADJUSTED IMPORTS P.4, SERIES
JPNIMP
STABLE SEASONALITY TEST
SUM OF DGRS. OF MEAN
SQUARES FREEDOM SQUARE F
BETWEEN MONTHS 3273.851 11 297.623 7.522
RESIDUAL 4668.700 118 39.565
TOTAL 7942.551 129
MOVING SEASONALITY TEST
SUM OF DGRS. OF MEAN
SQUARES FREEDOM SQUARE F-VALUE
BETWEEN YEARS 4969412.9357 9 552156.992854 3.130
ERROR 17464937.2345 99 176413.507419

COMBINED TEST FOR THE PRESENCE OF IDENTIFIABLE SEASONALITY:
IDENTIFIABLE SEASONALITY NOT PRESENT
1 JPIMP SHORT: UNADJUSTED IMPORTS P.5, SERIES
JPNIMP
D 9. FINAL REPLACEMENT VALUES FOR EXTREME SI RATIOS

YEAR	JAN	FEB	MAR	APR	MAY	JUN	JUL	AUG	SEP	OCT	NOV	DEC	AVGE
1974	*****	*****	105.07	*****	97.36	100.10	*****	*****	*****	*****	*****	*****	*****
1975	*****	*****	*****	*****	*****	*****	*****	*****	*****	*****	*****	*****	*****
1976	*****	*****	*****	*****	*****	*****	*****	*****	*****	*****	95.12	*****	*****
1977	*****	*****	*****	*****	*****	*****	100.07	108.50	*****	*****	*****	*****	*****
1978	104.00	*****	*****	*****	*****	*****	*****	*****	*****	*****	*****	*****	*****
1979	*****	*****	99.59	*****	*****	*****	*****	*****	*****	*****	*****	*****	*****
1980	*****	*****	*****	*****	*****	*****	*****	*****	*****	96.90	*****	*****	*****
1981	*****	81.70	*****	*****	*****	*****	*****	*****	89.23	*****	*****	*****	*****
1982	*****	*****	*****	110.29	*****	*****	*****	106.91	*****	*****	*****	*****	*****
1983	*****	85.58	*****	*****	*****	*****	*****	*****	91.97	*****	*****	*****	*****
1984	*****	*****	*****	*****	*****	*****	100.24	101.81	*****	109.99	*****	*****	*****

D9A. YEAR TO YEAR CHANGE IN IRREGULAR AND SEASONAL COMPONENTS AND
MOVING SEASONALITY RATIO

	JAN	FEB	MAR	APR	MAY	JUN	JUL	AUG	SEP	OCT	NOV	DEC
I	3.678	4.309	3.897	3.595	4.741	3.703	3.783	4.350	4.773	3.793	5.363	3.726
S	0.452	0.894	0.778	0.822	0.664	0.677	0.836	0.571	0.564	1.115	0.629	1.436
RATIO	8.13	4.82	5.01	4.37	7.14	5.47	4.52	7.62	8.46	3.40	8.52	2.59

OVERALL MOVING SEASONALITY RATIO: 5.266
1 JPNIMP SHORT: UNADJUSTED IMPORTS P. 6, SERIES
JPNIMP
D10. FINAL SEASONAL FACTORS

YEAR	JAN	FEB	MAR	APR	MAY	JUN	JUL	AUG	SEP	OCT	NOV	DEC	AVGE
1974	105.63	88.03	106.60	99.48	95.18	102.50	105.63	104.72	96.94	98.86	93.04	103.15	99.98
1975	105.40	88.32	106.51	99.77	95.67	102.35	105.47	104.54	97.12	98.82	93.02	102.34	99.94
1976	105.49	88.60	106.04	100.66	96.17	102.66	104.82	104.43	97.34	98.86	93.43	100.73	99.94
1977	105.41	89.28	105.03	101.84	97.15	103.20	103.81	103.54	97.85	98.63	94.30	98.89	99.91
1978	105.96	89.29	103.94	103.20	98.48	103.57	102.43	103.33	97.66	99.23	95.22	96.64	99.91
1979	106.66	89.00	103.40	104.84	99.34	103.04	101.21	102.96	97.43	100.89	96.09	94.51	99.95
1980	107.47	87.80	103.71	106.56	99.52	102.20	99.87	103.39	96.30	103.31	96.97	92.55	99.97
1981	108.01	86.63	104.91	107.28	99.78	100.95	98.82	103.52	95.69	105.40	97.43	91.66	100.01
1982	108.29	85.05	106.68	107.42	100.20	99.74	97.88	104.32	94.70	107.40	97.56	91.06	100.03
1983	108.27	84.05	108.17	107.25	100.48	98.32	97.62	104.53	94.40	108.87	97.44	90.69	100.01
1984	108.20	83.43	109.14	107.51	100.25	97.73	97.29	104.75	94.15	109.70	*****	*****	101.21

TABLE TOTAL- 13007.88 MEAN- 100.06 STD. DEVIATION- 5.91

D10A. SEASONAL FACTORS, ONE YEAR AHEAD

YEAR	JAN	FEB	MAR	APR	MAY	JUN	JUL	AUG	SEP	OCT	NOV	DEC	AVGE
1984	*****	*****	*****	*****	******	*****	*****	*****	*****	*****	97.39	90.51	93.95
1985	108.17	83.11	109.63	107.64	100.13	97.43	97.12	104.85	94.03	110.12	*****	*****	101.22

1 JPNIMP SHORT: UNADJUSTED IMPORTS P. 7, SERIES

JPNIMP

D11. FINAL SEASONALLY ADJUSTED SERIES

YEAR	JAN	FEB	MAR	APR	MAY	JUN	JUL	AUG	SEP	OCT	NOV	DEC	AVGE
1974	7909.	8697.	7592.	9600.	10826.	9520.	11131.	11048.	11631.	11952.	12083.	11622.	10301.
1975	11298.	10375.	9449.	9312.	8449.	8384.	9032.	8758.	8655.	9493.	9322.	10210.	9395.
1976	10965.	11231.	12338.	12231.	12317.	13632.	12923.	13481.	13667.	13117.	15273.	14025.	12933.
1977	13392.	13415.	14678.	13863.	15907.	15695.	14648.	17031.	16599.	16430.	16533.	18275.	15539.
1978	16840.	20633.	20239.	21142.	20411.	19784.	21645.	19990.	21143.	21368.	21263.	20632	20424.
1979	21069.	20959.	19198.	21943.	21059.	22514.	21571.	22107.	22464.	22795	24447.	22595.	21893.
1980	23230.	25626.	22999.	24068.	26694.	26197.	26168.	24580.	27435.	24866.	26729.	29323.	25659.
1981	29590.	27026.	29102.	30044.	30370.	31181.	31781.	34223.	30411.	35094.	34144.	32747.	31309.
1982	34351.	31842.	33621.	34998.	29344.	29749.	29504.	36568.	30667.	30483.	27624.	27304.	31338.
1983	27276.	34436.	31803.	32666.	32777.	33831.	33389.	34762.	31521.	37389.	41313.	41977.	34428.
1984	42641.	43562.	43597.	43140.	48771.	46090.	64340.	48542.	52468.	46261.	*****	*****	479.41
AVGE	21687.	22527.	22238.	23001.	23357.	23357.	23325.	25103.	24644.	24242.	24477.	22873.	22871.

TABLE TOTAL- 3038059. MEAN- 23370. STD. DEVIATION- 11278.

TEST FOR THE PRESENCE OF RESIDUAL SEASONALITY

NO EVIDENCE OF RESIDUAL SEASONALITY IN THE ENTIRE SERIES AT THE 1 PER CENT LEVEL. F= 0.48

NO EVIDENCE OF RESIDUAL SEASONALITY IN THE LAST 3 YEARS AT THE 1 PER CENT LEVEL. F= 0.39

NO EVIDENCE OF RESIDUAL SEASONALITY IN THE LAST 3 YEARS AT THE 5 PER CENT LEVEL.

NOTE: SUDDEN LARGE CHANGES IN THE LEVEL OF THE SEASONALLY ADJUSTED SERIES WILL INVALIDATE THE RESULTS OF THIS TEST FOR THE LAST THREE YEAR PERIOD.

END OF X-11.2 RUN

Appendix C:
Sources for
Business Statistics

1. Personal income by source and disposition of personal income
   U.S. Department of Commerce, Bureau of Economic Analysis,
   National Income and Wealth Division, BE-54, 1441 L Street, NW,
   Washington, DC 20230 (202-606-5304)
2. Industrial production
   Jerry Storch, Board of Governors of the Federal Reserve System,
   Division of Research and Statistics, Industrial Output Section,
   Eccles Building, Room 3212-D, 20th & Constitution Avenue, NW,
   Washington, DC 20551 (202-452-2932)
3. Business sales, inventories, inventory-sales ratios, and retail trade
   Ronald Piencykoski, U. S. Department of Commerce, Bureau of the
   Census, Business Division, Current Retail Sales and Inventories
   Branch, FOB 3, Room 2626, Washington, DC 20233 (301-763-5294)
4. Manufacturing and trade sales, inventories, and ratios in 1987 dollars
   U.S. Department of Commerce, Bureau of Economic Analysis,
   National Income and Wealth Division, BE-54, 1441 L Street, NW,
   Washington, DC 20230 (202-606-5304)
5. Manufacturers' shipments, inventories, and orders
   Steve Andrews or Kathy Menth, U.S. Department of Commerce,
   Bureau of the Census, Industry Division, M3 Branch, FOB 4,
   Room 2232, Washington, DC 20233 (301-763-2502 or 763-2575)

6. Business incorporations and industrial and commercial failures
The Dun & Bradstreet Corporation, Economic Communications Department, 299 Park Avenue, New York, NY 10171 (212-593-4163)

7. Prices received and paid by farmers
Herb Vanderberry, U.S. Department of Agriculture, National Agricultural Statistical Service, Commodity Prices Section, Economic Statistics Branch, South Building, Room 5912, 14th & Independence Avenue, SW, Washington, DC 20250-2000 (202-720-5446)

8. Consumer prices and purchasing power of the dollar
U.S. Department of Labor, Bureau of Labor Statistics, Office of Consumer Prices and Price Indexes, Postal Square Building, Room 3615, 2 Massachusetts Avenue, NE, Washington, DC 20212 (202-606-7000)

9. Producer prices and producer price indexes for all commodities
U.S. Department of Labor, Bureau of Labor Statistics, Division of Industrial Prices and Price Indexes, Postal Square Building, Room 3840, 2 Massachusetts Avenue, NE, Washington, DC 20212 (202-606-7705)

10. Construction put in place and construction cost indexes
George A. Roff, U.S. Department of Commerce, Bureau of the Census, Construction Statistics Division, Progress Branch, Iverson Mall, Room 301-03, Washington, DC 20233 (301-763-5717)

11. Construction contracts
Laura Pelzer, McGraw-Hill Construction Information Group, F. W. Dodge Division, Paramount Plaza, 13th Floor, 1633 Broadway, New York, NY 10019 (212-512-3523)

12. Housing starts and permits
U.S. Department of Commerce, Bureau of the Census, Construction Statistics Division, Construction Starts Branch, Iverson Mall, Room 300-15, Washington, DC 20233 (301-763-5731)

13. Boeckh indexes
Janet Olson, BOECKH, Division of Mitchell International, P.O. Box 51291, New Berlin, WI 53151-0291 (800-809-0016, ext. 2808)

14. Engineering News-Record and construction hourly wages
Rona Nadi, McGraw-Hill Construction Information Group, Engineering News-Record, 41st Floor, 1221 Avenue of the Americas, New York, NY 10020 (212-512-3418)

15. Federal Highway Administration—highway construction
Claretta, Duren, U.S. Department of Transportation, Federal

Highway Administration, Interstate and Programs Support Branch, HNG-13, Nassis Building, Room 3128, 400 7th Street, SW, Washington, DC 20590 (202-366-4636)

16. Real estate
Zenora Hines, U.S. Housing and Urban Development, Federal Housing Administration, Information Systems Division, Room B 133, 451 7th Street, SW, Washington, DC 20410 (202-755-7500, ext. 107)

17. Federal Home Loan Banks, outstanding advances to member institutions
Phil Quinn, Federal Housing Finance Board, District Bank Directorate Division, Financial Report Branch, 4th Floor, 1777 F Street, NW, Washington, DC 20006 (202-408-2865)

18. Newspaper advertising expenditures
Miles Groves, Newspaper Association of America, Newspaper Center, 11600 Sunrise Valley Drive, Reston, VA 22091 (703-648-1339)

19. Wholesale trade
Nancy Piesto, U.S. Department of Commerce, Bureau of the Census, Business Division, Current Wholesale Branch, FOB 3, Room 2747, Washington, DC 20233 (301-763-3916)

20. Labor force and population
U.S. Department of Labor, Bureau of Labor Statistics, Office of Employment and Unemployment Statistics, Current Employment Analysis Section, Postal Square Building, Room 4675, 2 Massachusetts Avenue, NE, Washington, DC 20212 (202-606-6378)

21. Employment, average hours per week, indexes of employee-hours, and hourly and weekly earnings
U.S. Department of Labor, Bureau of Labor Statistics, Office of Employment and Unemployment Statistics, Monthly Industry Employment Statistics, Postal Square Building, Room 4860, 2 Massachusetts Avenue, NE, Washington, DC 20212 (202-606-6555)

22. Aggregate employee-hours
U.S. Department of Labor, Bureau of Labor Statistics, Division of Productivity Research, Postal Square Building, Room 2150, 2 Massachusetts Avenue, NE, Washington, DC 20212 (202-606-5606)

23. Employment cost index
Wayne Shelly, U.S. Department of Labor, Bureau of Labor Statistics, Office of Compensation and Working Conditions, Division of Employment Cost Trends, Postal Square Building, Room 4170, 2 Massachusetts Avenue, NE, Washington, DC 20212 (202-606-6199)

24. Help-wanted advertising
Ken Goldstein, The Conference Board, Inc., 845 3rd Avenue, New York, NY 10022 (212-339-0331)
25. Work stoppages
U.S. Department of Labor, Bureau of Labor Statistics, Division of Developments and Labor Management Relations, Postal Square Building, Room 4175, 2 Massachusetts Avenue, NE, Washington, DC 20212 (202-606-6288)
26. Unemployment insurance
Cindy Ambler, U.S. Department of Labor, Employment and Training Administration, Unemployment Insurance Service, Suite S-4519, 200 Constitution Avenue, NW, Washington, DC 20210 (202-219-5922)
27. Bankers' acceptances
Thomas Brady, Board of Governors of the Federal Reserve System, Division of Monetary Affairs, Stop 81, Eccles Building, 20th & Constitution Avenue, NW, Washington, DC 20551 (202-452-3363)
28. Commercial and financial company paper
Federal Reserve Bank of New York, 33 Liberty Street, New York, NY 10045 (212-720-6143)
29. Loans of the Farm Credit System
Federal Farm Credit Banks Funding Corporation, Suite 1401, 10 Exchange Place, Jersey City, NJ 07302 (201-200-8000)
30. Federal Reserve Banks condition
Kim Jefferson, Board of Governors of the Federal Reserve System, Information Resource Management, Stop 170, Martin Building, 20th & C Streets, NW, Washington, DC 20551 (202-452-2398)
31. All member banks of Federal Reserve System, average daily figures
Board of Governors of the Federal Reserve System, Division of Monetary Affairs, Stop 72, Eccles Building, 20th & Constitution Avenue, NW, Washington, DC 20551 (202-452-3577)
32. Large commercial banks reporting to Federal Reserve System
Dennis Farley, Board of Governors of the Federal Reserve System, Division of Monetary Affairs, Stop 81, Eccles Building, 20th & Constitution Avenue, NW, Washington, DC 20551 (202-452-3021)
33. Commercial bank credit
Virginia Lewis, Board of Governors of the Federal Reserve System, Division of Monetary Affairs, Stop 84, Eccles Building, 20th & Constitution Avenue, NW, Washington, DC 20551 (202-452-3012)

34. Money and interest rates and taxable U.S. Treasury bonds
    Deborah McMillian, Board of Governors of the Federal Reserve
    System, Division of Monetary Affairs, Stop 81, Eccles Building,
    20th & Constitution Avenue, NW, Washington, DC 20551
    (202-452-2851)

35. Home mortgage rates
    Travis King, Federal Housing Finance Board, 1777 F Street, NW,
    Washington, DC 20006 (202-408-2967)

36. Consumer installment credit
    Mark Pierce, Board of Governors of the Federal Reserve System,
    Division of Research and Statistics, Stop 93, Eccles Building, 20th &
    Constitution Avenue, NW, Washington, DC 20551 (202-452-3760)

37. Federal Government finance
    Sherry Sherrod, U.S. Department of the Treasury, Financial Man-
    agement Service, Room 749, 941 North Capitol Street, NE, Wash-
    ington, DC 20227 (202-208-2456)

38. Gold, monetary stock
    Donald Adams, Board of Governors of the Federal Reserve
    System, Division of International Finance, Stop 43, Eccles Build-
    ing, 20th & Constitution Avenue, NW, Washington, DC 20551
    (202-452-2364)

39. Gold and silver prices at New York
    Platt's Metals Week, McGraw-Hill, Inc., 42nd Floor, 1221 Avenue
    of the Americas, New York, NY 10020 (212-512-2823)

40. Monetary statistics
    Board of Governors of the Federal Reserve System, Division of
    Monetary Affairs, Stop 72, Eccles Building, 20th & Constitution
    Avenue, NW, Washington, DC 20551 (202-452-3577)

41. Currency in circulation
    Bernadette Derr, U.S. Department of the Treasury, Financial
    Management Service, 401 14th Street, SW, Washington, DC 20227
    (202-208-1374)

42. Profits and dividends
    Paul Zarrett, U.S. Department of Commerce, Bureau of the Cen-
    sus, Economic Census and Survey Division, FOB 3, Room 2578,
    Washington, DC 20233 (301-763-2718)

43. State and municipal securities issues and domestic municipal
    bond yields
    The Bond Buyer, Statistics Department, 31st Floor, 1 State Street
    Plaza, New York, NY 10004 (212-943-8542)

44. Bond prices, domestic municipal bond yields, and stock prices and yields
    Standard & Poor's Corporation, Central Inquiry, 25 Broadway, New York, NY 10004 (212-208-1199)

45. Bond sales
    Mike Hyland, New York Stock Exchange, Inc., Fixed Income Markets, 20 Broad Street, New York, NY 10005 (212-656-5868)

46. Bond yields
    Moody's Investors Service, Corporate Rating Desk, 99 Church Street, New York, NY 10007 (212-553-0377)

47. Stock prices, Dow Jones averages
    Dow Jones & Company, Inquiry Department, 200 Liberty Street, New York, NY 10281 (212-416-2676)

48. Stock prices, stock sales, and shares listed, New York Stock Exchange (NYSE)
    Bethann Ashfield, New York Stock Exchange, Inc., Research Library, 17th Floor, 11 Wall Street, New York, NY 10005 (212-656-2491)

49. Stock prices and stock sales, NASDAQ over-the-counter
    Mike Shokouhi, National Association of Securities Dealers, Inc., Economic Research Department, 1735 K Street, NW, Washington, DC 20006 (202-728-8274)

50. Stock sales on all registered exchanges (SEC)
    William Atkinson, Securities and Exchange Commission, Office of Economic Analysis, Stop 9-1, 450 5th Street, NW, Washington, DC 20549 (202-272-7360)

51. Value of exports, value of imports, and merchandise trade balance
    Richard Preuss, U.S. Department of Commerce, Bureau of the Census, Foreign Trade Division, Trade Data Services Branch, FOB 3, Room 2279, Washington, DC 20233 (301-763-7754)

52. Export and import price indexes
    Michelle Vachris, U.S. Department of Labor, Bureau of Labor Statistics, Division of International Prices, Branch of Index Methods, Analysis, and Evaluation, Postal Square Building, Room 3955, 2 Massachusetts Avenue, NE, Washington, DC 20212 (202-606-7155)

53. Shipping weight and value
    Norman Tague, U.S. Department of Commerce, Bureau of the Census, Foreign Trade Division, Transportation Branch, FOB 3, Room 2266, Washington, DC 20233 (301-763-7770)

54. Air carriers
    Paul Gavel, U.S. Department of Transportation, Research and

Special Programs Administration, Office of Airline Statistics, DAI-20, Washington, DC 20590 (202-366-4391)

55. Urban transit industry
Terry Bronson, American Public Transit Association, Suite 400, 1201 New York Avenue, NW, Washington, DC 20005 (202-898-4129)

56. Motor carriers
Andrew Lee, Interstate Commerce Commission, Office of Economics, Section of Costing and Financial Information, Room 3310, 12th & Constitution Avenue, NW, Washington, DC 20423 (202-927-6387)

57. Freight carried—volume indexes, class I and II intercity truck tonnage
Mike Arendes, American Trucking Association, Trucking Information Services, 2200 Mill Road, Alexandria, VA 22314-4677 (703-838-1791)

58. Class I railroads
David Miller, Association of American Railroads, Economics and Finance Department, Room 5404, 50 F Street, NW, Washington, DC 20001 (202-639-2304)

59. Foreign travel
Pat Harrington, U.S. Department of Transportation, Volpe National Transportation Systems Center, Center for Transportation Information, Kendall Square, Cambridge, MA 02142 (617-494-2450)

60. Passports issued
David Brown, U.S. Department of State, Passport Services, Office of Program Support, Room 584, 1425 K Street, NW, Washington, DC 20522-1705 (202-326-6075)

61. National parks, recreation visits
Tom Wade, U.S. Department of Interior, National Park Service, Socio-Economic Studies, 12795 West Alameda Parkway, Denver, CO 80225-0287 (303-969-6977)

62. Inorganic chemicals
Lissene Hafenrichter, U. S. Department of Commerce, Bureau of the Census, Industry Division, Wood and Chemical Products Branch, FOB 4, Room 2212, Washington, DC 20233 (301-763-2541)

63. Sulfur
Pamela Shorter, U.S. Department of Interior, Bureau of Mines, Branch of Industrial Metals, MS-9705, 810 7th Street, NW, Washington, DC 20241 (202-501-9506).

64. Inorganic fertilizer materials
Walter Hunter, U.S. Department of Commerce, Bureau of the

Census, Industry Division, Wood and Chemical Products Branch, FOB 4, Room 2212, Washington, DC 20233 (301-763-4490)

65. Potash, sales
Connie Holcomb, Potash and Phosphate Institute, Inc., Suite 110, 655 Engineering Drive, Norcross, GA 30092 (404-447-0335)

66. Industrial gases
Suzanne Pasdar, U.S. Department of Commerce, Bureau of the Census, Industry Division, Wood and Chemical Products Branch, FOB 4, Room 2212, Washington, DC 20233 (301-763-4485)

67. Organic chemicals and plastics and resin materials
Gwen Bennett, International Trade Commission, Energy, Chemicals, and Textiles Division, Suite 513B, 500 E Street, SW, Washington, DC 20436 (202-205-3357)

68. Glycerin, production
David Gromos, U.S. Department of Commerce, Bureau of the Census, Industry Division, Food, Textiles, and Apparel Branch, FOB 4, Room 2132, Washington, DC 20233 (301-763-7809)

69. Alcohol and alcoholic beverages
U.S. Department of the Treasury, Bureau of Alcohol, Tobacco, and Firearms, Industry Compliance Division, Market Compliance Branch, 650 Massachusetts Avenue, NW, Washington, DC 20226 (202-927-8128)

70. Paints, varnish, and lacquer
Kim Ciurca, U.S. Department of Commerce, Bureau of the Census, Industry Division, Wood and Chemical Products Branch, FOB 4, Room 2212, Washington, DC 20233 (301-763-5602)

71. Electric power production
U.S. Department of Energy, National Energy Information Center, Forrestal Building, Room IF-048, 1000 Independence Avenue, SW, Washington, DC 20585 (202-586-8800)

72. Electric power sales and revenue from sales
Edison Electric Institute, 701 Pennsylvania Avenue, NW, Washington, DC 20004-2696 (202-508-5000)

73. Gas
American Gas Association, 1515 Wilson Boulevard, Arlington, VA 22209-2470 (703-841-8507)

74. Dairy products
Daniel Buckner, U.S. Department of Agriculture, National Agricultural Statistical Service, Estimates Division, Livestock

Branch, South Building, 14th & Independence Avenue, SW, Washington, DC 20250-2000 (202-720-4448)

75. Fluid milk, utilization in manufactured dairy products
    LaVerne T. Williams, U.S. Department of Agriculture, Economic Research Service, Livestock, Dairy, and Poultry Branch, Room 808D, 1301 New York Avenue, NW, Washington, DC 20005 (202-219-0769)

76. Fluid milk wholesale prices
    James Hand, U.S. Department of Agriculture, National Agricultural Statistical Service, Economic Statistics Branch, Commodity Prices Section, South Building, Room 5927, 14th & Independence Avenue, SW, Washington, DC 20250-2000 (202-690-3236)

77. Grain and grain products
    Charles Van Lahr, U.S. Department of Agriculture, National Agricultural Statistical Service, Estimates Division, Crops Branch, South Building, Room 5175, 14th & Independence Avenue, SW, Washington, DC 20250-2000 (202-720-2127)

78. Rice
    Dan Kerestes, U.S. Department of Agriculture, National Agricultural Statistical Service, Estimates Division, Crops Branch, South Building, Room 5175, 14th & Independence Avenue, SW, Washington, DC 20250-2000 (202-720-9526)

79. Rye and wheat
    Vaughn Siegenthaler, U.S. Department of Agriculture, National Agricultural Statistical Service, Estimates Division, Crops Branch, South Building, Room 5175, 14th & Independence Avenue, SW, Washington, DC 20250-2000 (202-720-8068)

80. Wheat flour
    John Miller, U.S. Department of Commerce, Bureau of the Census, Industry Division, Food, Textiles, and Apparel Branch, FOB 4, Room 2132, Washington, DC 20233 (301-763-7837)

81. Poultry, slaughter
    Joel Moore, U.S. Department of Agriculture, National Agricultural Statistical Service, Estimates Division, Livestock, Dairy, and Poultry Branch, South Building, Room 5906, 14th & Independence Avenue, SW, Washington, DC 20250-2000 (202-720-3244)

82. Cold storage stocks of poultry, eggs, total meats, beef and veal, lamb and mutton, and pork
    John Lang, U. S. Department of Agriculture, National Agricultural Statistical Service, Estimates Division, Livestock, Dairy, and Poultry

Branch, South Building, Room 5906, 14th & Independence Avenue, SW, Washington, DC 20250-2000 (202-720-0585)

83. Poultry and egg prices
Debra Kenerson, U.S. Department of Agriculture, National Agricultural Statistical Service, Estimates Division, Economic Statistics Branch, South Building, Room 5912, 14th & Independence Avenue, SW, Washington, DC 20250-2000 (202-690-3234)

84. Egg production
Robert Little, U.S. Department of Agriculture, National Agricultural Statistical Service, Estimates Division, Livestock, Dairy, and Poultry Branch, South Building, Room 5913, 14th & Independence Avenue, SW, Washington, DC 20250-2000 (202-720-6147)

85. Cattles and calves
Glenda Shepler, U.S. Department of Agriculture, National Agricultural Statistical Service, Estimates Division, Livestock, Dairy, and Poultry Branch, South Building, Room 5906, 14th & Independence Avenue, SW, Washington, DC 20250-2000 (202-720-3040)

86. Hogs
Tom Kurtz, U.S. Department of Agriculture, National Agricultural Statistical Service, Estimates Division, Livestock, Dairy, and Poultry Branch, South Building, Room 5901, 14th & Independence Avenue, SW, Washington, DC 20250-2000 (202-720-3106)

87. Sheep and lambs and meats
Linda Simpson, U.S. Department of Agriculture, National Agricultural Statistical Service, Estimates Division, Livestock, Dairy, and Poultry Branch, South Building, Room 5871, 14th & Independence Avenue, SW, Washington, DC 20250-2000 (202-720-3578)

88. Coffee, U.S. Import Price Index
Rob Frumkin, U.S. Department of Labor, Bureau of Labor Statistics, Division of International Prices, Branch of International Indexes, Postal Square Building, Room 3930, 2 Massachusetts Avenue, NE, Washington, DC 20212 (202-606-7106)

89. Fish
Barbara O'Bannon, U.S. Department of Commerce, National Oceanic and Atmospheric Administration, National Marine Fisheries Service, Fisheries Statistics Division, 1315 East West Highway, Silver Spring, MD 20910 (301-713-2328)

90. Tobacco
Greg Preston, U.S. Department of Agriculture, National Agricultural Statistical Service, Estimates Division, Crops Branch, South

Building, Room 5175, 14th & Independence Avenue, SW,
Washington, DC 20250-2000 (202-720-3843)

91. Tobacco leaf stocks
Henry Martin, U.S. Department of Agriculture, Agricultural
Marketing Service, Tobacco Division, Market Information and
Program Analysis Branch, Annex Building, Room 502, 300 12th
Street, SW, Washington, DC 20250-2000 (202-205-0489)

92. Leather manufactures
Nat Shelton, U.S. Department of Commerce, Bureau of the Census, Industry Division, Food, Textiles, and Apparel Branch, FOB
4, Room 2132, Washington, DC 20233 (301-763-5809)

93. Lumber—all types, southern pine, and western pine
Kathy Shaffer, American Forest and Paper Association, Suite 800,
1111 19th Street, NW, Washington, DC 20036 (202-463-2754)

94. Softwoods
Western Wood Products Association, Yeon Building, 522
Southwest Fifth Avenue, Portland, OR 97204-2122 (503-224-3930)

95. Hardwood flooring
Patsy Davenport, National Oak Flooring Manufactures Association,
P.O. Box 3009, Memphis, TN 38173-0009 (901-526-5016)

96. Iron and steel; pig iron and iron products; steel, raw and semifinished; and steel mill products
Janet Nash, American Iron and Steel Institute, Suite 1300, 1101
17th Street, NW, Washington, DC 20036-4700 (202-452-7203 or
452-7201)

97. Iron and steel scrap and pig iron consumption
David Kulha, U.S. Department of Interior, Bureau of Mines,
Branch of Metals, MS-9703, 810 7th Street, NW, Washington, DC
20241 (202-501-9520)

98. Ore
William S. Kirk, U.S. Department of Interior, Bureau of Mines,
Branch of Metals, MS-5208, 810 7th Street, NW, Washington, DC
20241 (202-501-9430)

99. U.S. and foreign ores: Receipts and consumption at iron and steel
plants and stocks at furnace yards and U.S. docks
Joy Earlywine, American Iron Ore Association, 915 Rockefeller
Building, 614 Superior Avenue West, Cleveland, OH 44113-1383
(216-241-8261)

100. Pig iron and iron products castings and steel castings
Renee Reda, U.S. Department of Commerce, Bureau of the Census,

Industry Division, Metals and Industrial Machinery Branch, FOB 4, Room 2207, Washington, DC 20233 (301-763-7865)

101. Producing steel mills, inventory
     Michele L. Chaney, U.S. Department of Commerce, Bureau of the Census, Industry Division, Metals and Industrial Machinery Branch, FOB 4, Room 2207, Washington, DC 20233 (301-763-7863)

102. Aluminum
     Patricia Plunkert or Cindy Lui, U.S. Department of Interior, Bureau of Mines, Branch of Metals, MS-5208, 810 7th Street, NW, Washington, DC 20241 (202-501-9419)

103. Aluminum products
     Mary Ellickson, U.S. Department of Commerce, Bureau of the Census, Industry Division, Metals and Industrial Machinery Branch, FOB 4, Room 2207, Washington, DC 20233 (301-763-7862)

104. Copper
     Dan Edelstein, U.S. Department of Interior, Bureau of Mines, Branch of Metals, MS-5208, 810 7th Street, NW, Washington, DC 20241 (202-501-9415)

105. Lead
     Jerry Smith, U.S. Department of Interior, Bureau of Mines, Branch of Metals, MS-5208, 810 7th Street, NW, Washington, DC 20241 (202-501-9444)

106. Lead producers' stocks and slab zinc production and producers' stocks
     Robert Clock, American Bureau of Metal Statistics, Inc., 400 Plaza Drive, P.O. Box 1405, Secaucus, NJ 07094-0405 (201-863-6900)

107. Tin
     James Carlin, U.S. Department of Interior, Bureau of Mines, Branch of Metals, MS-5208, 810 7th Street, NW, Washington, DC 20241 (202-501-9426)

108. Zinc
     Bob Reese, U. S. Department of Interior, Bureau of Mines, Branch of Metals, MS-5208, 810 7th Street, NW, Washington, DC 20241 (202-501-9422)

109. Industrial heating equipment
     Data not available for public distribution.

110. Materials handling equipment
     Elizabeth Baatz, Cahners Economics, Cahners Building, 275 Washington Street, Newton, MA 02158-1630 (617-630-2114)

111. Industrial supplies, machinery, and equipment
     Chuck Moore, American Supply & Machinery Manufacturers' Association, Inc., 1300 Sumner Avenue, Cleveland, OH 44115-2851 (216-244-7333)
112. Industrial suppliers distribution of machinery and equipment
     Steve Hern, Industrial Distribution Association, Suite 201, 3 Corporate Square, Atlanta, GA 30329 (404-325-2776)
113. Fluid power products shipments indexes
     Steven Latin-Kasper, National Fluid Power Association, Suite 311, 3333 North Mayfair Road, Milwaukee, WI 53222 (414-778-3358)
114. Machine tools
     Steve Bell, Association for Manufacturing Technology, 7901 West Park Drive, McLean, VA 22102-4269 (703-827-5262)
115. Tractors used in construction, shipments
     Richard Wiesler, U.S. Department of Commerce, Bureau of the Census, Industry Division, Metals and Industrial Machinery Branch, FOB 4, Room 2207, Washington, DC 20233 (301-763-7867)
116. Battery shipments
     Mary Warmowski, Smith Bucklin & Associates Inc., 401 North Michigan Avenue, Chicago, IL 60611-4267 (312-644-6610)
117. Radio factory sales and television set production
     Tom Godsman, Electronic Industries Association, 2001 Pennsylvania Avenue, NW, Washington, DC 20006-1813 (202-457-4958)
118. Household major appliances and ranges
     Alane Mackay, Association of Home Appliance Manufacturers, 20 North Wacker Drive, Chicago, IL 60606 (312-984-5800, ext. 315)
119. Vacuum cleaners
     Clifford J. Wood, Vacuum Cleaner Manufacturers Association, Box 2642, North Canton, OH 44720 (216-499-5998)
120. Furnaces
     Gary Thibeault, Gas Appliance Manufacturers Association, Inc., 1901 North Moore Street, Arlington, VA 22209 (703-525-9565)
121. Water heaters
     Frank Stanonik, Gas Appliance Manufacturers Association, Inc., 1901 North Moore Street, Arlington, VA 22209 (703-525-9565)
122. Coal and coke
     U.S. Department of Energy, National Energy Information Center, Forrestal Building, EI-231, 1000 Independence Avenue, SW, Washington, DC 20585 (202-586-8800)

123. Petroleum coke production and stocks and petroleum and products
    Morris Rice, U.S. Department of Energy, Office of Oil and Gas,
    EI-424, Forrestal Building, Room 2E068, Washington, DC 20585
    (202-586-4634)
124. Pulpwood, waste paper, wood pulp, and paper and paper products
    American Forest and Paper Association, Paper Information Cen-
    ter, 1111 19th Street, NW, Washington, DC 20036 (1-800-878-8878)
125. Newsprint
    Jan Liddy, American Forest and Paper Association, 11th Floor, 260
    Madison Avenue, New York, NY 10016 (212-340-0649)
126. Paper products
    Peggy Gilmore, Fibre Box Association, 2850 Golf Road, Rolling
    Meadows, IL 60008 (847-364-9600)
127. Tires and tubes
    Dan Mustico, Rubber Manufacturers Association, 1400 K Street,
    NW, Washington, DC 20005 (202-682-4863)
128. Portland cement
    Cheryl Solomon, U.S. Department of Interior, Bureau of Mines,
    Branch of Industrial Minerals, MS-5209, 810 7th Street, NW,
    Washington, DC 20241 (202-501-9393)
129. Clay construction products
    Robert Miller, U.S. Department of Commerce, Bureau of the
    Census, Industry Division, Wood and Chemical Products Branch,
    FOB 4, Room 2212, Washington, DC 20233 (301-763-4484)
130. Flat glass shipments
    Susan Sundermann, U.S. Department of Commerce, Bureau of
    the Census, Industry Division, Wood and Chemical Products
    Branch, FOB 4, Room 2203, Washington, DC 20233 (301-763-2376)
131. Glass containers
    Sheila Proudfoot, U.S. Department of Commerce, Bureau of the
    Census, Industry Division, Wood and Chemical Products Branch,
    FOB 4, Room 2203, Washington, DC 20233 (301-763-7574)
132. Gypsum and products
    Lawrence Davis, U.S. Department of Interior, Bureau of Mines,
    Branch of Industrial Minerals, MS-5209, 810 7th Street, NW,
    Washington, DC 20241 (202-501-9386)
133. Cotton production
    Roger Lathan, U.S. Department of Agriculture, National Agricul-
    tural Statistical Service, Crops Branch, Room 5175, 14th & Indepen-
    dence Avenue, SW, Washington, DC 20250-2000 (202-720-5944)

134. Cotton consumption and spindle activity
     Karen Harshbarger, U.S. Department of Commerce, Bureau of
     the Census, Industry Division, Food, Textiles, and Apparel
     Branch, FOB 4, Room 2132, Washington, DC 20233
     (301-763-4476)
135. Cotton stocks in the United States
     Tim Barry, New York Cotton Exchange, Market Surveillance
     Division, 8th Floor, 4 World Trade Center, New York, NY 10048
     (212-938-7909)
136. Cotton farm prices, American upland
     Debra Kenerson, U.S. Department of Agriculture, National Agri-
     cultural Statistical Service, Estimates Division, Economic Statis-
     tics Branch, Commodity Prices Section, 14th & Independence
     Avenue, SW, Washington, DC 20250-2000 (202-690-3234)
137. Cotton prices, strict low middling
     Leslie Meyer, U.S. Department of Agriculture, Economic
     Research Service, Commodity Economics Division, Crops
     Branch, Room 1034, 1301 New York Avenue, NW, Washington,
     DC 20005-4788 (202-219-0840)
138. Cotton cloth broadwoven goods and production of wool broad-
     woven goods
     Keith Featherstone, U.S. Department of Commerce, Bureau of
     the Census, Industry Division, Food, Textiles, and Apparel
     Branch, FOB 4, Room 2132, Washington, DC 20233 (301-763-2553)
139. Manmade fibers and manufactures
     Kim Costa, Fiber Economics Bureau, Inc., 101 Eisenhower Park-
     way, Roseland, NJ 07068 (201-228-1107)
140. Wool consumption
     Maria Dixon, U.S. Department of Commerce, Bureau of the
     Census, Industry Division, Food, Textiles, and Apparel Branch,
     FOB 4, Room 2132, Washington, DC 20233 (301-763-5895)
141. Wool imports and wool prices
     John Lawler, U.S. Department of Agriculture, Economic
     Research Service, Commodity Economics Division, Crops
     Branch, Room 1034, 1301 New York Avenue, NW, Washington,
     DC 20005-4788 (202-219-0840)
142. Floor coverings
     Amelia Williams, American Textile Manufacturers Institute, Inc.,
     Office of Chief Economist, Suite 900, 1801 K Street, NW,
     Washington, DC 20006 (202-862-0547)

143. Apparel
     Andrew Kraynak, U.S. Department of Commerce, Bureau of the
     Census, Industry Division, Food, Textiles, and Apparel Branch,
     FOB 4, Room 2132, Washington, DC 20233 (301-763-7108)
144. Hosiery shipments
     Mary Ann Blansett, National Association of Hosiery
     Manufacturers, 200 North Sharon Amity Road, Charlotte, NC
     28211-3004 (704-365-0913)
145. Aerospace vehicles, truck trailer and chassis shipments, and
     trailer chassis sold separately
     Lynn Sizemore, U.S. Department of Commerce, Bureau of the
     Census, Industry Division, Electrical and Transportation Branch,
     FOB 4, Room 2231, Washington, DC 20233 (301-763-5547)
146. Passenger cars, trucks, and buses factory sales and retail invento-
     ries of trucks and buses
     American Automobile Manufacturers Association, Suite 300,
     7430 Second Avenue, Detroit, MI 48202 (313-872-4311)
147. Passenger car retail sales, inventories, and inventory-sales ratios
     U.S. Department of Commerce, Bureau of Economic Analysis,
     National Income and Wealth Division, BE-54, 1441 L Street, NW,
     Washington, DC 20230 (202-606-5304)
148. Passenger car imports
     Mike Hagey, U.S. International Trade Commission, Machinery
     and Transportation Division, 500 E Street, SW, Washington, DC
     20436 (202-205-3392)
149. Registrations of passenger cars, trucks, and buses
     R. L. Polk & Company, Statistical Services Division, 1155 Brewery
     Park Boulevard, Detroit, MI 48207-2697 (313-393-0880)
150. Retail sales of trucks and buses
     U.S. Department of Commerce, Bureau of Economic Analysis,
     National Income and Wealth Division, BE-54, 1441 L Street, NW,
     Washington, DC 20230 (202-606-5304)
151. Railroad equipment
     Association of American Railroads, Communications
     Department, 50 F Street, NW, Washington, DC 20001-1564
     (202-639-2555)

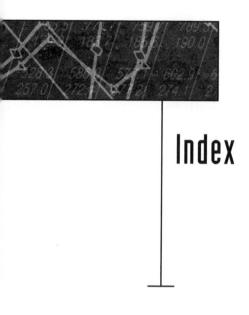

Index

THE AMERICAN MARKETING ASSOCIATION is the world's largest and most comprehensive professional association of marketers. With over 45,000 members, the AMA has more than 500 chapters throughout North America. The AMA publishes nine major marketing publications and sponsors 25 major conferences per year, covering topics ranging from the latest trends in customer satisfaction measurement to business-to-business and service marketing, attitude research, and sales promotion.